The
Bozeman Trail
Volume II

JOHN M. BOZEMAN
Pathbreaker of the Bozeman Trail.

The Bozeman Trail

Historical Accounts of the Blazing of the
Overland Routes into the Northwest,
and the Fights with Red Cloud's
Warriors

VOLUME II

by
Grace Raymond Hebard and
E. A. Brininstool

with Introduction by
General Charles King, U.S.V

Introduction to the Bison Book Edition
by John D. McDermott

University of Nebraska Press
Lincoln and London

First Bison Book printing: 1990
Most recent printing indicated by the last digit below:
10 9 8 7 6 5 4 3 2 1

Library of Congress Cataloging-in-Publication Data
Hebard, Grace Raymond, 1861–1936
The Bozeman trail: historical accounts of the blazing
of the overland routes into the Northwest,
and the fights with Red Cloud's warriors /
by Grace Raymond Hebard and E. A. Brininstool:
with introduction by Charles King.
p. cm.
"Introduction to the Bison Book
edition by John D. McDermott." Reprint.
Originally published: Cleveland: A. H. Clark, 1961.
ISBN 0-8032-7249-9 (v. 1).—ISBN 0-8032-7250-2 (v. 2).
1. West (U.S.)—History.
2. Bozeman Trail. 3. Indians of North
America—West (U.S.)—Wars. 4. Overland journeys
to the Pacific. 5. Red Cloud, 1822–1909.
I. Brininstool, E. W. (Earl Alonzo), 1870–1957.
II. Title.
F591.H4 1990 978'.02—dc20
90-12364 CIP

Reprinted by arrangement with the Arthur H. Clark Company

An introduction by General Charles King, which originally
appeared in Volume I only, is repeated in Volume II of the
Bison Book edition.
The original index, which appeared at the end of Volume II, has been
divided, in the Bison Book edition, into separate indexes for the two
volumes.

TO THE PIONEER

[*by Theodore O'Hara*]

A dirge for the brave old pioneer!
The patriarch of his tribe!
He sleeps—no pompous pile marks where,
No lines his deeds describe.

They raised no stone above him here,
Nor carved his deathless name;
An empire is his sepulchre,
His epitaph is fame.

Contents of Volume II

INTRODUCTION TO THE BISON BOOK EDITION ... 1

INTRODUCTION BY GENERAL CHARLES KING ... 9

JOHN PHILLIPS, A HERO OF FORT PHIL KEARNEY ... 15

THE WAGON BOX FIGHT ... 39

PERSONAL EXPERIENCES IN AND AROUND FOR PHIL
KEARNEY ... 89

ROUTE OF THE BOZEMAN TRAIL; DESCRIPTION OF FORTS
RENO, C. F. SMITH, AND FETTERMAN ... 113

A PRIVATE'S REMINISCENCES OF FORT RENO ... 149

FORT C. F. SMITH AND THE HAYFIELD FIGHT ... 159

RED CLOUD, THE GREAT OGALLALA SIOUX WAR CHIEF ... 175

JIM BRIDGER – "THE GRAND OLD MAN OF THE ROCKIES" ... 205

AFTERWORD ... 253

INDEX ... 267

Illustrations, Volume II

JOHN M. BOZEMAN, THE PATHFINDER OF THE BOZEMAN
TRAIL . . . . *Frontispiece*

JOHN ("PORTUGEE") PHILLIPS 17

SERGEANT SAMUEL GIBSON 41
From a photograph taken at Camp Proctor, on the Yellowstone River, September, 1891

GENERAL HENRY B. CARRINGTON, U. S. A. . . . 41
From an original photograph, in possession of his son,
James B. Carrington, Esq.

WAGON BOX FIGHT, AUGUST 2, 1867 (PLAN) . . . 55
From original sketch by Sergeant Samuel Gibson, redrawn
by Grace Raymond Hebard

FORT C. F. SMITH, MONTANA TERRITORY, 1867 . . 112
From a sketch by Captain I. D'Isay, after drawing by Anton
Schonborn. The original is in possession of Captain John A.
Perry. It is reproduced here by courtesy of Charles N. Kessler,
Esq.

FORT RENO, DAKOTA TERRITORY, 1867 123
Reproduced from the original drawing by Anton Schonborn,
now in possession of Captain John A. Perry

FORT RENO (PLAN) 129
Prepared by Grace R. Hebard from information furnished by
A. B. Ostrander, Vie Willits Garber, F. G. Burnett, and Ed-
ward Parmelee

RUINS AT FORT C. F. SMITH, 1920 133

PART OF THE RESERVATION OF FORT C. F. SMITH (PLAN) 137
Redrawn by Grace R. Hebard from a map made January 27,
1881, by Captain Edward L. Hartz, secured through the
courtesy of Senator F. E. Warren

FORT C. F. SMITH (PLAN) 141
Drawn by Grace R. Hebard from information furnished
by Vie Willits Garber, and F. G. Burnett

HAY FIELD FIGHT, AUGUST 1, 1867 (PLAN) . . . 163
Prepared by Grace R. Hebard from data furnished by F. G.
Burnett

CAPTAIN JAMES H. COOK, IN SCOUTING RIG, 1879 . . 183

CHIEF RED CLOUD AT THE AGE OF 75 201
    From a copyrighted photograph by D. F. Barry

JIM BRIDGER – "THE GRAND OLD MAN OF THE ROCKIES" . 207

THE SUTLER'S OLD ADOBE STORE AT FORT LARAMIE . . 255

MAP

THE BOZEMAN TRAIL . . . . . . x–xi

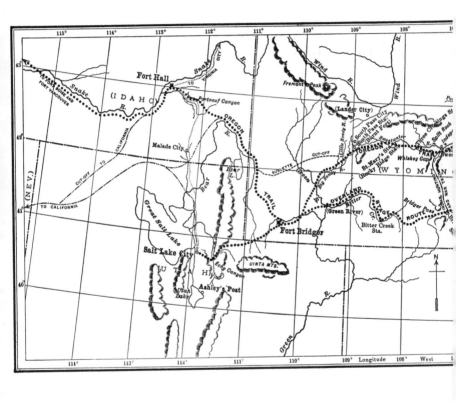

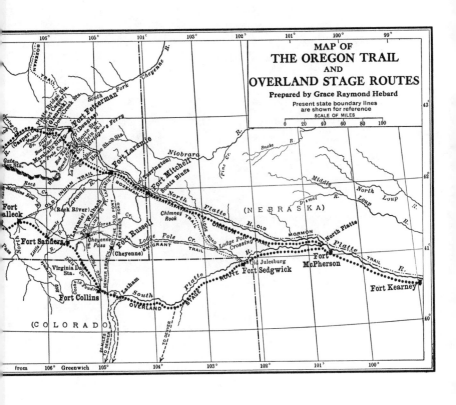

MAP OF
THE OREGON TRAIL
AND
OVERLAND STAGE ROUTES

Prepared by Grace Raymond Hebard

Present state boundary lines
are shown for reference

SCALE OF MILES

0   20   40   60   80   100

(N E B R A S K A)

(C O L O R A D O)

Fort Halleck

Fort Sanders

Fort Collins

Virginia Dale Sta.

Fort Russell

(Cheyenne)

Fort Laramie

Fort Fetterman

Fort Mitchell

Scotts Bluff

Chimney Rock

Fort Sedgwick

Old Julesburg

Fort McPherson

Fort Kearney

North Platte

Niobrara

Bridger's Ferry

Horse Shoe Sta.

Torrington

OREGON TRAIL

MORMON TRAIL

LODGE POLE TRAIL

OVERLAND STAGE ROUTE

SOUTH OVERLAND STAGE

OLD INDIAN TRAIL

BOZEMAN TRAIL

Lodge Pole Cr.

North Platte R.

South Platte R.

Snake R.

Pine Cr.

Middle Loup R.

North Loup R.

Cheyenne R.

South Fork

Dismal R.

TO DENVER

from   106°   Greenwich   105°

Introduction to the Bison Book Edition
By John D. McDermott

As might be expected, in the seven decades since the publication of Volume II of *The Bozeman Trail* other scholars have added a great deal to our knowledge of the period and its dramatic events. For example, we now have Cecil Alter's two biographies of Jim Bridger for reference.[1] In *Indian Fights: New Facts on Seven Encounters,* published in 1966, J. W. Vaughn pioneered in utilizing archaeological evidence in discussing the Fetterman and Hayfield Fights.[2] But perhaps the greatest advances have been in the results of research dealing with the Indian side of the conflict. The volumes by George Hyde and the more recent work of James C. Olson on Red Cloud give balance to the story, and anthropological writings by George Bird Grinnell, Royal Hassrick, Robert Lowie, and many others help us to understand Indian motivation and perspectives.[3]

Although a product of its time, Volume II retains permanent value, since it is here that Hebard and Brininstool present much of the primary source material underpinning their previous narratives. The lasting worth of *The Bozeman Trail* depends primarily on the eyewitness accounts of Samuel Gibson, Max Littman, Frederic Claus, F. M. Fessenden, A. B. Ostrander, and Finn G. Burnett, who participated in the pivotal events of the 1866–68 period and possessed the ability to recapture the past through oral and written expression.

It is also in Volume II that the authors present the

story of of John "Portugee" Phillips, long lauded as the
savior of Fort Phil Kearny. Every schoolchild in Wyoming now knows how Phillips rode 236 miles in four
days, traveling only at night through subzero tempera-
tures, to interrupt the revelers at Fort Laramie and
supposedly send them rushing to the relief of the beleaguered command.

Although Phillips had been properly praised by
Margaret Carrington in *Absaraka* (1868) and by
Frances Carrington in *My Army Life on the Frontier*
(1910), it was Hebard and Brininstool who raised him
to near deification. "It was a ride," they wrote, "beside
which that of Paul Revere . . . was a mere summer's
day canter." In a dramatic passage, the authors bring
the tale to its heroic climax at an officers' ball at Fort
Laramie: "Phillips staggered into the room—a swaying, gigantic figure, swathed in a buffalo-skin overcoat,
with buffalo boots, gauntlets and cap. He was covered
with snow, and his beard trailed icicles. Gasping out
that he was a courier from Fort Phil Kearney, with important dispatches for the commanding officer, he
dropped senseless to the floor from the terrible privation, exposure and exertion which he had faced so
bravely."[4]

There were a few early deflators of the story, principally the telegrapher at Horse Shoe Station, John C.
Friend, who reported Phillips arriving on December
25 in the company of Daniel Dixon and "Captain" Bailey (see p. 21, this volume). While acknowledging this,
Hebard and Brininstool stress that Phillips made the
most dangerous part of his journey, from Fort Phil
Kearny to Fort Reno, "absolutely unaccompanied." (p.
33, this volume).

However, they were mistaken. When he visited

Sheridan, Wyoming, in 1908 to participate in ceremonies dedicating the monument on Fetterman Battlefield, Henry Carrington brought with him a copy of a history of his service at Fort Phil Kearny, a vindication in typescript resembling a lawyer's brief. On page seven appears this entry: "A citizen, John Phillips, with one of my own horses and his intimate companion, supposed to be a half-breed, volunteered to risk all danger, and they left the postern gate behind my Headquarters that night."[5] In his testimony before a Special Commission in March 1867, Carrington stated that he had hired two men to carry dispatches the evening of December 21, and quartermaster records show that Phillips and Daniel Dixon were so employed on that day.[6] In his annual report for June 30, 1867, Quartermaster George B. Dandy stated that in the early hours of December 23 two couriers from Phil Kearny arrived at Fort Reno in exhausted condition, having been traveling all night in the mountains.[7]

Although Phillips did not ride alone, he was certainly of the stuff from which heroes are made, and the fact that his friend also made the ride ought not to deprecate the remarkable feat but rather raise Dixon to adulation and respect. Furthermore, the records of the Mountain District for 1867 contain a letter written by Phillips to Quartermaster George B. Dandy on May 16 describing a journey from Fort Laramie to Fort Phil Kearny that adds to his heroic stature. One morning in mid-April when he found his mule missing, Phillips went out alone looking for it. Suddenly, he found himself surrounded by fifteen Sioux in war paint. With humorous self-deprecation that was typical of him, he wrote that he escaped, but "without the aid of my faithful horse, and a good revolver, [I] would have lost my hair, the part of my body I feel most anxious about on the prairies."[8]

Perhaps the most interesting eyewitness account in this volume is that of Finn Burnett, an employee of the post sutler, who participated in the so-called Hayfield Fight of August 1, 1867, not far from Fort C. F. Smith, the most northerly of the Bozeman Trail forts. In this particular case, Hebard and Brininstool tampered with the original document prepared by Burnett. In it, the frontiersman had given the name of the fort's commander, Lt. Col. Luther P. Bradley, whom he accused of cowardice for not sending troops immediately to relieve the men under attack. In the 1960 reprint of *The Bozeman Trail* by the Arthur H. Clark Company, the publisher printed an excerpt of a letter from E. A. Brininstool that explained what had happened. "General King told me personally," he wrote, "that it was a forbidden topic in army circles (for the plain reason that the commander, Gen. Bradley, played the coward in refusing to allow a relief party to leave the fort to aid the nineteen men in the hayfield)." Brininstool stated that he had been asked by King not to mention Bradley's name because they had always been close friends, so he had withheld it. "Burnett insisted that I flay Bradley good and hard and give the public his name," Brininstool wrote, "but we both (Dr. Hebard and myself) decided not to do it" (see p. 174, this volume).

In 1927 Burnett wrote a letter to Clarence Reckmeyer in which he told of another damning incident not included in the version published in this volume. Repeating that Bradley had denied Captain Hartz's request to lead a force to the rescue and ordered everyone inside the fort, Burnett revealed that the group had sent the post commander this message via a soldier courier: "We have three dead and five wounded. We will be unable to defend the corral after dark if you are *a man send us relief, if you are a Devil Go to Hell where you ought to be.*" D. A. Colvin, who had assumed command after Lieutenant Sternberg's death and the wounding of Sergeant Horton, was the author of the note, which he wrote on the leaf of a small day book with a sharpened bullet from a .44 caliber Henry cartridge. It was this message, according to Burnett, that finally caused Bradley to send the relief column.[9] Most recent scholarship agrees that Bradley was aware of the plight of the nineteen about 1 p.m. and that he had ample numbers of men to effect a rescue.[10]

In their concluding essay, Hebard and Brininstool describe the contemporary scene, noting how little the landscape had changed in five decades since Red Cloud and his warriors met in combat with the officers and men of the frontier army. The site of Fort Phil Kearny was a productive alfalfa field, but the site of Fort Reno remained nearly as it was in the 1860s, "an open unpeopled territory," cattle herds enjoying the sun-cured grass as did the buffalo of yore (p. 262, this volume).

Although nearly seven decades have passed since the publication of *The Bozeman Trail*, the description of the route by Hebard and Brininstool still fits in many respects. Interstate Highways 90 and 26 cut through the foothills of the Big Horns, paralleling the Bozeman Trail at times, and ranch roads wander thither and yon in the rolling grassland, but the region still retains much of its nineteenth-century integrity. In 1893 historian Frederick Jackson Turner reported that the U. S. Census Bureau could no longer trace a line on the map showing a continuous frontier, defined as an area inhabited by less than two people per square mile. In 1990, Johnson County, Wyoming, still meets Turner's definition of the frontier, most of its sparse population centered in Buffalo and its many acres of prairie seen only by a few. The site of Fort Reno, so peacefully isolated in 1922, remains remote and undisturbed, watched over by Pumpkin Buttes and preserved in public ownership for posterity.

The state of Wyoming now controls the site of Fort Phil Kearny, much of Fetterman Battlefield, and an acre of the Wagon Box Fight Site. A nonprofit organization, the Fort Phil Kearny/Bozeman Trail Association donated a building for a museum at Fort Phil Kearny and is in the process of acquiring another nineteen acres of land at the Wagon Box Fight Site. In 1989 nine little-known properties important in the Bozeman Trail story were entered in the National Register of Historic Places and identified so that they might not be harmed through ignorance or heedless federal action. A matching grant from the Peter Kiewit Foundation will make archaeological investigation possible, and an appropriation from the Wyoming legislature will support a plan for a regional museum in Buffalo.

Consequently, on the eve of the 125th anniversary of the fortification of the Bozeman Trail, the memory of the past lingers. Most important, the story now about to be commemorated is a two-sided one, and planning for forthcoming events involves relatives of soldiers who served in the frontier army, descendants of the Plains Indian warriors who fought there, and historians of both races who strive for understanding and appreciation of differing views and cultures.

The soldier and civilian accounts found in *The Boze-*

man Trail provide the data needed to assist in interpretation and planning of new developments and commemorative events. In these stories, we learn the views of those who stood on the front line—of the common soldier and civilian laborer—whose opinions often differed from those in command and whose insights give us a more balanced perspective of the difficulties and risks of life on the frontier at midcentury. Therein, *The Bozeman Trail* retains its freshness and keeps its place in western historiography.

NOTES

1. Cecil Alter, *James Bridger, Trapper, Frontiersman, Scout and Guide* (Salt Lake City, 1925) and *Jim Bridger* (Norman: University of Oklahoma Press, 1962).

2. J. W. Vaughn, *Indian Fights: New Fights on Seven Encounters* (Norman: University of Oklahoma Press, 1966).

3. George Hyde, *Red Cloud's Folk: A History of the Oglala Sioux Indians* (Norman: University of Oklahoma Press, 1937) and *Spotted Tail's Folk: A History of the Brule Sioux* (Norman: University of Oklahoma Press, 1961); James C. Olson, *Red Cloud and the Sioux Problem* (Lincoln: University of Nebraska Press, 1965); Royal Hassrick, *The Sioux: Life and Customs of a Warrior Society* (Norman: University of Oklahoma Press, 1964); George Bird Grinnell, *The Cheyenne Indians: Their History and Ways of Life*, 2 vols. (New Haven: Yale University Press, 1923) [Bison Book reprint 1972]; Robert Lowie, *Crow Indians* (New York: Holt, Rinehart and Winston, 1935).

4. See pp. 23–24, this volume. Capt. David S. Gordon who witnessed Phillips's entrance did not mention a collapse. See "The Relief of Fort Phil Kearny," *Journal of the Military Service Institution of the United States* 48 (September–October 1911): p. 281.

5. Carrington, "Wyoming Opened," unpublished ms, Sheridan County Fulmer Public Library, Sheridan, Wyoming, p. 7.

6. "Testimony of Henry B. Carrington," Fort McPherson, March, 1867, p. 238, Records of the Special Commission to Investigate the Fetterman Massacre and the State of Indian Affairs, 1867," Records of the Bureau of Indian Affairs Record Group 75, National Archives; Robert A. Murray, "The John "Portugee"

Phillips Legend, A Study in Wyoming Folklore," *Annals of Wyoming* 40 (April 1968), reprinted in Murray, *The Army on the Powder River* (Bellevue, Nebr.: The Old Army Press, 1969), p. 15.

7. George B. Dandy, "Annual Report, June 30, 1867," Records of the Office of the Quartermaster General, Record Group 94, National Archives.

8. Letter from Phillips to Quartermaster George B. Dandy, Fort Laramie, May 16, 1867, Letters Received, Records of the Mountain District, Record Group 393, National Archives. The writer recently discovered these long-thought-lost records misfiled under "Kansas Area."

9. Letter to Clarence Reckmeyer, Ennis, Texas, May 1, 1927, Wagon Box Fight File In2-bat-wb, American Heritage Center, Laramie, Wyo. In 1937, the Arthur H. Clark Company published *Finn Burnett, Frontiersman* by Robert B. David, in which the story of the letter and the feelings toward Bradley were included. See David, *Finn Burnett, Frontiersman* (Glendale, Calif.: Arthur H. Clark Co., 1937), p. 189.

10. Jerome E. Greene, "The Hayfield Fight: A Reappraisal of a Neglected Action," *Montana* 22 (Autumn 1972): p. 11. Reprinted by the Big Horn Canyon Natural History Association, Fort Smith, Montana, n.d., p. 11.

Introduction by General King

My first look at the Powder River was in the heat and glare of a July morning, in the fateful summer of '76. Custer and nearly half his regiment had been annihilated only a long day's march "as the crow flies" beyond that other fateful field where, ten years earlier, Fetterman and his men had been surrounded and slowly massacred. "Covering the hills like a red cloud" the warriors of Makh-pi-ya-luta had swarmed about the hated soldiery, and there was left no white man to tell the tale.

The folly of going after Indian braves in unknown numbers, with forces both unskilled and inadequate, having been thrice demonstrated, our leaders stopped to think. Within three months, and three days' march, of the scene where Red Cloud had earlier taught us the first lesson, Reynolds, Crook, and Custer had successively met defeat or death. Crook, realizing conditions, fell back upon his entrenched camp in the northeast foothills of the Big Horn and sent for reinforcements. We were the reinforcements.

The Fifth Cavalry had then never encountered Red Cloud. We were on terms of comradeship with his great rival, Spotted Tail, chief of the Brulé band. We came freighted with anything but favorable impressions of the chief who had so defiantly parted from the Great Father's representatives in '66, and had so contemptuously dealt with their successors at Fort Robinson in '75. We knew when we forded the Platte at Fetterman that Red Cloud had given fair warning ten years earlier that he would kill every white man who ventured to invade his hunting grounds beyond Cantonment Reno, and we were now beyond. We knew that he was not present in person the blistering Sunday morning six weeks earlier, on which Custer had dared to attack an Indian village six miles in length. Between the outspoken leader of the Ogallalas and the sly, scheming politician who headed the Uncpapas, and through them the young men of the six confederated tribes, there could never be alliance or accord. Red Cloud, the soldier, Sitting Bull, the schemer, were chiefs of totally different mould, though we had not then the appreciation of Red Cloud's virtues that came with long later years.

We knew him only as the inspiration of the most brilliant and daring battles the Sioux had fought, and as the trainer of so many of the young warriors who had gone to swell the ranks of Sitting Bull. We remembered his warning as we dismounted to bivouac for the night on the banks of this ash-colored, turbid, sluggish stream. We were choked with alkali dust and faint with heat, and we gazed with longing, burning eyes on the snow-clad summits far to the west where Cloud Peak towered above the fir-crested heights of the Big Horn. We again recalled it when, three days later, we drew rein and gazed at the palisaded ruin of little Fort Phil Kearney, and pictured, silently, the scene within those wooden walls where the puny garrison and the affrighted, trembling women and children listened, appalled, to the crash of musketry, a mile away to the west, where, beyond that screening ridge, the pitiable force sent out to drive away skulking Indians who were annoying their wood choppers, found themselves presently hemmed in by countless hordes. Oh, well for those poor women that Carrington, post commander, refused to listen to the few hot-heads who urged him to send forth his remaining companies to the support of Fetterman! That would have inevitably led to the massacre of the last man – to the martyrdom of the last woman. We spent ten weeks that summer hunting those red warriors over the prairies of Wyoming, Montana, and the Dakotas, finding them once in such force at Slim Buttes, in September, that we were glad to get away with their pony herd and a handful of prisoners. We "went through the motions," as soldiers say, of deposing Red Cloud from his high estate and designating "Old Spot" to reign in his stead as chieftain of the whole Sioux nation, but it was *"brutum fulmen."* In the hearts of his tribesmen Red Cloud lived and reigned long years thereafter, while Spotted Tail died at the hands of the assassin.

Before ever the ghost dance craze of 1890 brought about the last of the Indian wars, we had begun to realize the truth of the adage that, red or white, you could not keep a good man down. There were fellow men whose character was beyond reproach, whose word was truth itself, and whose experience and knowledge none of our number could question, and of such was Captain "Jim" Cook, the chosen associate, guide and scout of such soldiers as Generals (S. S.) Sumner and Fountain in the trying Geronimo campaigns of the mid eighties. Time was, in the old days of '75 and '76, we left Fort Laramie at daybreak and marched away east by north, over the rolling divide, bound for the Sioux reservation, with a parting glance at Laramie Peak sinking toward the horizon in our wake, and Rawhide Butte at long intervals peeping warily at us from the north of west, and along in the afternoon we would bivouac on the treeless banks of the Niobrara. Something less than a mile away eastward a conical, mound-like butte overlooked the country in every direction, and thither, under careful guard, would go our signal officer and men, while the troop horses and pack mules, shed of their burdens, rolled and kicked on the scanty turf. Look whithersoever you would, in those days, not a sign of foliage was in sight, not even the cottonwood. But, forty-three years thereafter, I rode, one August morning, into a veritable oasis, a bower of beautiful foliage, of shaded vistas and softened lights, where all had been bare and almost barren. Now, soft green turf, vine-clad arbor, rippling streamlets and a modern homestead marked the spot where so often we rolled in our blankets for a night's rest under the summer stars, and not until I had climbed that signal height and gazed over miles and miles of bare ridge and divide, of broad and shrubless valley, could I realize the truth. There were the old landmarks, Laramie Peak dimly visible in the far southwest, Rawhide Butte, storm-scarred and hoary, twenty miles away to the west. Tumbling waves of wind-swept uplands stretched from horizon to horizon, east, west, and north, broken only on the northward skyline by jagged sawteeth—"Inyan Kara" and the kindred cliffs of the Black Hills of Dakota—the Black Hills old Red Cloud would have died to keep, if he could, forever free from the intruding paleface.

And that evening, with all the comforts of home about us, with a fine portrait of old Red Cloud himself, and with many of his prized belongings, in the heart of the family circle, we sat for hours and listened to Captain Cook's story of his years among the Indians, his long intimacy with Red Cloud and his deliberately-formed conception of the old chieftain's actual character. If there were any among us who had come to scoff, they remained to pray.

We heard at last the Red Cloud side of the long controversy. And those of us who had served under, and honored, General Crook—"Wichahnpi Yamoni" as the Sioux called him, not "Gray Fox," as the newspapers had it—wished that he, too, could have known the truth, both as to Red Cloud and to that fierce, untamable but most gallant warrior, Crazy Horse. Crook was the last man to permit injustice to the Indian.

The story of the old Bozeman Road around the Big Horn and through Indian Fairy Land is or was "a tale that is told." The sorrows and sacrifices of the army ordered to hold and defend it, our people have long forgotten, if indeed they ever knew. Solemnly had Red Cloud given his word and warning. It was scoffed at by the powers at Washington, and the army paid with its lifeblood for the blunders of the Interior Department. In the thankless duty to which so many of my comrades gave their last full measure of devotion, there was neither honor nor glory. It meant death, perhaps by torture, if a battle went against us, and unlimited abuse at the hands of the Eastern press and pacifists if the victory were ours. It involved more peril, privation and hardship than did service in the Civil War, and yet, for years, our senators, in Congress assembled, refused to confer brevets bestowed for bravery, on the ground that it was *not* warfare! We were the pioneers of civilization, the defense of the emigrant and settler, the real agency that made possible the development of a continent, yet, east of the Mississippi we had hardly a defender.

In the ten years of profound peace enjoyed by the nation after the final muster-out of the last volunteers of the Civil War, we, the regulars, lost scores of officers and hundreds of men in battle to the death with our red wards. It is comfort to know that there are those in civil life who, even in their sympathy for the cause of the Indian, have learned to estimate at something like its true worth the service rendered to the people of the United States by, and the sacrifices demanded of, their little army of the old frontier, especially along that line of battle and humiliation, the Bozeman Trail by way of Powder River.

CHARLES KING
Brig.-General, U. S. V.

August, 1921

John Phillips, a Hero of Fort Phil Kearney

If ever a roll of honor is made of the unnumbered heroes of the great American Western Frontier who performed deeds of valor without thought of recompense or reward, but whose sole thought was "duty," prompted by the necessity for instant action, that the lives of others might be saved, the name of John ("Portugee") Phillips should be written high on the scroll of fame. For lofty self-devotion and sacrifice it stands unparalleled, and for bravery and physical endurance has seldom, if ever, been equaled. And this is the story of "Portugee" Phillips' courageous deed:

The Fetterman disaster of December 21, 1866, had dropped like a thunderbolt on the little garrison at Fort Phil Kearney. Eighty-one men from the "hated fort on the Little Piney" had fallen victims to Red Cloud's strategic cunning in less than a brief half-hour of combat. Glutted and drunken with their bloody victory over Fetterman's command, the triumphant Sioux now felt that it would be a matter of hours only before the balance of the already-depleted force behind the log stockade would be in their power. And doubtless nothing but the awful, yet providential, severity of the weather prevented this.

The night of December 21st, the weather became unprecedented in its Arctic-like fierceness, as if to add to the horror of the great tragedy. The temperature dropped to more than twenty-five degrees below zero, and a terrible blizzard swept down from the Big Horn Mountains, while the swirling snow piled high about the log stockade, as the winds howled and shrieked in wild glee. So heavy was the snowfall that it was necessary to keep a continual force of men shoveling away the huge drifts that formed against the stockade, least it should pile so high as to form a foundation over which the Indians might easily climb the log barricade. So intense was the cold that it was necessary to relieve the sentries every fifteen minutes. Even then, many of the soldiers were badly frost-bitten.

The situation of the little garrison was desperate indeed. None knew at what moment Red Cloud's exultant savages might descend in swarms upon the stricken post. It was a question whether they would attack the fort, or if they would consider that, by the overwhelming of Fetterman's brave men, their thirst for blood had been satiated for the time. In any event, relief was urgent and of the greatest necessity, if Fort Phil Kearney was to be expected to defy the Sioux hordes and maintain its position as one of the defenses of the Bozeman Trail.

In all the quarters lights were burning, in anticipation of an attack at any moment. There was no sleep for anyone. There were many women and helpless children at Fort Phil Kearney that awful night to protect, and the total defensive force at the post had now been reduced to but one hundred and nineteen, including all civilian employes. Outside were three thousand exultant Sioux warriors, only waiting for the opportune moment to finish their bloody work.

The nearest point from which relief could be had was Fort Laramie, two hundred and thirty-six miles

John ("Portugee") Phillips

southeast. Where was the man brave enough to attempt to slip through the Sioux cordon in such an hour of peril and in such Arctic weather? Capture could mean but one fate – death by torture in its most agonizing form. Men looked at one another in helpless dismay. The emergency arose; the man appeared.

Colonel Carrington had made known to all the desperate plight of his little handful of men, women and children. Impressed by the gravity of the situation, John Phillips – better known to everyone in the Powder River country simply as "Portugee" Phillips, a brave frontiersman in the employ of the post quartermaster, stepped into the breach and voluntarily offered to attempt to break through the Sioux lines on horseback and ride to Fort Laramie for the sorely-needed relief. It was a ride beside which that of Paul Revere – lauded in song and story – was a mere summer's day canter. Phillips scorned the idea of remuneration for his services on this dangerous mission, but stipulated that in making the attempt he be allowed to use the fastest and best horse at the post – a thoroughbred belonging to Colonel Carrington himself. This request was immediately granted by the commander.

Among the women at Fort Phil Kearney was the young wife of Lieutenant George W. Grummond. The lieutenant had been numbered with the Fetterman victims. She was utterly prostrated with grief over the awful death of her husband, who had, on the sixth of the same month, barely escaped with his life in a desperate encounter with the Indians. While the beleaguered garrison-folk were talking in whispers of their dangerous situation, and speculating as to the outcome, "Portugee" Phillips knocked at the door of the quarters occupied by Mrs. Grummond and asked to see the

bereaved woman, to whom he was an utter stranger.
Over his arm he carried a choice wolf-robe which he
had long cherished. He said to Mrs. Grummond:
"For your sake I am going to attempt to bring relief
from Laramie. I may not get through the Indian lines,
but in case I fail, I want you to keep this robe as a
slight remembrance of me."

While Phillips was preparing for his dangerous ride,
Colonel Carrington penned the following dispatch:

FORT PHIL KEARNEY, D.T., Dec. 21, 1866 – (By courier
to Fort Laramie) – Do send me reinforcements forthwith.
Expedition now with my force is impossible. I risk everything but the post and its store. I venture as much as anyone
can, but I have had a fight today unexampled in Indian warfare.
My loss is ninety-four (81) killed. I have recovered forty-
nine bodies and thirty-two more are to be brought in in the
morning that have been found. Among the killed are Brevet
Lieutenant-Colonel Fetterman, Captain F. H. Brown, and
Lieutenant Grummond.

The Indians engaged were nearly three thousand, being
apparently the force reported as on Tongue River in my dispatches of the 5th of November and subsequent thereto. This
line, so important, can and must be held. It will take four
times the force in the spring to reopen if it be broken up this
winter. I hear nothing of my arms that left Fort Leavenworth September 15; additional cavalry ordered to join have
not reported their arrival; would have saved us much loss today; the Indians lost beyond all precedent; I need prompt
reinforcements and repeating arms. I am sure to have, as
before reported, an active winter, and must have men and arms;
every officer of this battalion should join it today. I have
every teamster on duty, and, at best, one hundred and nineteen
left at the post. I hardly need urge this matter; it speaks for
itself. Give me two companies of cavalry, at least, forthwith,
well armed, or four companies of infantry, exclusive of what I
need at Reno and Fort Smith. I did not overestimate my early
application; a single company, promptly, will save the line;
but our killed show that any remissness will result in mutila-

tion and butchery beyond precedent. No such mutilation as that today on record. Depend on it that this post will be held so long as a round or a man is left. Promptness is the vital thing. Give me officers and men. Only the new Spencer arms should be sent. The Indians desperate and they spare none.

HENRY B. CARRINGTON,
Colonel Eighteenth Infantry, commanding.

It was expected that Phillips would file and send these dispatches at Horseshoe Station, a good three days' ride from Fort Phil Kearney, where was situated the first available telegraph station between Phil Kearney and Fort Laramie. It was near midnight when Phillips, after looking to his arms and equipment, and stowing away in his saddlebags supplies of biscuit only, with a scant amount of feed for his horse, reported to Colonel Carrington that he was ready to start. He shook the commander's hand, mounted his horse, and the colonel himself unbarred and opened the sally-port gate, out of which horse and rider slipped into the midnight storm, followed by the God-speed of every person who witnessed his departure, to face expected perils which would appall the stoutest heart. Those inside the stockade listened intently for some time, momentarily expecting to hear the dreaded war-whoop, which would indicate that the brave courier had been detected leaving the fort, but only the roar of the blizzard was to be heard.

John C. Friend, now of Rawlins, Wyoming, was, in 1866, the telegraph operator at Horseshoe Station, where Phillips arrived at 10 a.m., on Christmas day. Mr. Friend states, in communication to the authors, that Phillips arrived at Horseshoe Station in company with two men – George Dillon and a Captain Bailey.[96]

[96] Bailey was leading a company of fifty miners who were operating in the vicinity of Fort Phil Kearney.

If Phillips had company on the route, it must have been after he had reached and passed Fort Reno, as it is certain that he passed through Reno *absolutely alone*. From Reno to Fort Laramie was the least dangerous part of the entire trip. Mr. Friend does not state where Phillips picked up the two men who rode into Horseshoe Station with him. Neither has it ever been stated if these two men accompanied the courier from Horseshoe Station to Fort Laramie. Mr. Friend states in his correspondence with the authors that Phillips filed two dispatches with him—one to the department commander at Omaha, and one to the post commander at Fort Laramie, and then continued on his way to Fort Laramie. The probability that Phillips had company along this route is not disputed, but that he left Fort Phil Kearney alone and rode the greater—and by far the most dangerous—part of the route alone is certain. The statement of A. B. Ostrander, further along in this chapter, and his conversation with John C. Brough, who was on guard duty at the gate through which John Phillips passed *alone* from Fort Phil Kearney, are unmistakable evidence that Phillips started absolutely unaccompanied.

Captain James H. Cook, of Agate, Sioux Co., Nebraska, whose entire life was spent on the frontier and among Indians, as a scout, guide and trailer, and who now owns and operates an extensive cattle ranch on the Niobrara River, also knew Phillips intimately. Capt. Cook has informed the authors that Phillips located a ranch on the Chugwater, some forty miles from his place, in the '70's. He has talked many times with Phillips about the ride to Fort Laramie, and states that Phillips never made any mention to him of having companions anywhere along the route. He says the courier related to him that just before he reached Horseshoe Station he was pursued by quite a large band of Indians, mounted on ponies, but that with the superb charger belonging to Colonel Carrington, which he was riding, he was enabled to outdistance the savages and gain a high hill, where he stood the Indians off, they not venturing to charge up the hill after him. Phillips said he stayed on the hill all night alone, keeping a constant lookout against surprise, ready to mount and flee at a moment's notice, but that with the first streaks of day he "made a run for it" passing through the Indian lines in safety, and soon reaching Horseshoe Station.

Phillips further told Capt. Cook that after leaving the fort, on the night of December 21st, he "steered clear of the trail," riding parallel to it at some little distance, as he realized it would be closely watched by the Indians. He made no attempt to pursue his journey in the daytime, well knowing he would be discovered by some of the keen-eyed savages who swarmed the country. Before daylight had fully appeared, Phillips would ride into a thicket where he could not be observed, and there spend the day, resuming his ride as soon as darkness had fully set in.

It was about eleven o'clock on Christmas night, December 25th, when Phillips arrived at Fort Laramie. The mercury was standing at twenty-five degrees below zero, and a brilliant Christmas levee was in full swing at "Bedlam," the large building at the post used as the officers' clubhouse, where all the dances and gay festivities were held. Phillips staggered into the room – a swaying, gigantic figure, swathed in a buffalo-skin overcoat, with buffalo boots, gauntlets and cap. He was covered with snow, and his beard trailed icicles. Gasping out that he was a courier from Fort Phil Kearney, with important dispatches for the commanding officer, he dropped senseless to the floor from the terrible privation, exposure and exertion which he had faced so bravely. The faithful horse which had carried him in safety through two hundred and thirty-six miles of zero weather, already was lying dead out on the parade ground, where the exhausted animal had dropped the moment Phillips reeled from the saddle.

"Portugee" Phillips placed no financial obligation upon the service which he had rendered. Even had the ride been made in moderate weather it was a feat which would stand unrivaled for heroic self-sacrifice to duty, but to ride two hundred and thirty-six miles through deep snow in zero weather, in the face of a blinding blizzard, and with thousands of savage enemies eager for his scalp; with no food but a pocketful of hard biscuit, was an act which calls for the highest possible praise and commendation.

A few lines about this brave man are worth remembering. John Hunton writes the authors that Phillips told him he was born and raised on the island of Fayal, and that his parents were Portugese. He first landed in America on the Pacific coast, later working his way eastward with a party of prospectors. During the summer of 1866 Phillips, with a party of four or five others, had arrived at Fort Phil Kearney, where all were there employed part of the time by contractors and the post quartermaster. During the forenoon of December 21st, when Captain Fetterman and his command left the post to go to the relief of the beseiged wood train, Phillips was engaged in driving a team attached to a water-wagon, presumably hauling water to be used at the fort. Two of the men who had arrived at the fort with him that summer, went out with the Fetterman party that ill-fated morning to "have a little brush with the redskins," and both were killed.

Phillips died in Cheyenne, November 18, 1883, aged fifty-one years. After his death, his widow lived on Laramie River, twelve miles west of Fort Laramie. It was thirty-two years after Phillips made his famous ride before the government – always tardy in its awards in an Indian campaign – took official recognition of this heroic act. About 1899 Senator F. E. Warren and Congressman F. W. Mondell succeeded in obtaining a compensation of five thousand dollars for Mrs. Phillips, as a partial recognition of the services of her husband on this hazardous ride, and as a settlement of claims for horses and cattle belonging to him which were shot or run off by Sioux and Cheyenne Indians, the savages ever holding a grievance against Phillips for slipping through their lines on the night of December 21, 1866, and bringing relief to the Fort Phil Kearney garrison. He was, in consequence, continually harrassed, hunted and persecuted by these tribes.

The following government report sets forth the claims of Mrs. Phillips:

. . . The bill proposes to pay for certain valuable services rendered by John Phillips in 1866, in rescuing the garrison at Fort Phil Kearney, and also a full settlement of claims against the government amounting to five thousand seven hundred and eighty-five dollars, for oxen, mules and horses taken from said Phillips while engaged in hauling wood for the government at Fort Fetterman in 1872. A part of this amount was allowed as an Indian depredation claim, passed upon by the Secretary of the Interior, and reported to Congress in 1874, and afterward passed favorably upon by the Court of Claims, but not paid because of a technicality regarding Mr. Phillips' naturalization papers.

The Committee on War Claims of the House of Representatives in the Fifty-fourth Congress, recommended the passage of a bill precisely similar to this bill, and we copy the following from the House report:

House Report No. 1913, Fifty-fourth Congress, First Session

. . . In all the annals of heroism in the face of unusual dangers and difficulties on the American frontier, or in the world, there are few that can excel in gallantry, in heroism, in devotion, in self-sacrifice and patriotism, the ride made by John Phillips from Fort Phil Kearney, in December, 1866, to Fort Laramie, carrying dispatches which gave the first intelligence to the outside world of the terrible massacre near the former post, and which saved the lives of the people garrisoned there – men, women and children – by starting reinforcements to their relief. On the 21st of December, 1866, Fort Phil Kearney, commanded by Col. Henry B. Carrington, under the shadow of the Big Horn Mountains, over two hundred miles from the nearest telegraph line, was the extreme outpost in that part of the northwest. The savage Sioux, under Red Cloud, had been hovering in the vicinity of the post for some time, and had been last seen in large numbers on Tongue River, northeast of the fort.

On the 21st of December the Indians made an attack upon the wood train a few miles north (west) of the fort. A detachment of troops under the command of Brevet Lieutenant-Colonel Fetterman, including two other officers and seventy-eight men, and a number of civilians, made a dash from the fort for the purpose of protecting the wood train. When some four miles from the fort they were surrounded by the Indians in overwhelming numbers, and every man of the detachment was killed. The heroism of their struggle for life can never be told, but the terrible slaughter which has since been confessed by the Indians of their braves, and the fact that the troops were only killed after their ammunition was exhausted, speaks eloquently of the horrible and bloody nature of the encounter. The triumphant and bloodthirsty Sioux, commanded by Red Cloud, and outnumbering the garrison by twenty to one, had then surrounded and entirely invested the fort. An attack was hourly expected. It was understood that if the

Indians were successful in taking the fort it mean death for the garrison and a worse fate for the women and children, who begged piteously to be placed in the powder house and blown up in the case of a successful attack by the Indians.

At this juncture, when brave men felt that the only possible hope for the garrison was in taking news of their beleaguerement to the nearest outside post, and not a soldier could be found who would brave the attempt to break through the savages and ride to the nearest outpost, a distance of two hundred and thirty-six miles, John Phillips, a scout and hunter, volunteered to take dispatches to Fort Laramie. Placing a few biscuits in his pocket, and tying to his saddle a small quantity of feed for his horse, he left the post at midnight on the night of the massacre and reached Fort Laramie with the dispatches five days later. The country across which he rode was absolutely uninhabited by white men, and the ground was covered with snow from three to five feet in depth; he had no food for himself or his horse, other than the meager amount he took with him, and it was necessary for him to travel entirely by night for fear of hostile Indians. The weather was exceedingly cold, the thermometer reaching twenty degrees below zero. When he delivered the dispatches at Fort Laramie, hardy frontiersman that he was, he fell in a dead faint. Immediately on receipt of the dispatches, troops were forwarded from Fort Laramie, and the garrison at Fort Phil Kearney was relieved. For this remarkable act of heroism John Phillips has never, in any way, been paid by the General Government, the only payment made him being the sum of three hundred dollars which was paid him for various scouting services.

In the years immediately following his heroic ride, John Phillips was employed in various capacities and engaged in business in connection with government posts, and he was continually hunted and harrassed by the Sioux, who always looked upon him as the man who had wrested from their grasp the garrison at Fort Phil Kearney. At one time he was lassoed by the Indians, in an attempt to capture him for the purpose of torture. At other times his cattle were shot down, undoubtedly through pure wantonness on the part of these Indian marauders. In 1872 John Phillips was engaged in hauling wood for the government at Fort Fetterman, when a band of Indians, supposed to be Ogalalla Sioux and Cheyennes, drove off and killed a considerable amount of stock belonging to him. The Sioux chief, Red Cloud, acknowledged this depredation, but insisted that the Indians belonged to another band than his. This claim was passed upon by the Court of Claims, and the evidence was overwhelming, including the evidence of army officers, Indian agents, special examiners and others, and the Court of Claims allowed and entered judgment for the sum of two thousand two hundred and ten dollars. (See House of Representatives Ex. Doc. No. 125, pp. 82 and 83, Forty-ninth Congress, first session.)

It subsequently transpired that at the time the above depredations occurred, John Phillips was not a fully naturalized citizen of the United States, and therefore the claim was not paid. As the court could not take into account the gallant and meritorious services to his country of this brave man, but could make its decision only on the finding of fact, the claim has never been recognized. Subsequently, John Phillips became a fully naturalized citizen of the United States. Broken in health by the exposure and strain of his long and perilous ride, he died in the prime of life, leaving a widow and child in straitened circumstances. There is no question but that John Phillips suffered from Indian depredations other than those at Fort Fetterman, which was passed upon by the Court of Claims, and that the Indians held a grudge against him for his action in saving the Fort Phil Kearney garrison.

The following affidavits, among those before the committee, relate to John Phillips' heroic ride:

Henry B. Carrington, United States Army, being duly sworn, makes oath and says: That on the 21st day of December, 1866, as colonel of the Eighteenth United States Infantry, and as commanding officer of the Rocky Mountain district, Military Department of the Platte, he found his whole district to be in a state of bitter warfare; that it became necessary to employ citizen scouts and messengers who were familiar with the country and with Indian methods.

That on the 21st of December, 1866, aforesaid, an action took place within six miles of Fort Philip Kearney, which post was his headquarters, in which, surprised by Red Cloud, a Sioux chief, and his band of overwhelming numbers, three officers and seventy-eight men were killed and mutilated in less than one hour; that several thousand Indians surrounded the post, rendering communication with Fort Laramie, the nearest post having troops at disposal, impracticable; that the garrison was so small that no troops could be sent back for assistance; that only by the utmost care, all troops being on guard constantly, supported by five pieces of artillery, was the post itself preserved intact; that ammunition had been reduced to less than twenty rounds per man, and neither officers nor men believed it possible to venture through the surrounding Indian forces for help with any hope of success.

At this juncture John Phillips, used to frontier life, the wiles of the Indians, and convinced that utter destruction awaited the command unless relief were promptly obtained, volunteered his services as dispatch bearer to Fort Laramie, two hundred and twenty-five (two hundred and thirty-six) miles distant, through a hostile country, absolutely without inhabitants or the possibility of aid or supplies en route. Confidential dispatches were intrusted to his care, with instructions how to meet emergencies, and during the night after the battle he started on his dangerous mission. Previous mail parties and another party of expert border scouts, which left later, were scalped and their bodies and the mails were found on the ground where they were overpowered.

Phillips, by riding nights and keeping under cover by day, safely reached a telegraph station forty miles from Fort Laramie, just before the Indians attacked and burned it, sent his dispatches, pushed on to Fort Laramie and found that his dispatches had been received and troops were preparing to go to the relief of the endangered garrison.

His heroism was without the promise of any special reward, but was executed with rare skill, patriotism and success. His mission practically rescued the whole country from Indian outrage and brought to that section immediate relief.

It is impossible to state more strongly the value of his services, which were never adequately requited: and affiant knows of no soldier of the Army whose services more absolutely demand recognition for the sake of the family than do those of the brave, modest, faithful John Phillips, since deceased, leaving his widow in a destitute condition.

The heroism of Phillips had a peculiarly tender and noble aspect. Lieutenant G. W. Grummond was among the massacred party, and his widow was the guest of the family of the affiant, and greatly overwhelmed with sorrow, while several other ladies with their families were exposed to the threatened attack. Mrs. Grummond several years later became the wife of the affiant, and her statement of particulars, specially within her knowledge, is furnished for information of those in authority and the consideration of Congress.

HENRY B. CARRINGTON, U.S.A.

Frances C. Carrington, resident of Hyde Park, state of Massachusetts, being duly sworn, makes oath and says:

That on the 21st day of December, 1866, her husband, Lieutenant George W. Grummond, of the Eighteenth United States Infantry, was killed in action with Sioux Indians near Fort Philip Kearney, in what is now the state of Wyoming; that she was the guest of General Carrington's family when all the troops were rallied for defense of the fort, and families were concentrated for convenience of defense; that during that terrible night, when an attack in overwhelming numbers was constantly expected, John Phillips called to express his sympathy with her; that, overcome by his interest in her condition and the imminent danger of all concerned, and weeping with sorrow over her loss, he said: 'If the general wishes I will go as messenger if it costs me my life.' He presented to affiant his wolf robe 'to remember him by if he was never heard of again.' His whole bearing was manly, brave, unselfish, self-sacrificing and beyond all praise. He had been respected by all the officers for the quiet courage he always exhibited, and was the only man of the garrison who realized the peril of the garrison to the extent of daring to expose his own life in the desperate attempt to cut through the savage hordes that surrounded us, with any faith in the success of such a mission. He left with the good wishes of all, and it is the smallest possible reward that Congress can offer to provide a suitable support for his widow in her lone and destitute condition.

FRANCES C. CARRINGTON.

"The name of John Phillips should be written among those heroic men the tales of whose heroism, devotion and patriotism illumined the story of savage warfare on our frontier. The committee believe that the Government does tardy justice to his memory in allowing this claim. It simply reimburses the widow for property actually lost, with a very slight recognition for the gallant and heroic services rendered."

That John Phillips stood high in the estimation of the "old-timers" of Wyoming is testified to from the action taken at the Old Pioneers' Meeting, following the death in November, 1883, of the Phil Kearney hero, when the following resolutions were adopted:

> WHEREAS, it is with unfeigned regret that we, the Old Pioneers of Wyoming, are called upon to follow to the grave the old time pioneer, scout and hero, John Phillips, who departed this life on Sunday, November 18, 1883, and
> WHEREAS, it is but fitting and proper that the Old Pioneers of Wyoming should attest to and pay a last tribute of respect to the memory of the hero, who rode a nobler ride than did Sheridan at Winchester, nearly twenty years ago, from Fort Phil Kearney to Fort Laramie to obtain assistance . . . in which ride he took his life in his hands, and . . . made his way through bands of hostile Indians . . . therefore, be it
> Resolved, that in the death of John Phillips the people of the far west have lost a true friend, and one who was ever in this life friendly to all the interests of the pioneers and settlers of this prosperous border-land, but which at the time of his advent here on the plains, was naught but Nature's unbroken solitude, disturbed only by the war cry of the Sioux and Arapahoes.
> Resolved further, that in the death of Mr. Phillips we have sustained an irreparable loss as a community, of one who has ever proved himself to be a true, honest, upright citizen, friend and neighbor.

This was followed by the following:

IN MEMORIAM JOHN PHILLIPS

A hero, I consider, has passed from our midst almost un-
heeded. Yes, he has even died in the field of his battles, but
not without victory. I suppose none have done more in this
vicinity to open the way for civilization, which so many of us
enjoy, as the deceased. A good many of the old settlers will
remember how often he has hazarded his life on many occasions on the frontier, from the Cache la Poudre to the con-
fines of Montana, and how he foiled the wily craftiness of the
red man, and secured succor to many who would have fallen
a prey to the savage. He played a very important part in the
drama of this country.

All honor, then, to the name of John Phillips! While
no costly monument marks the spot where he lies, and
there is nothing to perpetuate his gallant deed, his
name will ever be remembered in the history of the
western frontier and Indian warfare as the hero whose
pluck, endurance and bravery saved from annihilation
scores of men, women and children of the beleagured
garrison at Fort Phil Kearney.

A. B. OSTRANDER[97] ON JOHN PHILLIPS' RIDE

Some Interesting Information From a Strictly Authentic Source

At different times and in various items contained in
magazines and newspaper articles, I have read accounts
of the wonderful ride made by John Phillips from
Fort Phil Kearney to Fort Laramie the night of the
Fetterman disaster. In all of these accounts, while all
due credit seemed to be given him for his self-sacrificing act, yet every story contained a sentence or more
that would seem to convey the idea that to others also
should be given some credit for participation in that
historical performance.

[97] Former private, Twenty-seventh U. S. Infantry.

I have seen a letter written and autographed by John C. Friend, the telegraph operator at Horseshoe Station in 1866, who received and forwarded the message handed him by Phillips, in which are given the names of two men who arrived at that station with Phillips. I believe the statement to be true and correct in every detail.

In Coutant, *History of Wyoming,* volume i, page 578, appears the following:

> Daniel McUlvane . . . tells me that John Phillips did not make the ride from Fort Phil Kearney alone, and that there were five men in the party. He is certain of this, as he saw and talked with them when they reached Bridger's Ferry, and rode with them a considerable distance toward Fort Laramie.

I believe that Mr. McUlvane was honest in his statement, but I know that he was ignorant of all the facts.

The words "John Phillips did not make the ride from Fort Phil Kearney alone," should be qualified, for, as a matter of fact, he started *alone* and passed over all of the most dangerous territory *absolutely unaccompanied.*

The following is my authority for this statement:

In 1917 I attended the National Encampment of the Grand Army of the Republic in Boston, Mass., and met a comrade on the street with a sunflower on the lapel of his coat. As I had been a member of the Kansas Legislature in 1874 and '75, the insignia appealed to me, and I hailed him with:

"Hello, you old Jayhawker! My name is Ostrander; what's yours?"

He replied, "My name is John C. Brough. What do you want to know for?"

I said, "Did you ever know D. R. Anthony, Tom

Moonlight, Col. Jenison, Tip Fenlon, Col. Carpenter, Governor Tom Osborne and—"

He shut me off before I could finish the state directory and said, "Let's go in and sit down."

On a tete in the lobby of the Vendome, we compared notes, and finally G.A.R. matters came up, and he remarked, "I served three years in the Fifth Kansas Cavalry, and in 1866 I enlisted in the Second U.S. Cavalry and served three years more."

I answered, "I served three years in the Second Battalion Eighteenth U.S. Infantry, from 1864 to '67."

"You must have been at Fort Phil Kearney, then?" he queried, and then for several minutes we were climbing over each other, trying to get answer to "Did you know—" "Do you remember—" etc., etc. Finally he remarked, "You are the first and only man I ever met that was at Fort Phil Kearney when I was there. Let's lubricate."

We did. Then we commenced to talk all over again.

Finally he said, "Do you remember John Phillips?" and after I answered, "You bet I do, and talked with him often," he related to me the following story. I will use his own language as near as I can remember it:

The morning of the day of the Fetterman fight, I was detailed for guard duty, and so did not take any part in the main occurrence of that day, but at regular intervals was on post, and rested in the guardhouse during relief. After sundown I was posted at the 'water gate,' and given a short beat. Some time after dark the Sergeant of the Guard and two men approached, and after the usual challenge and replies, they leaned up against the gate and I continued to walk my beat.

Pretty soon we saw two men walking toward us, their heads close together, seemingly in earnest conversation, and one of them leading a horse. When they got within twenty or twenty-five feet, I put myself in position and prepared to challenge, when the sergeant said, 'Attention! It's the Commanding Officer.' General Carrington interrupted and said, 'Never mind, sergeant; open the gate.'

The sergeant unlocked the padlocks, and the two men pulled out the bars and pushed the gate open. In the meantime I stood in a position to obstruct their passage, when, in a low tone, the general gave the countersign.

I recovered arms, stepped back and stood at 'Present,' while the two walked forward to the opening.

They conversed for a minute or two, and finally one of them mounted the horse, which was restive and prancing around. The other man, General Carrington – he was Colonel Carrington then – reached up, took his hand and spoke a few words. I could not hear all he said, but did hear him say, 'May God help you.'

The horseman wheeled and started off on a trot. For about thirty seconds we could hear the hoof beats, and then they ceased. The general stood with his head bent one side, as if listening intently, and then straightening up, and speaking to no one in particular, said, 'Good! He has taken softer ground at the side of the trail.'

Turning back, he proceeded toward quarters. He was alone. Not even his personal orderly was with him. The two men closed the gates and put up the bars. The sergeant snapped the locks and went back toward the guardhouse, and I continued to walk my beat.

That man was *John Phillips,* and he went from Fort Phil Kearney *alone.*

Eliminating dates and hour in the night, because I have forgotten them, I will add:

As one of the headquarters clerks at Fort Reno, I slept in a bunk located in a room adjoining, and in the rear of the adjutant's office. It was against the wall and under a window of the building which was built about six or eight feet from the palisades comprising the stockade. The Bozeman Trail ran alongside that stockade, not over fifteen or twenty feet from my bunk.

The northeast bastion of the fort was not to exceed one hundred feet directly west, and I could hear, every night, the sentry call out the hours.

One night I heard the sentry yell, "Corporal of the guard, post number ——" (I have forgotten the number). At the same time there were hoof-beats and a shout. I could not distinguish the words but being in English I was immediately relieved from an Indian scare. In a few seconds I heard hoof beats passing along the trail at a smart trot. They did not stop at the gate, near headquarters, but proceeded toward the east gate of the lower fort. I thought it was the "down mail" carrier and did not worry, although I heard some commotion and talking outside headquarters.

But in the morning the story was told. Shortly after reveille the officers began to congregate in the adjutant's office, and I heard the story. They all looked and felt serious.

That horseman was John Phillips. He had come to, and passed through, Fort Reno alone.

Listening to the officers, I gathered up what information they had received from him during his short rest, while waiting for his horse to feed and recuperate.

I distinctly remember one officer's remark, "How did he ever get through Crazy Woman's Fork? The Indians must have been laying for him there." Captain Proctor spoke up, saying, "He didn't come through Crazy Woman's Fork. He told me he left the trail at Buffalo Wallows and came around five miles south of the Forks."

It was a very serious crowd of officers, and comments were numerous as to the possibilities of his getting through to Fort Laramie.

But the one fact remains and stands out the truth:

John Phillips made the ride from Fort Phil Kearney alone.

He started alone; passed Fort Reno alone and that was the most dangerous part of his ride.

The Indians knew that a messenger would be sent, and every foot of the trail was under surveillance. How he ever got through was a miracle. Their own runners had an outline of the news in Fort Laramie before Phillips got there with the facts.

I believe all the statements made by men as to the company he had when he arrived at Bridger's Ferry, Horseshoe Station and Fort Laramie are true, but I am sure he picked them up away down on the trail somewhere, and not on the real dangerous part of his ride.

In the month of April, 1867, some of us civilians were having a good meal in Mrs. Washington's cabin outside the fort (Phil Kearney), and I heard one of the men say to Phillips, who was present, "John, did you stick close to the trail all the way down?"

I never forgot Phillips' answer. "Hell no! More'n once I was more'n ten miles off the trail."

Before I left Phil Kearney, some of our boys used to "sit around" and try to figure it out; how did he make it, etc. And the concensus of opinion was that after he passed Fort Reno, Dry Fork of the Powder, Humphrey's camp and Sage Creek, he picked his own way and came out on the Overland Trail somewhere between Fort Caspar and Bridger's Ferry, where he was liable to pick up the company who were with him on his further journey. His story alone at that time was sufficient to attract adventurous spirits who would ride with him to note the results, and "be in at the death."

There must be some person alive in Wyoming or in

its vicinity who knew Phillips, and who can verify the facts and give further information as to his wonderful performance, and while they are living and accessible they should be induced to give their testimony.

Citizens of the New England states, and especially of Massachusetts, cherish the memory of "Paul Revere's Ride," and have perpetuated it in song and story. All histories of that state mention it, and tablets have been placed along the line at certain points. He made that ride to warn patriots of an impending raid on their homes and property, and if intercepted he could only expect punishment by imprisonment.

But John Phillips faced death if intercepted, and horrible torture if captured. His object was to bring aid to a garrison in which men, women and children were besieged, and upon him alone they depended for assistance.

His act was equally as patriotic and important as was that of Paul Revere, and it is to be hoped that the state of Wyoming will see to it that his memory is kept green and his act not forgotten.

The Wagon Box Fight[98]

The outcome of the Fetterman disaster of December 21, 1866, was the transferring of the command of Fort Phil Kearney from Colonel Henry B. Carrington to General H. W. Wessels. The latter came up from Fort Laramie with four companies of the Eighteenth Infantry and one troop of cavalry in response to Colonel Carrington's courier, Phillips, who brought the first news of the disaster to Fetterman's party, and requests for immediate aid, more troops and better arms. General Wessels arrived at Fort Phil Kearney on the 17th of January, 1867, after a most exhausting march, in which his men were often wading through snowbanks four feet in depth.

I had been a member of Carrington's expedition from Fort Kearney, Nebraska, in May, 1866, and was at Fort Phil Kearney (then situated in the territory of Dakota, which included the present state of Wyoming) from the time of its erection until the post was ordered abandoned by the government early in the fall of 1868. After the arrival of General Wessels, the winter continued one of unusual severity, with the thermometer down to twenty-five and forty degrees below zero most of the time. We had no fresh meat, no vegetables. We did get one small loaf of bread issued to us daily — just about enough for one meal, and after that was gone we had to fall back on musty hardtack, salt pork and

[98] By Sergeant Samuel S. Gibson (retired), Omaha, Nebr., former private, Twenty-seventh U. S. Infantry.

black coffee. Occasionally we had bean soup. We had no place in barracks to wash, and after the creeks were frozen over we could not take a bath until they thawed out the following spring.

The Indians did not bother us at all the balance of the early part of the winter of 1867, although we were in mortal terror that they would try some new deviltry every day that we were in the pinery, getting out logs, as it was necessary to do this to furnish firewood to cook our rations and warm our barracks.

Colonel Carrington and his family, with Mrs. Grummond, the widow of Lieutenant Grummond, who had been killed in the Fetterman fight, together with the Eighteenth Infantry band, left the post the latter part of January, 1867, for Fort Caspar, leaving General Wessels in command at Fort Phil Kearney. He had nineteen sentries posted on and around the stockade every day and night, there being three reliefs of the guard. Fifty-nine men mounted guard every day, besides the officer of the day and four non-commissioned officers. This large detail of men for guard duty worked great hardship on us, for in addition, we had to saw wood for our stoves in quarters. Then, many of our comrades were sick with scurvy, and the hospital was filled with invalids, many of whom died.

As soon as spring opened, the bull trains commenced to come up from Fort Laramie, and with them came Red Cloud and his red devils, the Sioux, again. They immediately began their tactics of the previous summer, attacking every train that passed over the Bozeman Trail, and harrying our wood trains every day or so.

During June, Gilmore & Porter's bull train arrived at the fort with wagons loaded with rations, forage, etc. We were mighty pleased to see them, but what

GENERAL HENRY B. CARRINGTON,
U. S. A.

SERGEANT SAMUEL GIBSON
From a photograph taken at Camp Proctor, on the Yellowstone River, September, 1891.

tickled us most was the seven hundred new breech-
loading Springfield rifles of fifty-caliber, with one hundred thousand rounds of ammunition, which they
brought to supersede the old muzzle-loaders with
which we had been previously armed.

Gilmore & Porter remained at the post all summer.
They had taken a contract from our quartermaster,
General George P. Dandy, to supply the fort with
logs for the sawmills, and firewood for the following
winter.

In order to protect their stock from night attacks
by Indians, the contractors improvised a corral six
miles west of the fort on a level plain. They removed
the boxes from their wagons, fourteen in number, and
formed them into an oval shaped enclosure into which
their stock was driven every night. The pinery where
the logs were being cut was at some little distance from
the wagon box corral. Several tents were pitched just
outside the corral where the woodchoppers and soldiers
bunked. Seven thousand rounds of ammunition were
arranged inside the corral, and everybody was instructed, in case of an Indian attack at the pinery, to retreat
to the corral, where it was considered that a good defense could be made until relief arrived from the fort.

It was early in July when the contractors formed the
corral, and Company A of my regiment, the Twenty-
seventh Infantry, was sent out with the train, as a
guard for the month, to do escort duty to and from the
fort daily, and also to protect the woodchoppers in
the pinery. Company A saw Indians but two or three
times during the entire month of July. On July 31st,
Company C, to which I belonged, relieved Company
A. Packing our wagons with a month's rations we
marched out from Fort Phil Kearney, across Sullivant

Hills, to the woodchoppers' camp near the lower pinery.

We pitched our tents around the outside of the corral. There were spaces between the wagon beds wide enough for a man to walk through, but not large enough for a steer to push outside. There were two of the wagon beds which had canvas covers on them – one at the extreme east end, holding the rations of the woodchoppers, and one on the south side which held our company rations and miscellaneous stores. There was also a wagon complete, with extra rations for the woodchoppers standing outside the corral at the west end, which contained the bedding of the woodchoppers. This wagon stood some ten feet from the wagon boxes which formed the corral. It had a canvas cover over the bows.

On August 1st I was with the detail guarding the woodchoppers at the lower pinery, and was on picket all day. Several of us, when questioned by the sergeant in charge of the detail as to whether we had seen any Indians, replied that we had not, but that we "thought we could *smell* them." The sergeant, McQuiery, gave us an incredulous look and gruffly exclaimed, "Smell hell!" with extreme contempt.

That night we, who had been on picket duty all day, formed the guard around the camp. Two sentinels were posted, one at the east end and one at the west end of the corral, with strict orders from Captain Powell to allow no one to enter the camp, and to challenge anyone or anything approaching; also, if there was the slightest suspicion in our minds, to open fire upon the approaching objects, or upon anything that looked like Indians.

The night was clear and starry above us, but toward

the mountains and down the Big Piney valley it looked awfully dark and ominous. Private Jack McDonough's dog, "Jess," was around with the sentinels all night, and although we could not see or hear anything suspicious, the animal would run furiously down the hill toward the Big Piney valley every few minutes, barking and snapping furiously.

I have always since believed that Red Cloud's warriors were in the valley and around our camp all that night of August 1st, waiting for a chance to surprise us during the night or at day-break, when we were supposed to be somewhat off our guard.

At day-break on August 2d, the cooks were called early to get up and prepare breakfast for the company. A detail of pickets was sent to the point on the banks of the Little Piney between the two camps. Our drummer-boy, Hines, beat the reveille first call, and fifteen minutes later the company fell in, and answered reveille roll call – some, alas, for the last time.

Breakfast was announced by Cook Brown calling "Chuck!" and immediately after, the company broke ranks and laid away their rifles. The whole company took breakfast, with the exception of two men still on picket around the corral. By this time the sun had risen, and we scanned the horizon and the foothills to the north and down the valley of the Big Piney.

We could not see the least sign of an Indian, although we learned afterward that they were watching our every movement from points of vantage in the hills. I was told this some years later by Chief Rain-in-the-Face while I was a sergeant of Company H, Twenty-second Infantry, at Standing Rock agency, during the Sioux Ghost Dance war of 1890-1891.

Immediately after breakfast the wagon trains started

for their different destinations – one going to the fort loaded with logs which had been brought out of the pinery the day before, with a detachment of twenty men, commanded by Lieutenant Francis McCarthy and Corporal Paddy Conley, who accompanied the train as an escort. If my memory serves me right, Mr. Porter who owned the bull train and had the contract for supplying the wood to the quartermaster at Fort Phil Kearney, went along.

The other train pulled out for the lower pinery with an escort of thirteen men. Jack McDonough, Dave Moore, McNally and McCumber are the names of some of this escort, which was commanded by Corporal Riley Porter. With Porter was "Portugee" Phillips, who had carried the dispatches of Colonel Carrington from Fort Phil Kearney to Horseshoe Station after the Fetterman disaster of December 21, the previous year. Phillips was accompanied by a man named Judd. Both Phillips and Judd had sub-contracts from Mr. Porter, the contractor.

About this time, 6:45, a.m., I was ordered by the first sergeant to proceed, fully armed and equipped, and relieve Private John Grady as lance corporal in charge of the picket-post on the banks of the Little Piney. Having relieved Grady, who instructed me to keep a sharp lookout for Indians, I fixed up a sort of shade from the hot sun with willows stuck in the ground and ponchos tied over the tops. I had laid under this canopy for perhaps fifteen minutes with a private named Deming, when suddenly Guard Garrett yelled "Indians!"

Deming and I jumped to our feet, and sure enough, away to the west of us we counted seven Indians, mounted, coming across the divide from the north on a dead run and in single file, riding toward the Little Piney and chanting their war song. As the Indians were coming in an oblique direction toward us, and as not a man in the company had yet fired a shot at an Indian from the new breech-loading fifty-caliber Springfield rifles with which we had just been armed, I sat down and adjusted my sights to seven hundred yards, and laying my rifle on top of a stone breastwork, took steady aim at the Indian in advance and fired. My bullet struck a stone in front of the Indian, ricocheted off and wounded his pony. The Indian was thrown off, but immediately sprang to his feet as his pony fell, and was taken up behind a mounted warrior who was following closely in his rear.

About this time Deming and I looked toward our main camp, and over the Big Piney, to the foothills toward the north, and there we saw more Indians than we had ever seen before. Deming exclaimed in an excited tone: "Look at the Indians!" and pointing toward the foothills across Big Piney Creek, he added: "My God! there are thousands of them!"

Hearing shots across the Little Piney, I ordered Garrett to watch for signals from the main camp, and sent Deming across the Little Piney to see what was going on at the other camp, which was a woodchoppers' camp consisting of seven or eight wagons. This camp was perhaps twelve hundred yards directly south of our main camp. Garrett and I watched the Indians coming across the foothills, like a big swarm of bees, on the north side of the Big Piney, feeling very uneasy the while about our failure to receive any signals to return to the main camp where the wagon boxes were corraled. Deming soon came back and reported that Indians had run off the herd, and that all the men, including four of our soldiers (Harris, Kittredge, Lang and Kilberg), who were guarding the small camp south of Little Piney, had run for the mountains, and that one of the civilians, a herder, was coming across the creek, leading his pony, to join us.

Looking toward the main camp we saw quite a commotion going on. The men were hurrying here and there. By this time the herder had come across the creek and joined us, and I told Deming and Garrett that we would start at once for the main camp, and that if the Indians got after us we would make a running skirmish for it. The plan was that we would stop alternately and fire two or three shots, following each other up closely, with myself in the rear.

We immediately started on a good brisk walk, but had retreated only about seventy-five or a hundred yards before the Indians commenced coming up out of the Little Piney Creek bottom by ones, twos and threes at different places. The first one I saw was coming up the bank of the creek sideways, and he carried an old Spencer carbine which he was waving excitedly. I immediately "pulled down" on him just as he was aiming at me. My bullet knocked him off his pony, and I heard his shot whizz past my head.

By this time Garrett had stopped and was down on one knee, firing at the Indians who had come up out of the creek higher up to the west of us. I ran past Garrett toward camp, and saw Deming on my right, shooting at the Indians. At this moment the citizen herder, who was leading his pony by the bridle-rein, told me to stick my bayonet in the animal's flanks to make him go faster. I told him to turn the pony loose and shoot at the Indians, who had by this time increased in numbers at such an alarming rate that they seemed to rise out of the ground like a flock of birds. All of them were naked, with the exception of the regulation "gee-string" around their waists, while some of them wore gorgeous war-bonnets; others had a single feather in their scalp-locks. Their bodies were painted white, green and yellow, which made them look hideous in the extreme.

All of us were now on the dead run. Even the herder's pony was clipping it off, with half a dozen arrows sticking in his flanks, and it seemed as if hell had broken loose. The Indians whooped and yelled as they rode hither and thither and backward and forward in their efforts to surround us by circling, endeavoring thereby to cut us off from the main camp. Each one of us knew full well that if we were hit by an arrow or bullet it would mean death – or something worse if captured alive. We realized that if disabled our scalps would soon be dangling at the scalp-pole of some Sioux warrior. We had seen and assisted in collecting the bodies of our comrades who were so horribly mutilated at the Fetterman fight, and knew that a similar fate awaited us if we were cut off. We kept on running and shooting, expecting every minute to feel a bullet or an arrow in our backs.

We soon saw one of our men run out to meet us from the main camp. He dropped on one knee about a hundred yards from the main corral and opened a rapid fire on the advancing hordes of savages. Several fell from their ponies under his accurate fire. This man proved to be one of our sergeants, Littman by name, who, by his courage and thoughtfulness in coming out to meet us, and the rapidity and effectiveness of his fire, saved us from being surrounded and cut off by the red devils. We were thus enabled to reach the main camp in the wagon box corral, although we were in a completely exhausted condition. The civilian herder who was leading his pony, was the last one to enter the corral.

Upon our arrival, completely winded from our long and dangerous run, I immediately reported to Captain Powell, who was standing outside and on the south side of the corral, where he had evidently observed our retreat and pursuit by the Indians. To him, in a panting and exhausted condition, I reported why we had left the picket-post without orders, as it was impossible for us to hold it against such overwhelming odds.

Looking me straight in the eye, Captain Powell exclaimed: "You have done nobly, my boy! You could not have done better!" Then addressing the three of us, he said "Men, find a place in the wagon boxes. You'll have to fight for your lives today!"

We saluted and turned to obey his orders, at the same time following his instructions to provide ourselves with plenty of ammunition.

To my dying day I shall never forget the fierce "do-or-die" look on Captain Powell's face that morning. Deming, Garrett and I split up, and each man carried into his wagon box plenty of loaded shells. The Indians were not aware that we had received new rifles, and supposed that after we had fired one shot they would be able to ride us down before we could reload.

Much has been said by historians and others who have written short accounts of this fight, regarding the wagon boxes inside of which we fought. Some have said that the boxes were made of boiler-iron, and others that they were lined with steel and had loopholes through the sides. All such statements are absolutely without foundation. They were the ordinary government wagon boxes, part of the same equipment used during the Civil War. They were built simply of thin wood, while some of them were make-shift wagons belonging to the contractor's bull train; the heaviest of them being made of but one inch boards. There was not a particle of iron about them anywhere, except the bolts, stay-straps and nuts used in holding the rickety concerns together. I also have read in some accounts that the wagon boxes were "a kind of traveling fort supplied by the government." Any statement that the wagon boxes used as protection in this fight of August 2, 1867, were other than plain, ordinary wood wagon boxes, is a fabrication pure and simple, no matter on what authority given.

I soon found a place in one of the wagon beds on the south side of the corral, and here I found Sergeant McQuiery and Private John Grady. Grady was the only one to speak to me, inviting me to come in with them, saying: "You'll have to fight like hell today, kid, if you expect to get out of this alive." I was the youngest boy in the company, being but eighteen years of age, and was always called "the kid," which appellation was given me by Dan Flynn, a member of Company H.

Leaning my rifle against the sides of the wagon beds, I carried a hundred rounds of ammunition to my place, and then took a walk around among the men who were standing in groups inside and outside of the corral watching the Indians assembling all around us. I spoke to some of the men, but no one answered me, and the expression of their faces will haunt me as long as I live. I had been in a score of fights and skirmishes with most of my comrades since we began to build

Fort Phil Kearney in July of 1866, and had been with
some of these same men when we went out with Colonel
Carrington on December 22d of that fatal year to
bring in the remainder of Fetterman's command from
Massacre Hill, where they were killed the previous day,
and had then seen the stern, revengeful looks on their
faces; but the looks in their eyes this morning was
altogether different. It was a look, not of despair or
desperation, but one of intense earnestness and resolution.

I saw Private Tommy Doyle piling up some neck-
yokes belonging to the bull train on top of one another
for the purpose of forming a breastwork, between the
ends of two of the wagon boxes. I saw another man,
Sergeant Frank Robertson, an old soldier who had
served in the old Seventh and Tenth Infantry, taking
the shoestrings out of his shoes and tying them together,
with a loop at one end, which he fitted over his right
foot, and a smaller loop at the other end to fit over
the trigger of his rifle. I did not ask him what he was
doing, because the awful horror of our isolated position seemed to dawn upon my mind, but I knew too
well the meaning of those grim preparations – that the
red devils would never get old Frank Robertson alive!

I then joined a group of five or six men outside the
corral at the southwest end, and in the midst of them
stood Lieutenant John C. Jenness, who was watching
the Indians through a field glass down the Big Piney
valley to the north, and on the highest point of the
hill on the ridge east of us. There seemed to be
hundreds of Indians, all mounted on their finest and
handsomest war ponies, riding here and there, chanting their war and death songs. In the valley, more
were assembling. Lieutenant Jenness seemed to be

watching the big bunch of Indians on the high hill about three-quarters of a mile distant, and I heard him say to Captain Powell, who soon joined us: "Captain, I believe that Red Cloud is on top of that hill," (pointing to the east). The captain made no reply, but hearing a commotion, accompanied by loud talking, among the men to the south of us, he turned, and seeing the Indians riding furiously about on the plains between Little Piney and Big Piney Creeks, he exclaimed:

"Men, here they come! Take your places and shoot to kill!"

And those were the only words of command given by him, save once, during the entire fight.

Each man quickly took his place in the wagon boxes. Not a word was spoken by anyone, and the silence was awful. When I took my place in the wagon box occupied by Sergeant McQuiery and Private John Grady, both of them had their shoes off, and were fixing their shoestrings into loops to fit over the right foot and from thence to the trigger of their rifles, for the same purpose that Sergeant Robertson had done – to kill themselves when all hope was lost, in the event the Indians passed over our barricade by an overwhelming force of numbers, when every man would stand erect, place the muzzle of his loaded rifle under his chin and take his own life, rather than be captured and made to endure the inevitable torture. I had just taken off my own shoes and made loops in the strings when the firing began.

Resting my rifle on the top of the wagon box I began firing with the rest. The whole plain was alive with Indians, all mounted and visible in every direction. They were riding madly about, and shooting at us with guns, bows and arrows, first on one side and then on the other of the corral. Then they would circle, and each time come in closer, uttering the most piercing and unearthly war cries. Some of the more venturesome would ride in close and throw spears at us. Others would brandish their war-clubs and tomahawks at us, and others, still more daring, would ride within a hundred yards, then suddenly drop on the off side of their ponies, and all we could see would be an arm or a leg sticking above the pony's back, and "whizz!" would come the arrows! They paid dearly for their daring, for we had a steady rest for our rifles, the Indians were all within easy point-blank range, and we simply mowed them down by scores.

The tops of the wagon beds were literally ripped and torn to slivers by their bullets. How we ever escaped with such a slight loss I never have been able to understand. After we had commenced firing, a great number of Indians rode in very close – probably within a hundred and fifty yards, and sitting on their ponies waited for us to draw ramrods for reloading, as they supposed we were yet using the old muzzle-loaders, but, thanks to God and Lieutenant-General Sherman, the latter had listened to the appeals of Colonel Carrington, commanding Fort Phil Kearney the previous year, and we had just been armed with the new weapon, and instead of drawing ramrods and thus losing precious time, we simply threw open the breech-blocks of our new rifles to eject the empty shell and slapped in fresh ones. This puzzled the Indians, and they were soon glad to withdraw to a safe distance.

The plain in front of us was strewn with dead and dying Indians and ponies. The Indians were amazed, but not by any means undaunted. They were there for blood, and came in such hordes that they were ready

WAGON BOX FIGHT. AUG. 2, 1867.

FROM SKETCH FURNISHED BY SERGEANT SAMUEL GIBSON

Figures indicate location of different soldiers and civilians.

(1) Sergt. Gibson; (2) Sergt. Hoover; (3) Major Powell; (4) Max Littmann (behind barrel of beans); (5) Private Condon (behind barrel of salt); (6) Spot where Lieut. Jenness was killed; (7, 8) Bullwhackers in wagon boxes; (9) Private Doyle killed; (10) Private Haggerty killed; (11) Somers wounded in wagon box. Big Piney Creek is to the north, and the covered wagons are at the west end of the wagon box corral.

for any sacrifice if they could but capture our little party. They made heroic attempts to recover their wounded. It was their lives or ours. We had not forgotten Massacre Hill. We were not fiends, gloating over the suffering of their wounded, but that bloody day of December 21st was fresh in our minds, and we were filled with a grim determination to kill, just as we had seen our comrades killed. There was no thought of wavering. We knew from their countless numbers that if they overwhelmed us they could easily capture the fort, but six miles distant, where there were helpless women and children. We were fighting for their lives as well as our own. It was not revenge but retribution.

After recovering a great number of their dead and wounded at a fearful sacrifice of life, the Indians withdrew to a safe distance, but while recovering their injured we witnessed the most magnificent display of horsemanship imaginable. Two mounted Indians would ride like the wind among the dead and wounded, and seeing an arm or leg thrust upward, would ride one on each side of the wounded savage, reach over and pick him up on the run, and carry him to a place of safety. This was done many times, and we could not help but admire their courage and daring.

During the lull in the firing, we got a fresh supply of cartridges out of the seven cases holding a thousand rounds each, which had been opened by order of Captain Powell some time before the firing started, and had been placed about the corral at convenient places. We had to crawl on our hands and knees to get the ammunition, and I saw several of the men, crawling like myself, to get cartridges. None of them spoke a word to me, and the utter silence was uncanny.

When I got back to my wagon bed I heard some man in the box next to me ask in a loud whisper for a chew of tobacco. While I had been getting my ammunition I asked a man named Phillips, who was also getting shells, if anyone had been shot. He shook his head and simply whispered, "Don't know." After I got back to my place I looked around and saw Captain Powell, who was in the second box west of me, with Sergeant Frank Hoover, and both of them were firing at some wounded Indians within sixty yards of the corral to the west.

Lieutenant John C. Jenness was leaning over the cover of the wagon bed at the west end of the corral, firing at some Indians on the northwest side, where they lay partially concealed under the brow of the hill where the land sloped down toward Big Piney valley. On the north side of the corral, in a very irregular form, the land on which we were encamped came to an abrupt termination, sloping down toward the Big Piney Valley. The nearest point from the corral was probably seventy-five yards northwest, and extended a greater distance toward the east. It was behind this ridge where the Indians on foot had placed themselves in scores, all armed with rifles, and all one could see of them would be the two sticks across which they rested their guns. When they raised their heads to take aim we could see the single feather sticking up in their scalplocks. It was these Indians who killed Lieutenant Jenness and Privates Doyle and Haggerty.

While watching Lieutenant Jenness I heard Sergeant McQuirey ask in a hoarse whisper if anyone had been killed or wounded. I answered that I did not know. The Indians, both mounted and on foot, were still trying to rescue their dead and wounded from the

plain in front of us; and on the plain to the southeast
a large body of Indians were signaling with pocket-
mirrors toward the big ridge east of us, while couriers
were observed riding furiously back and forth at break-
neck speed, going and coming by way of Big Piney
valley. We did not know what to expect, but we knew
they would attack us again soon. Something desperate had evidently been determined upon by the savages. All we could do was to wait and watch. Not a
word was spoken. It was a moment of suspense that
was simply terrible.

As we sat and waited for what we thought would
be the finish of us, I looked along the wagon beds and
saw my comrades sitting there watching the assembling
of the Indians. Every man had his jaws firmly closed,
with a grim determination to fight until we were overpowered. We did not know what time it was and nobody cared.

The fight had commenced about seven o'clock in the
morning, and I did not hear any man ask about the
time of day during the fight. Nearly all of us were
bareheaded, as we had used our caps and hats to hold
ammunition. The sun beat down with a pitiless glare
that terrible August day, and it seemed like eternity to
us all.

Suddenly someone on the north side of the corral
yelled, "Look out! they're coming again!" We could
see the Indians to the east, south and southwest of us
galloping about and circling toward us, coming nearer and nearer. All at once some soldier shouted in a
loud voice: "The tents!"

The line of tents were in front of us on the south
side and had been left standing all the time of the first
fierce charge, and we had simply fired through the

spaces between them. No one had thought of pulling them down until that moment. Then two men leaped out of a wagon bed to the east of us, ran toward the tents but a short distance away, and began pulling them to the ground.

At this moment Private John Grady, who sat near me in my wagon bed, yelled: "Come on, kid!" As he leaped over the wagon bed I followed him, with the bullets zipping about us and the arrows swishing past and striking into the ground on all sides of us. We loosened the loops around the tent-pins at the corners, working together, until all but the last of the tents dropped; and as Grady and I started toward the last one – an officers' tent, sixty or seventy feet in front of ours, to the south, we heard Sergeant Hoover shout: "Come back here! you'll get hit! Never mind the captain's tent! Get into your wagon box and shoot!" We dropped everything, and amid a perfect hail of balls and arrows rushed back and leaped over into our wagon beds again. How we escaped has been the mystery of my life, but neither of us were even hit.

With the tents down, we could see the Indians to much better advantage, and were enabled to deliver a more effective fire. The whole plain was again alive with countless swarms of the warriors, assembling for another grand charge upon us. Our fire was terribly destructive and deadly in accuracy, and we repulsed them again, but our gun-barrels were so overheated from the rapidity of our fire that the metal burned our hands, and we were obliged to open the breech-blocks during this lull to allow the barrels to cool off. During one of these momentary lulls Grady asked me to go after more ammunition. I crawled out of the wagon box westward, and saw several other men after more ammunition, and as I looked toward the west end I saw the body of Lieutenant Jenness lying where he had fallen, shot through the head and heart. Within a few feet of the corpse, Private Jim Condon was fighting behind a barrel of beans placed in the interval between Captain Powell's wagon bed and the one with a cover on.

Having secured the ammunition, I crawled back in my wagon bed. Here I told Sergeant McQuiery and Private Grady that Lieutenant Jenness had been killed, and of the manner in which he had apparently been shot. They both exclaimed: "Good God! Anyone else?" I answered that I did not know, and as the Indians were still making false charges toward us to recover their dead and wounded, we opened a desultory fire upon them.

About this time word was passed around that Privates Henry Haggerty and Tommy Doyle had been killed on the north side of the corral. The brave little Jerseyman, Haggerty, had been shot through the left shoulder earlier in the fight, but the fact had been kept secret by the other men in the same wagon bed, lest some men become disheartened. The men in the box with Haggerty wanted him to lie down after getting shot through the shoulder, but with his left arm hanging useless at his side, he had used his good right, and kept on loading and firing for over two hours, until the Indians on the north ridge finally killed him by sending a bullet through the top of his head. Doyle had been killed some time after the first charge, while bravely fighting behind a breastwork of ox-yokes. He was struck in the forehead.

It was now becoming a question of water. Men were everywhere asking for it, and the supply was getting woefully scarce, and the suffering from the terrific heat and nervous strain was intense. Added to this, the Indians had rained fire-arrows inside the corral, which set fire to the dry manure within the enclosure, and the stench from this was abominable. I had filled my canteen in Little Piney Creek that morning and had brought it back to the corral on the retreat from the picket-post, so that we three in my wagon box had all the water we desired up to that time, and there was still some left. Grady took up the canteen and drank a mouthful, but immediately spat it out again, exclaiming that it was too hot for him. Sergeant McQuiery then washed out his mouth with some, remarking: "It *IS* pretty warm, but water is too precious to waste just now."

Soon after this Sergeant Robertson started crawling on his hands and knees, coming from the east end of the corral toward the west end, poking aside with his head the arrows that were sticking up in the ground. When he arrived at the place where the body of Lieutenant Jenness was lying, he placed a wagon cover over it, and then returned to his wagon bed at the east end of the corral.

There was a barrel half full of water standing outside the corral at the west end when the fighting began. It was about twenty feet away from the wagon beds. During the fighting it had been struck by bullets and the water had nearly all leaked out. Under the covered wagon, close to the west end of the corral, were two camp kettles in which our coffee had been made for breakfast, and Brown, the cook, had filled them with water on top of the old coffee grounds, intending to use the coffee for the company supper. Private Jim Condon had seen the water leaking from the barrel, and had passed the word around the corral that the barrel was empty, or nearly so. Then Cook Brown volunteered the information that the camp kettles had been filled with water, and as they were but a short distance away, we immediately planned to secure them.

My comrade, Johnny Grady, who sat next to me in our wagon bed, was crazy for water. He said: "Kid, let's go and get one of those kettles." I replied, "All right." We took a careful look about and then commenced crawling on our stomachs through the arrows that lined the corral, and as we reached the wagon bed with the cover on at the west end, Jim Condon, from behind the barrel of beans where he was fighting, cautioned us to be on the lookout or the Indians would get us sure.

The men on the north side seemed to divine our purpose, and word was passed along to keep up a steady fire on the Indians along the ridge. We crawled through the opening between the wagon beds, hugging the ground as closely as possible, and soon reached the place where the kettles stood without having apparently been detected. We each grabbed a kettle and then commenced crawling back, pulling the kettles along. We had gotten about half-way to safety, when "bang! bang! bang!" came several shots from the Indians to the north of us, and "z-zip! p-i-n-g-g-g!" we heard some of the bullets strike the kettles, but, fortunately without injuring us. We both thought our time had come, but we finally got back inside the corral with those kettles of dirty black water. When I looked at mine, there were two holes clean through it, and consequently I had lost some of the water, but we left them both with Private Condon, who gave each man a good drink when he crawled out of his wagon box for it.

The time between each charge dragged heavily, and the day seemed almost endless. Yet, the Indians on the north side of us, hidden under the ridge, kept us constantly on the alert, and some of them at the east end of the ridge, about two hundred yards from the east side of the corral, would run out toward us once in a while, armed with spears and tomahawks, each carrying a big shield made of buffalo-hide. There they would brandish their weapons in a menacing manner and utter shrill war cries. There was one big giant of an Indian who had thus run out several times from the ridge to the east, and he always managed to escape our fire, until he apparently thought he bore a charmed life, and that we could not kill him. He was truly a magnificent specimen of Indian manhood, nearly seven feet tall and almost wholly naked. He had led all of the previous charges from the east end of the ridge, and must have been a sub-chief. The last time he appeared must have been about two o'clock in the afternoon, and this time he came out slowly but grandly, with his big buffalo shield in front of him, brandishing his spear and chanting a war-song. Then he would hold his shield on one side and run toward us, jumping into the air and alternating this movement by dodging to one side. The sight was fascinating, and we could not but admire his superb courage. Several of us had fired at him but without effect, when one of the boys at the east end remarked: "We have simply got to get that fellow, as he thinks we can't hit him." We carefully adjusted our sights, taking accurate aim, and just as he shifted his shield aside and began running toward us, we fired together, and he leaped into the air and came down as limp as a rag, fairly riddled with bullets. We all breathed easier after this warrior was killed, for his death seemed to put a stop to any more charges from that direction.

The Indians had withdrawn out of range, except those concealed under the brow of the ridge on the north side. These would take a shot at us every few minutes. The main body of Indians was around the big hill at the end of the ridge east of us, where Red Cloud was stationed in supreme command, and we could plainly hear him or some other chief haranguing them in a loud voice. Presently a great number of Indians rode down the Big Piney valley out of sight. Another party, several hundred in number, rode out on the plain toward us, evidently for another charge. We all knew that they had lost scores of their braves in killed and wounded, and in their maddened frenzy would make another attempt to overwhelm us by force of superior numbers, and would take horrible revenge upon us if they captured us.

It must have been after three o'clock in the afternoon when, straining our eyes for the sight of that line of skirmishers in the glorious blue uniform (which appeared later) we could distinctly hear a sort of humming sound, seemingly made by many voices, below us in the Big Piney valley. Some of us thought it was the squaws wailing over their dead warriors, and as the sound grew louder some of the men on the north side of the corral rose to their feet to see if they could discern anything below them in the Big Piney valley, but they had no sooner risen to their feet than others yelled at them, "Down, down, or you will get hit!"

As we waited in silent wonderment at this strange sound, unlike anything we had ever heard before, the echo appeared to come from the northwest of the corral. The Indians to the east and south of us had come out on the plain, where they were circling and coming nearer all the time, brandishing their spears and war clubs at us and giving voice to their war cries. Those of the warriors who were armed with guns immediately opened fire again upon us, and we at once replied, killing and wounding many more of them. During this time, that awful humming, chanting sound grew in volume and intensity, coming nearer and nearer, now directly from west of us. The Indians to the south had withdrawn out of range, and seemed to be waiting for something to happen.

And something *DID* happen! Suddenly there was a cry from the west end of the corral: "Here they come!" We all looked in that direction, and saw a sight which none of those yet alive will ever forget to their dying day. It chilled my blood at the time. We saw the naked bodies of hundreds upon hundreds of Indians swarming up a ravine about ninety yards to the west of the corral. They were all on foot, formed in the shape of a letter V, or wedge, and were led by Red Cloud's nephew, who wore a gorgeous war bonnet. Immediately we opened a terrific fire upon them, under which nothing could stand, and at the very first volley Red Cloud's nephew fell, pierced by many bullets. Nothing daunted, the forces came on slowly, and in .great numbers, the places of those who fell under our fire being taken immediately by others.

So close were the Indian hordes by this time that the heavy rifle bullets from our guns must have gone through two or three bodies. They were so near us that we could even see the whites of their eyes. As they swarmed toward us with shrill cries and piercing whoops, Private Jim Condon jumped to his feet from behind his barrel of beans, and shouted, as he waved his rifle over his head: "Come on, you blatherin' sons av guns! We kin lick th' hull damn bunch av yez!" Captain Powell, who was close by Condon, at once ordered him to lie down.

And now the Indians were so close that it seemed as if nothing could prevent their swarming over our barricade and into the corral, when it would have been all over with us in no time. Our fire was accurate, coolly delivered and given with most telling effect, but nevertheless it looked for a minute as though our last moment on earth had come. Just when it seemed as if all hope was gone, the Indians suddenly broke and fled. They could not stand before the withering fire we poured into their ranks. The several hundred mounted Indians, on the plain to the south of us, who were intently watching this foot-charge, never offered to assist their red brothers by making a mounted charge, but discreetly remained out of rifle range.

During all these charges against our corral, Red Cloud who was in supreme command, stood (or sat on his horse) on top of the ridge due east of our little improvised fort. Some of the boys estimated it to be three-quarters of a mile away. After this last charge of the Indians on foot from the west, and while we were waiting to see what the red devils would try next, some six or eight of us elevated the sights on our rifles to the full extension of long range firing, and let loose five or six volleys at Red Cloud and his crowd on top of the hill, and we all fully believed, from the sudden scattering of Indians, that some of our bullets found lodgment and made "good Injuns" of some of them.

Suddenly the Indians on the big hill at the top of the

ridge started down the steep decline into Big Piney valley by twos, threes and fours. We took a few long range shots at them, which served to accelerate their speed very effectively. We did not understand this maneuver for a few minutes.

Just then someone at the east end of the corral cried out: "Hark! did you hear that?" Everybody ceased firing, and in another moment we distinctly heard the boom of a big gun to the east of us. It was indeed heavenly music to all of us. It was the sorely needed relief from Fort Phil Kearney. They had heard the sounds of battle and started reinforcements, with a howitzer, to our succor. It was this big gun that was driving the savages off the big hill. The Indians on the plain south of us could also be seen disappearing into the pinery to the west. We knew what the commotion meant, but waited, with nerves and senses wrought almost to a frenzy. Suddenly one of the men jumped to his feet, shouting: "Here they come, boys! Hurrah!" and as we looked toward the east we could see those glorious old McClelland caps on the heads of our comrades as they appeared in a long skirmish line.

Then we all jumped to our feet and yelled. We threw our caps in the air. We hugged each other in the ecstacy of our joy. We laughed, cried and fairly sobbed like little children in the delirium of our delight. The awful strain was over.

Captain Powell suddenly ordered everybody back into the wagon beds, lest another charge be made by the Indians before our rescuers should reach us. We obediently returned to our places, and sat watching the skirmish line advancing, while the boom of the big gun was the sweetest sound that ever fell on our ears.

The gunners were throwing shells into a big bunch of Indians in the Big Piney valley.

The redskins began scattering rapidly across Big Piney Creek and were soon out of range. The skirmish line continued to advance, and in a few minutes we saw the main body marching in front of a small wagon train of ten or twelve six-mule teams of empty ambulances and wagons, with the big brass cannon in front of the teams.

By this time everybody was talking and waving their arms as we recognized well known comrades from the fort. We recognized Major Smith as in command of the rescue party, and also our genial post surgeon, Dr. Samuel M. Horton, and when they arrived within two hundred yards of us we ran out to meet them, and such a shaking of hands as there was. The first question he asked us was, "Who's hit? Who's killed or wounded?" Our rescuers told us they had not expected to find a man of us alive.

Dr. Horton—God bless him!—for he was also so kind and considerate of every man, woman and child at the post, had his ambulance driven near to the west end of the corral, and with the consent of Captain Powell he gave every man—soldier and civilian—a big drink of whiskey out of a small keg which he had brought along.

Then we tenderly laid the body of Lieutenant Jenness in the ambulance, and the bodies of Doyle and Haggerty in one of the wagons, and having packed our tentage, bedding and rations in the empty wagons, marched back to the fort. When we arrived at the big hill at the west end of the ridge east of the corral, we halted, and as we looked back up Big Piney valley, we saw a long train of Indian ponies, three and four deep and fully a quarter of a mile long. They were carrying off their dead and wounded.

As we approached the commanding officer's quarters, he stepped from the house and halted us. We came to attention and the general removed his cap and complimented Captain Powell and all of us for our splendid victory against such overwhelming odds. He furthermore added that we had displayed such heroic courage and bravery that he would recommend every one of us for a medal of honor. The recommendation was made, but for some reason none of us ever received the medal.

As to the number of Indians killed in the fight, that is a hard question to answer. Captain Powell, in his official report, estimated the Indian loss at over three hundred killed and wounded, but we – the men of Company C – estimated that there must have been seven or eight hundred killed and wounded. The late General Grenville M. Dodge said that about thirty years ago, in an interview with Chief Red Cloud at Pine Ridge Reservation, the chief placed the total loss of the Sioux, Cheyennes and Arapahoes at over eleven hundred in killed and wounded. It was utterly impossible to keep any account of the individual Indians each man saw fall, because as fast as an Indian dropped, others would ride up and carry him away. Chief Rain-in-the-Face told me at Standing Rock agency in 1895, through an interpreter, that he did not care to talk about the Wagon Box fight.

I have served in the army forty-eight years, taking active part in the Sioux campaign of 1876 and also in the Wounded Knee campaign of 1890-'91 at Pine Ridge agency, but never before or since have my nerves ever been put to the test they sustained on that terrible 2d of August, 1867, when we fought Red Cloud's warriors in the wagon box corral.

Referring back to the Fetterman disaster of December 21, 1866, eight months previous to the Wagon Box fight, I want to state that on that day I was Sentry Number Two of the first relief, and was on guard at gate Number Two (or the west gate) on that fatal day, and I saw Captain Fetterman and his party march through the gate, and heard Colonel Carrington tell Fetterman not to go by Lodge Trail Ridge, and Fetterman replied: "Very good, sir." I did not go out with Captain Ten Eyck when he was sent to ascertain the cause of the heavy firing beyond Lodge Trail Ridge, where Fetterman was then being annihilated, but I did go out on the morning of December 22d with Colonel Carrington's command to bring in the remainder of our dead and mutilated comrades. The poor fellows were stark naked, their bodies filled with arrows and scalped. It was a most gruesome task, I can assure you.[99]

A COMPLIMENT TO CAPTAIN POWELL BY COLONEL JAMES B. FRY

Brevet Major-General U. S. Army

In a modest little volume entitled *Army Sacrifices*, by Colonel James B. Fry, Brevet Major-General Unit-

---

[99] List of names of members of Company C, Twenty-seventh Infantry, engaged in the Wagon Box fight on the Piney, near Fort Phil Kearney, Dakota Territory, August 2, 1867. Compiled July, 1920, by Samuel Gibson, U.S.A., retired, one of the survivors: Captain James Powell, First Lieutenant John C. Jenness, First Sergeant John M. Hoover and John H. McQuarie (McQuiery), Corporals Max Littmann, Francis Robertson, Privates William A. Baker, Ashton P. Barton, William Black, Charles Brooks, Denis Brown, Alexander Brown, John Buzzard, James Condon, Frederick Claus, Nolan V. Deming, Thomas Doyle, Samuel Gibson, John Grady, John M. Garrett, Henry Gross, Henry Haggerty, Mark Haller, Philip C.

ed States Army, is the following sketch of Captain James W. Powell:

> The principal actor in the heroic defense above recounted (referring to the Wagon Box fight) deserves more than a passing notice, and we feel our task would be incomplete were we to close without adverting to him. Captain Powell entered the army as a private soldier at the opening of our late Civil War. Soon after the commencement of the war, being then a sergeant of First Dragoons, he was appointed a second lieutenant in the Eighteenth Infantry, and was promoted first lieutenant in 1861 and captain in 1864; and in 1868 was placed upon the retired list of the army, being incapacitated for active service, the result of gunshot wounds received at the battle of Jonesboro on the first of September, 1864. He received the brevet of captain in 1863 for gallant and meritorious conduct during the Atlanta campaign and at the battle of Jonesboro, Ga. He was brevetted a major September 1, 1864, for gallant service at Chickamauga, and lieutenant-colonel August 2, 1867, for gallant conduct in a fight with Indians on that date near Fort Phil Kearney. This last brevet was the reward for bravery and endurance. It is a remarkable illustration of courage and endurance of this brave soldier that, while he was fighting against overwhelming numbers of savage Indians on the 2d of August, 1867, he was then a sufferer from wounds received in battle in September, 1864, and which ultimately necessitated his retirement from the career he loved so well. Honor to whom honor is due.

THE WAGON BOX FIGHT AS I SAW IT[100]

I enlisted in the United States Army March 20, 1866, having emigrated from Germany but a short time previously. From New York I was sent to Jefferson Barracks, St. Louis, where all recruits were sent at that time. Here we received our guns. From St. Louis

---

Jones, Freeland Phillips, John L. Somers, Charles A. Stevens, and Julius Strache.

[100] By Max Littmann (living in St. Louis, Mo., 1920) former sergeant, Twenty-seventh U.S. Infantry.

we were sent to Fort Leavenworth, and we marched from that post in full battalion. We rested for a time at Fort Kearney, Nebraska, then moved up the North Platte River to Julesburg, or old Fort Sedgwick, as it was then known. From that point we were sent to Fort Laramie, where we again rested. We then marched almost due north to the site of Fort Reno, and from there to the site of Fort Phil Kearney.

I was twenty-one years of age at that time and unable to speak the English language at all. However, I was desirous of seeing something of the country to the west before making any attempt to establish myself in business. In seven months after I enlisted I was made sergeant of my company, although I had not by any means mastered the language. All my orders for my company were written down for me in English, which I memorized word for word.

Passing over different events which happened at Fort Phil Kearney during my stay there, I will come down to the famous Wagon Box fight of August 2, 1867. My company had been detailed to guard the wood-choppers in the pinery while getting out logs to finish some of the fort buildings, and also to use for fuel. On the morning of August 2, I was stationed at the wagon box corral, which was under the command of Captain James Powell. Part of the men were off guard, myself among the number, and we were lounging in our tents on the south side of the corral. Suddenly we heard a commotion, followed by a cry of "Indians!" We who were in the tents immediately ran out to see what was the matter. I looked to the south where the pickets were stationed, and saw Captain Powell running up from the creek where he had been taking a bath. Upon seeing the Indians swarming down over the hills, he hurried to give the alarm, as did those who were on picket duty.

We were immediately ordered into the corral. There were twenty-five soldiers, two officers and five civilians, or teamsters, making thirty-two men all told. Captain Powell reported that there were several thousand rounds of ammunition in boxes, besides which, every man had forty rounds in his belt, so that we had plenty of ammunition to use. The gun we were using was a breech-loading Springfield rifle – a style of weapon entirely unknown to the Indians up to that day, and we had only received them two or three weeks previously, but had not had an opportunity to try them against the Indians. It was the rapidity with which we were enabled to deliver our fire that puzzled and drove back the vast hordes of savages which repeatedly charged us. In addition to our rifles, every man also was armed with a revolver, but we did not use them – not, at least to my knowledge.

After being ordered into the corral, most of the men at once got inside the wagon boxes to fight it out with the Indians from behind this slight barricade. It occurred to me, however, that those wagon boxes – which were nothing but very thin planks – were mighty poor protection when it came to stopping a bullet, so I hastily looked around for some better protection. I found a barrel half full of salt. This I wheeled into position, and on the top I piled several neck-yokes used on the oxen, which afforded me some better protection than the wagon boxes alone. Flat on my stomach behind this barrel of salt, I did all my fighting, and another soldier named Jim Condon was lying next to me behind a barrel of beans, where he used his rifle in a most determined and dextrous manner.

An erroneous impression has been made by some historians and other writers who have attempted to give to the public the details of this most extraordinary engagement. They have stated that the wagon boxes used in this fight were lined with boiler iron and had loop holes in the sides. It also has been said that the wagon boxes were made entirely of iron. All of this is absolutely untrue. They were just the ordinary wooden wagon box, without a bit of iron or any other protection about them. They stood about four or five feet high, and the fighting was all done over the tops of the boxes, and not through any loopholes or any other such contrivance. If there was any wagon box in that fight that had been specially fortified or made bullet proof, I did not see it nor hear anything about it. There were no sacks of corn nor grain stuffed between the boxes to stop bullets, either. There were sacks of grain for the oxen and mules inside the corral, but there was no time to pile up such a barricade before the savages descended in hundreds upon us.

The reader must remember that two persons will often see things in an entirely different light; and for that reason I am stating only what came under my own personal observation in this fight. Some of our men were facing to the west, some to the north and others to the south, consequently different things were happening at different points of the compass, and some men saw and noted things which did not come under the observation of their comrades. This was due to the fact that this corral was oblong in shape, and we faced in different directions.

When we saw the hundreds upon hundreds of savage warriors pressing forward against our little improvised fort, not a man in the entire command expected to come out of that fight alive. The battle could not positively have lasted half an hour longer than it did, for we were almost completely exhausted by the awful heat of the day, and from the smoke occasioned by the fire arrows which the savages shot into the corral, and which ignited with scattered bits of hay and dry manure which had collected – for it was inside this corral where our animals were kept at night to prevent their being stampeded and run off by the Indians. This terrible stench and smoke nearly strangled us at times.

All the charges that I saw made against us by the Indians were on foot. True, they were on their ponies when they came down the mountain-sides and across the country, but the ponies were left out of rifle range, with their squaws to attend them, and the advances were all made without them – at least all that came under my observation. Many of the Indians circled us on their ponies and shot arrows into the corral in this manner, but they did not make a direct charge on horseback.

The first advance against us was made from the north hills. There were about three hundred Indians in this initial advance. They were stripped naked, save for breech-cloth and moccasins, and were all hideously painted for the fray. Their surplus clothing and fancy decorations were laid aside during the battle. They advanced on foot, very slowly at first, and after the first volley fired by our men on the north side of the corral – ten to fifteen in number – the savages advanced on the run. At the second volley the Indians still came on with wild cries and shrill warwhoops, thinking, no doubt, that once our guns were empty they could break over the corral and score an easy victory. But at the third volley they broke and fled for the hills out of rifle range. They had expected a time to expire after the first volley was delivered, and could not understand the rapid and continuous shooting without, apparently, stopping to reload. They advanced to within two hundred feet of the corral before the third volley sent them scattering. Had they advanced steadily with their entire force – which could not have numbered much under three thousand braves – the fight would not have lasted five minutes. It would have been simply impossible on our part to have loaded and fired rapidly enough to have prevented hundreds of them passing over our slight barricade, and had they once got inside the corral, it would have been all over in no time. It was perhaps a pardonable timidity on their part, as they had never before encountered breech-loading guns – and I am not speaking of repeating rifles, such as are used in the present day, but of single-loaders.

I kept my gun pretty well heated up during the conflict. I observed one huge Indian who seemed to have singled me out as his special foe. He was armed only with bow and arrows, but he certainly knew how to use his primitive weapons in a most skillful manner. Every time he sent a shaft at me he would leap into the air as high as he could, and would deliver his arrow at the apex of the leap. He was located not to exceed thirty to fifty feet away from me, but was in a slight depression into which I could not send an effective bullet. The only chance I had to return his fire would be when he jumped into the air to shoot at me. I fired at him a great many times before I finally managed to send a bullet where it would do the most good to all concerned.

I was stationed at the southwest corner of the corral, and in the excitement of the fight some of the Indians managed to get within five or six feet of us before falling under the withering fire we poured into them. These bodies falling so close to the corral, were not removed by their companions. Indians always recover their dead whenever possible, but these warriors were too close to our dead-line for any such attempt at rescue by their companions.

Early in the fight Lieutenant Jenness fell. He was standing behind the wagon boxes at the extreme west end of the corral, and was looking toward the west. He was just remarking, "Boys, look out! There are a good many Indians here, but—" The sentence was never finished. A bullet struck him in the head, killing him instantly. I was just at his left, kneeling to fire from behind my salt barrel when he received the fatal shot.

During the fight many of the men suffered greatly for want of water, of which we had no time to get a supply when attacked. As for myself, I was not thirsty, and did not use a drop of water during the entire battle; neither did the man stationed at my left.

Just after Lieutenant Jenness was killed, a mule was shot directly to my right. I worked my way over to the carcass and tried to pull it over where it would protect the body of my lieutenant from further mutilation, as a great many shots were being fired from the north. The mule, however, was too heavy for me to budge, and I had to give it up.

So far as I know, there were no blankets placed over the tops of the wagon boxes as protection from flying arrows. These shafts, more often than not, had burning pitch tied to them. Many of them dropped inside the corral and started the loose hay into flame and smudge. There was at least a smouldering fire burning in the center of the corral most of the time, and, as stated elsewhere, this smudge, smoke and stench would almost strangle us at times. The Indians not only were armed with bows and arrows, but they had guns as well. They had the eighty-one weapons secured from the Fetterman fight of December 21 the previous year. They also had obtained firearms from the wagon trains which they had successfully attacked along the Bozeman Trail, for the white man's tragedy along this road afforded the red men many weapons. Isolated trappers and frontiersmen also had been killed at various times and their guns secured. The Indians had further managed to acquire rifles from white traders while trafficking for buffalo robes and other peltries.

No person inside the corral was killed by an arrow. It was always a bullet that did the deadly work. However, our losses were very slight, and it seems almost beyond belief that it was a case of but thirty-two desperate men against three thousand infuriated Sioux. They must have lacked the right sort of leader, for had they attacked us in full force at any one time, not a man of us would have been spared – except to be reserved for torture.

I have seen somewhere a statement that one man used eight guns throughout this fight. This may have been true, but I did not see it myself, if any such incident occurred.

The first news we had that relief was coming from the fort was about one o'clock in the afternoon. We heard a cannon-shot and a shell exploded very close to where the main body of savages were congregated. At this shot the Indians fled from the field, going toward the northwest, from which direction they had first appeared.

The Indians were very brave in this fight, but seemed to lack a good leader, and did not use judgment in their attacks. I did not see any of our men jump to their feet and hurl any augurs or tools or stones into the faces of the Indians, as some writers have pictured.

No such battle as this has ever been recorded in all the Indian engagements of the west – I mean, where the whites were so overwhelmingly outnumbered – and we were outnumbered nearly a hundred to one. Neither has there been such a successful combat with Indians anywhere in the United States as to numbers killed in comparison to those fighting against them. The closest approach to it was the Beecher Island fight on the Arickaree Fork of the Republican River in 1868, where fifty men stood off about seven hundred Cheyennes for several days before relief came. The more one goes into the details of the fight, the more deeply is one impressed that it was the greatest Indian battle of the world. Thirty-two men struggling for six hours against three thousand well trained, dogged Indians – and the lesser number without any entrenchments, and with but the most meager protection. It cannot be emphasized too strongly that there was no intrenching done from the time of the sounding of the alarm to the time of the bursting of the first shell fired by the relief party from Fort Phil Kearney.

Referring to other matters of interest about old Fort Phil Kearney, I should state that I not only helped construct this post, but was one of the soldiers who stayed through its entire existence. I left the post with my company during August, 1868. From there we marched on foot to Cheyenne, and cheer after cheer went up when we heard the whistle of a locomotive, which the year before had made its appearance in that frontier town. From Cheyenne we took a train to a point in Nebraska. It must be remembered that we walked all the way from Fort Leavenworth to Fort Phil Kearney two years before. My company was mustered out at Plum Creek, Nebraska, and I was then detailed to Elm Creek, twelve miles east.

In speaking of the signals which Colonel Carrington installed for use at Fort Phil Kearney, I would state that the hill known today as Pilot Hill was the spot where these signals were displayed. On this point was a platform, and the back of the platform was in the manner of an intrenchment. The Indians signaled from their vantage points with mirrors. The soldiers signaled to the fort and other points with flags. Two of the signals were as follows: If a train of emigrants was seen on the Bozeman Trail, either going northwest or returning southeast, the flag was started at the ground and raised ninety degrees to zenith, and then wagged back to the ground again and furled back over the heads of the soldiers. If Indians were sighted on the trail or elsewhere, the flags executed a circle of one hundred and eighty degrees, starting from the ground on one side and going to the zenith and over to the ground on the reverse side, then back again and over again.

I knew old Jim Bridger, the famous scout and guide, very well, as he was the government guide for our battalion. He was at that time dressed in buckskin clothing. He was five feet, ten or eleven inches tall, of slim build, and was then sixty-two years of age. When one looked into his eyes they were wonderfully keen, and he could turn them down almost to a bead. He was silent when scouting, and knew every Indian sign and indication of the surrounding foe.

After 1869 my army life on the plains was a thing of the past. I was a young man and had my living to make. From that time until 1908 I had practically forgotten everything in connection with my army and Indian experiences. That year my son, who lives in St. Louis, saw something in the papers about a reunion which General Carrington was attending at Sheridan, Wyoming, in connection with the Fetterman Massacre Memorial monument and the battleground near old Fort Phil Kearney on the Bozeman Trail. Until I saw this notice, I did not know the general was still alive. I wrote to him at Hyde Park, Mass., where I found he was then living. Later, I learned that Sergeant Samuel Gibson, with whom I fought Indians on the plains, was living in Omaha. Gibson was in my company, and was himself in the Wagon Box fight. After that, he paid me a visit at St. Louis, and there we re-fought the Wagon Box battle in memory.

The United States government at one time promised that all the survivors of this wonderful engagement against hostile Indians would be rewarded with appropriate medals. Recognition, however, of the bravery and gallantry of our little handful of soldiers never has been made, and doubtless never will be. In any event, the Wagon Box fight seems to have been totally forgotten, save by the very few now alive who participated in that thrilling engagement.

MY EXPERIENCE IN THE WAGON BOX FIGHT[101]

Your letter with request for what I remember of the Wagon Box fight has been received, and I will oblige you, as far as my memory will permit.

---

[101] By Frederic Claus (living in Lincoln, Neb., 1920) former private, Twenty-seventh U.S. Infantry.

I arrived in New York City from Germany at the age of twenty-six. Times were hard, and so, early in 1867, I enlisted in the army. I was sent immediately to Fort McPherson, and from there, as soon as possible, with reinforcements, to Fort Phil Kearney, going over the road on foot, via Fort Laramie, Fort Fetterman and Fort Reno. The Eighteenth Regiment U.S. Infantry was at that time stationed—one battalion at Fort Reno and the other at Fort Phil Kearney. Part of our reinforcements were put in the Eighteenth, at Fort Reno and the balance at Fort Phil Kearney, where they were made into the Twenty-seventh U.S. Infantry.

When our reinforcements reached Fort Phil Kearney, I and some others were attached to Company C, Twenty-seventh U.S. Infantry, under Captain James W. Powell. Company C was detailed to the woods to protect the woodchoppers and the wagon train, which carried the logs from the pinery to the fort, also accompanying the empty wagons back. The wagon boxes were not used, but were taken off the gears and formed into an oval shaped corral. These wagon boxes were placed a little north of our tents.

On that memorable 2d of August, 1867, after the wagon train with the guards had been gone perhaps a couple of hours, the pickets gave the alarm of "Indians!" Captain Powell was down at the creek, taking a bath, I believe. He came toward the corral on the run, shouting: "Boys, the Indians are here! It will be a hard day for you all. You know what your orders are!"

Lieutenant Jenness called the company—or what was left of it, to fall in line, and the orderly-sergeant told us to take the ammunition out of the wagons and distribute it around in the wagon boxes, and to seek shel-

ter in them at once. The lieutenant had not been very
long in the country, and had had no experience in fighting Indians. He was instructed to also get in one of
the wagon boxes where he would be sheltered from the
fire of the Indians, but he replied that he knew how to
fight redskins as well as anyone. This was his last sentence, for just then he fell dead with a bullet through
his brain. That was in the first charge the Indians
made, where they posted their sharpshooters in front
of the wagon boxes with bows and arrows and tried to
set them on fire.

We had to contend with a rifle with which we were
not acquainted. They were breech-loaders, and we had
received them only about two weeks previously. We
knew that our only salvation was in keeping the Indians
from getting inside the corral. Once there, and they
could easily have cleaned us all up. The air was so
full of smoke from our guns that it was seldom that we
could see further than a few rods, and we had to be
very careful in putting our heads above the wagon
boxes in order to shoot.

Sometimes a box was set on fire by the Indians when
they would shoot fire arrows into them. Large bodies
of the savages were lying close in front of the wagon
beds, where they could easily reach our position with
their primitive weapons, and large numbers of them
were also armed with rifles.

These wagon boxes from which we were fighting
were just the old fashioned prairie schooner style. None
of them were lined with boiler iron, nor anything else
which would serve to protect us. I have read stories
by some writers that these wagon boxes were especially
prepared for just such a fight as we were engaged in,
but they were not. None of them had sides which were

more than an inch thick, through which bullets whizzed as easily as if we had no protection at all.

At the beginning of the fight, our tents were pulled down by some of the men to give us better observation to the south, and which left no place behind which the Indians could skulk up closer to us.

The woodchoppers who had been cut off in the woods and were unable at the time to reach our wagon box fort, hid out in the timber until the fight was over, and then they came in and went to the fort with us.

When the reinforcements arrived from the fort, we were indeed a happy lot of men. None of us ever expected to come out of that fight alive. There was a howitzer with the relief party, and it dealt death and destruction to the savages and put them quickly to flight.

I have read somewhere in some magazine about the number of Indians which are said to have been killed in this fight, and the figures given were between twelve hundred and thirteen hundred. This sounds to me pretty unreasonable and overdrawn, and I cannot believe their loss was so great as that. As I remember it, we found only one wounded Indian which they were unable to carry away with them. There was also a dead mule inside our corral. Our own loss was two or three killed and several wounded, but it was very slight in comparison to the Indian loss which must have amounted to several score. It must also be remembered that we had only thirty-two men fighting, and the Indian force was in the neighborhood of three thousand warriors.

Some months after the battle I and another comrade spoke to an Indian who had come to the fort. He could speak a little English. We asked him how many warriors Red Cloud had in the Wagon Box fight, and the Indian gave the number as over two thousand five hundred fighting men. Then we asked him how many Red Cloud lost. He could not – or would not – tell, but stated that the chief had declared that he lost the flower of his nation, and we came to the conclusion that their loss must have been a couple of hundred at least. I said always that it was impossible for our thirty-two men to have killed thirteen hundred out of their two thousand five hundred warriors.

On another occasion, about six weeks after this battle, our company was out on guard duty with the wood-choppers. As we were preparing to go back to camp again, one of the men returned to the creek to get a drink. We heard a shot in the direction in which he had gone, and when some of the men went to reconnoiter, we found his dead body lying where he had knelt down to drink. Of course an Indian had waylaid him.

Another time a soldier was pretty nearly killed by a big black bear. He had gone a little ahead from his station, being attracted by a peculiar noise in the underbrush. Suddenly he was confronted by an enormous bear. He shot at the animal, but must have missed. The bear sprang on him, knocked him down, and tore his cheeks open on both sides of his face. They were both hanging down, with the blood streaming from his wounds, when a couple of us reached him. We killed the bear and bandaged the man up as best we could, and brought him back to the fort. In the hospital he said his name was Haller. In about another month or so he came out of the hospital, but he had two terrible scars on his face, and was nicknamed "Bear" Haller ever after.

As to the Fetterman disaster that happened before I

had arrived at Fort Phil Kearney, and all I know about it is what I heard from others after reaching there, and I do not care to make any statement about it for that reason.

There were many interesting happenings at Fort Phil Kearney, as well as sad ones, but after a lapse of fifty years and more, many of them have escaped my memory and I am unable to recall them. The Wagon Box fight, however, is something that can never be effaced from my memory while time shall last.

Personal Experiences in and around Fort Phil Kearney[102]

My first enlistment in the United States army was in the Forty-ninth Illinois Infantry, January 1, 1862, for the War of the Rebellion. However, as this story deals with my Indian experiences on the plains, I will pass over my first enlistment. After my discharge, I re-enlisted in the Eighteenth United States Infantry, on March 28, 1864, and was sent west to help quell the Indian disturbances, which had become very numerous, owing to the fact that Uncle Sam's soldiers were busy putting down the Rebellion, and had but little time to fool with Indians.

This was in the stagecoach days of 1865 to 1867, when that whole expansive territory was a howling wilderness. We arrived at Fort Kearney, Nebraska, on the fifth of December, 1864. Passing over events which transpired there, will state that I started for the northwest with Colonel Henry B. Carrington's Expedition for the Big Horn and Powder River country, May 19, 1866. We followed the Platte River on the south side until we reached Julesburg, about May 29th. The last twenty miles of this march we found that the country had been settled by ranchers, but the Indians had swooped down upon them and killed men, women, and children, and destroyed the buildings.

From Julesburg we moved on to Fort Sedgwick,

102 By F. M. Fessenden, Chattanooga, Tenn., former sergeant and principal musician, Eighteenth U. S. Infantry Band at Kearney.

which was but a short distance. Here I was left behind the command with my wife—who, by the way, was with me on this entire trip and went through all the sufferings and privations of that frontier life, on the march and at Fort Phil Kearney. A daughter was born to us here at Fort Sedgwick. She was a great favorite with Captain Fetterman, who wanted us to name her "Sedgwick," after Fort Sedgwick. After a rest of about four weeks we both went to Fort Laramie in an army ambulance, with two men to drive and guard. Some new officers joined us at Laramie, and when we finally started on for Fort Phil Kearney we had a detachment of twenty-one men and officers, seven wagons, two ambulances, three women, five children and one colored woman, a servant for the wife of Lieutenant Wands.

At our first camp after leaving Fort Laramie, a number of Indians came to our command. They appeared very friendly—so much so that it excited our curiosity. We soon discovered the reason. The squaws wanted to buy our baby, offering beads, furs and trinkets of all kinds in exchange. When we refused they acted very sullen, and told us plainly that they would steal her if they got the chance.

After a toilsome journey we finally arrived at Fort Reno, situated on Powder River. Here we remained a few days. We had a three days' march ahead of us before we could reach Fort Phil Kearney, our destination. Our first camping ground after leaving Reno was on Crazy Woman's Fork of Powder River, on July 20th. On arriving at this camp we found the weather very warm. In our party there was a saddle horse which the officers took turns in riding. Lieutenant Daniels rode on ahead to find a good camping ground.

He was about a half-mile in advance. Just as we started to descend a hill, the horse came running back, riderless, with the saddle turned under him. Several Indians were pursuing the animal. The men all jumped from the wagons and opening a rapid fire upon the savages, succeeded in scattering them. We then managed to get down the hill and corraled. Here the Indians attacked us fiercely. We had formed the wagons into a hollow square, placing the women and children inside for protection.

There were about one hundred and sixty of the Indians as near as we could estimate, and only twenty-one of our party capable of fighting, but we kept those savages at a distance. We noticed among the Indians one whom we took for a chief. He was stationed on a little hill directing the fight by signals with a flag. Lieutenant Link had a Henry rifle, a sixteen shooter. He asked me to go with him and try to kill the chief. We crawled along a ravine until we got within rifle-shot, where Lieutenant Link, by a well directed shot, dropped the chief. As he started to fall from his horse, two Indians rode up, one on each side of him, and led him away out of rifle range.

After the death, or wounding, of this chief, the Indians went down the stream into some timber. In the meantime, we prepared to get into a better fighting position. Before we could carry out these plans, however, the Indians came out of the timber, with loud yells, and again attacked us. We reached the foot of another hill and intended to fight it out from that position, but we saw they had the timber, while we were fighting in the open. Then it was suggested that we make a rush up this hill and form for defense. After some sharp skirmishing, we accomplished this, reaching the top of the hill, where we again formed in a hollow square. Some of the men began to hastily dig rifle pits. We had a hot skirmish with the Indians here, and it looked for awhile as if it were all off with our brave little party. Soon we saw a heavy dust cloud arising over a nearby bluff, and felt sure it was reinforcements for the Indians. It happened, however, to be the wagon train of a man named Hugh Kirkendall on its way to Fort Reno. Nothing but the timely arrival of this train saved our hair. That night we sent two men back to Reno, for a relief party, and by daylight Lieutenant Kirtland, with a company of Infantry and a mountain howitzer, had arrived. Then we had a chance for the first time to hunt for Lieutenant Daniels. We found his body. It had been pierced by three bullets, and there were twenty-two arrows sticking in it. I have yet one of those arrows in my possession which went through the lieutenant's body; also an arrow which was shot at me, and which narrowly missed me.

After burying the lieutenant we again started for Fort Phil Kearney. This time we were fortunate in having a large force. The Indians bothered us all along the route that day. Some of them, pretending to be friendly, came into our camp, but we could see that they meant mischief. One buck offered me five ponies for my Colt revolver. When I told Lieutenant Wands about this, he ordered the Indians out of our camp.

After arriving at Fort Phil Kearney we pitched our tents, in which we lived while building quarters for our men. We had at that time plenty of supplies, including seven hundred beef cattle; the commissary was well filled, and we had plenty of ammunition and tools with which to operate. We had two portable sawmills. The fort was on a slight elevation. A fine stream ran on the south side of the stockade on which the saw-mills were set up. There was excellent grazing for the stock, and a more ideal spot for a fort could not be imagined. Less than half a mile to the west there was another elevation, which was on the route to the mountains where we got out our timber. To the east, the hills arose to a considerable height. The highest peak was called Picket Point, or "Pilot Hill." On this point a man on horseback was stationed in the daytime as a lookout for Indians. Several men would accompany the picket to this hill. Here an unobstructed view of the country could be had, and the atmosphere was so clear one could discern a wagon approaching while it was yet miles distant. If the lookout happened to see Indians, he would ride in a circle in plain view of the fort and stop his horse with its head in the direction of the savages. As soon as he began to "circle," several mounted men would start to his rescue, and the lookout himself would "dig out" at top speed. On several occasions these lookouts brought in arrows in their bodies as trophies of their retreat.

Out at the pineries where we cut our timber, we built two blockhouses, one at each cutting, we having what was known as the "upper" and "lower" cutting. This was six miles from the fort, and detachments of men went out and cut timber each day. Every morning twenty wagons were sent out for this purpose. About half a mile before reaching the timber, the road forked at an angle of about forty-five degrees, one road running to each cutting. Here we found trees that were ninety feet to the first limb, and as straight as an arrow.

The fort was planned by Colonel Carrington, who was an engineer, as well as our commander. There were six acres enclosed in the fort. Around this six acres a trench was dug three feet deep, in which the stockade posts were set. These posts were about sixteen inches in diameter and eleven feet long, and were tamped three feet in gravel. They were hewed on two sides so they would touch. The top of each post was sharpened, and a port hole cut every few feet, being largest on the outside, so that the guns could be aimed right or left. A platform was built at every port-hole, so that in case of an attack, a man could fire, then step aside and reload while another man took his place for a shot. Colonel Carrington was a very busy man, and took great interest in the building of Fort Phil Kearney. He was always out early in the morning and saw that everyone was in charge of their special departments, doing their duty. He took great interest especially in the construction of the magazine, to see that it was built according to detail.

To build a fort like this took time and timber. It was late in the fall before it was completed, as we had Indians to contend with every day. They delighted to harrass and torment us. They would make raids on our stock, and they eventually succeeded in getting away with six hundred out of our seven hundred beef cattle. We would have our horses and mules out grazing, with men herding them, and the Indians would appear as suddenly as though they had sprung from the earth, like so many grasshoppers. They would run through the herd, yelling, whooping and waving blankets or buffalo hides, and stampede the animals, thus getting away with much stock. We kept fifty horses saddled all the time with which to go after the stampeded animals, but none of them were ever recovered.

The company buildings were very nice for log structures. Posts were hewn and a mortise cut the whole length and set every ten feet. The logs were hewn on two sides, with a tenent on each side, and dropped in from the top, so as to fit closely. When finished it was in panels of about ten foot lengths, the bark side of the logs being turned to the weather. The roof was of poles about four inches thick, put close together, then covered with corn sacks or grass, with about six inches of earth over this for "shingles." Such a roof seldom leaked.

There were several married people at the fort, and a number of children as well. Colonel Carrington had his wife and two boys. Then there were Dr. Horton and wife; Lieutenant Grummond and wife; Lieutenant Wands, wife and boy; Bandmaster Curry, wife and two boys; John Maurer and wife; a man named Murray, wife and one daughter; a man named Hannibal, wife and three girls; another man named Laughlotts, wife and daughter, and myself, wife and daughter.

There was seldom a day that we were not harrassed by the Indians. They very often attacked the wood train, running off the teams and occasionally killing a soldier. Teamsters sitting by their camp fires were fired on at night by the red devils. They would often prowl around the fort and shoot arrows at the guards, and on one occasion killed a guard in that manner.

We had with us at Fort Phil Kearney an interpreter by the name of Jack Stead, who was taken along with the command when it left Fort Kearney, Nebraska. He had lived with the Pawnees for several years, but they had been at war with the Sioux for a long time. The Sioux knew Stead, and a price was put on his scalp by them, so he told me. He was so afraid of the Indians that I don't believe he ever went outside the stockade. He was very much excited when there was anything doing in the nature of an Indian fight.

There was a special artist at the fort for Frank Leslie's Illustrated Weekly, by the name of Professor Glover.[103] He had a camera outfit and was taking views for his paper. While taking pictures he would go around alone on the mountains, and sometimes would not be seen for five or six days at a time. He made his headquarters with the woodchoppers. He had long yellow hair, and I had often told him that the Indians would delight to clip that hair for him some day. He said he was safe, as the Indians would take him for a Mormon.

One Monday morning two other men and myself concluded to start out early ahead of the wagon train, steal our way into the timber and try for a couple of deer, which we had often observed crossing the road a short distance ahead of the wagons. We started before daylight, and had gone but a short distance when I observed something white lying across the wagon trail. I remarked, "What is that?" The other men thought at first that it was a mountain wolf, as the light was yet quite indistinct. "Watch out for Indians," I exclaimed. We cautiously approached the object, with our guns cocked, and as we got close to it we saw that it was the body of Professor Glover of Leslie's Weekly. It was the work of Indians, and they had clipped that long hair, taking the entire scalp. He was lying on his face, and his back was slit the entire length. Several arrows were sticking in the body. Poor Glover had met the white man's fate.

---

[103] There is some dispute over this artist's name. The Carrington books give it as Grover.

My surmise that there might be Indians about was correct. They had killed Glover, and were mighty near us at the same time. We at once rushed to the top of the steep ridge, where we laid low until the wagon train came along; then we lost no time in getting among the men. Here the Indians attacked us, and we were forced to corral the train and send to the fort for reinforcements. This was just about at the spot where the road to the two pinery cuttings divided. We stood them off until a detachment of cavalry came to our rescue; after which we got our train in order and proceeded to the upper cutting. On this day we lost so much time fighting the Indians that we did not get back from the pinery until dark.

Poor Glover, the artist, was told on Sunday, the day before he was killed, by the men at the cuttings, not to attempt to go to the fort alone, as the Indians were always keeping a sharp lookout for stragglers. The woodchoppers tried to get him to remain and wait for the wood train Monday. He left one cutting and said he would go to the other, which he did. The men at this cutting also warned him of the danger, and almost certain death, if he attempted to go on to the fort alone. He told these choppers that he would return to the other cutting–which he did not do, as he was on his way to the fort alone, when he met the certain fate which overtook every man caught alone away from the garrison. Glover had escaped so many times that he apparently thought he was Indian proof.

About this time of the year a company of miners appeared on the scene, searching for gold in the hills. A man by the name of Bailey was their captain, and they camped near the fort, where they were often of great assistance, as they were all crack rifle shots. There were about fifty of them in the party. One time one of Bailey's miners was out hunting and the Indians got after him. He succeeded in getting into the thick brush on the ridge of which I have spoken, and which was a rendezvous for lone men when Indians approached, because the thick underbrush afforded good concealment. The Indians surrounded this miner so closely that it was twenty-four hours before his companions rescued him.

The fort was now finished, with the exception of a few minor details. We now began to feel safer. We were well aware, however, that it behooved us to be on our guard every minute of the time. Vigilance is the price of life when surrounded by hostile Indians. We began to have some few enjoyments. We had church services, which were well attended every Sunday. The ground was fine for dress parades, which we had every afternoon. We had guard mount in the morning. We had a most excellent band, and they gave us concerts to remind us of the dear ones back home in civilization. All this served to help break the awful monotony of our lives in that desolate country.

The climate was very healthful, and we had no sickness of any consequence until our provisions ran low that winter. I do not remember that we buried but one man here who was not killed by the Indians, and that man was our band leader. The night he died I well remember how the wolves howled and made the night hideous, and we could hear them scratch at the stockade posts. When we buried the body we had to dig very deep, place heavy planks over the box, and then haul heavy stones and fill the grave to prevent the wolves from digging the body out.

In preparing for winter, we had wood to cut and hay

to haul. We contracted with civilians to cut the hay. They came from the settlements further east, and brought mowing machines. Remember, no white men were in that country then, except those passing through – and these were not always successful, by any means. We furnished soldiers to guard the haycutters, but soon the Indians began to burn the hay. We had to discontinue the haycutting, as the Indians were becoming too numerous. It was a queer thing about the numerical strength of the savages. Sometimes only a few would be seen, but at the psychological moment, it appeared that hundreds of them would rise out from the level of the prairie. As they became more numerous, they also grew bolder. Orders were given that none of our men should ever go out of the fort alone. The chaplain bought a cow, for which he paid seventy-five dollars. He told me if I would milk her, I could have all the milk that was left after he was served. I remember how I used to arm myself and go out hunting after that cow. I presume the Indians also wanted her, for they eventually got her, anyway. Orders finally became so strict that I did not dare go outside the stockade. Conditions were becoming more alarming every day. The Indians were becoming more numerous than ever in every direction, and they also were desperate.

As we kept fifty horses constantly saddled, there were now no idle moments, but plenty of anxiety. On December 6th, Colonel Carrington, Lieutenant Grummond and some others were in a desperate skirmish with the Indians, in which Lieutenant Bingham and Sergeant Bowers were both killed. Lieutenant Grummond told me afterward that he shut his eyes and literally slashed his way out, as did many of the others. Grummond said he could hear his saber "click" every time he cleaved an Indian's skull. The savages attempted to catch several of our boys by trying to put their strung bows over their necks and drag them off their horses.

Conditions now were so hazardous that the colonel doubled the number of guards sent out with the wagon trains to the pinery. The weather was getting cold, and feed for the stock was scarce, as the Indians had forced us to stop the haycutting before getting in a good crop, and they had destroyed all they possibly could. It was positive suicide for a man to go outside of the stockade. It was getting time for the Indians to go into winter quarters themselves, and we realized that whatever move they made would have to be done in short order.

On the 21st of December the train had gone out for timber. Just at nine o'clock, during guard mount, the picket on Pilot Hill gave the alarm that the Indians were attacking the wood train. Immediately the fifty saddle horses were mounted. At the same time two Indians made their appearance across the stream near the fort. They dismounted and sat down near a tree. Both were wrapped in red blankets. The cavalry had gone to the assistance of the wagon train, as mentioned. Captain Fetterman offered his services, and with Lieutenant Grummond and some soldiers, started out. Instead of going to protect the wood train, they started after the two Indians across the stream. The direction they had to go led them over a hill some little distance away. At the foot of this hill, but on the opposite side, were two ravines which came to a point. Over this point was a very large rock. The company of cavalry, not finding the Indians attacking the wood train, as expected, followed them over this point. Fetterman's men went over this hill, and followed them over this point, where the two ravines intersected. As soon as they were all over, the Indians swarmed out and closed in on them. The battle commenced. We could plainly hear every volley fired.

Captain Ten Eyck, with an ambulance and a few men, was sent out at once. By the time these men reached the top of the hill, the firing had ceased and the battle was over. Captain Ten Eyck sent a messenger back to the fort that our men were all annihilated. He could hear nothing but the groans of the dying. He requested that more men and a piece of artillery be sent to him. He said there were from three thousand to five thousand of them. Colonel Carrington sent back word: "Come back; I have lost men enough." There were eighty-one men killed in that awful fight. Nearly all died around the big rock mentioned. They found the body of brave Captain Brown, who had accompanied Fetterman's detail without the knowledge or consent of Colonel Carrington, some distance in advance of the other men, scalped, and his body cut in a horrible manner. They had even scalped his horse, their hatred for him was so extreme. Strung along this road behind him, some of his men fell. They scalped every man, stripped them and slashed them with their own sabres. They placed powder in the ears of some of the soldiers and touched it off. They gathered grass which was dried, and placed it on the stomachs of others and lighted it. Here your imagination must rest for the horrifying details.

That night was the most exciting one I have ever experienced. All was hustle and bustle. We expected they would attack the fort that same night. We had orders to bar up our windows and doors, but to leave port-holes in the windows to fire through. There was a magazine in one corner of the parade ground, which was a large hole in the ground, well supported with heavy timbers and covered with earth and sodded over. This magazine was well supplied with ammunition of all kinds. Wagons were hauled in; the beds taken off their gears and placed on their sides and surrounded this magazine. Then more wagons were placed in a circle, until we had three circles surrounding the magazine. The soldiers were then placed three in number at every port-hole around the inside of the stockade.

We had ten women and several children with us. The colonel gave orders that as soon as the Indians made the expected attack, the women and children should enter the magazine, and the men should hold the fort as long as possible. When they could hold it no longer, they were to get behind the wagons that surrounded the magazine, and when the colonel saw that all was lost, he would himself blow up the magazine and take the lives of all, rather than allow the Indians to capture any of the inmates alive.

I heard Colonel Carrington utter those words. The colonel's wife and two boys were with him. The young wife of Lieutenant Grummond, who had lost her husband in the fight of December 6th, was also with us. During the evening, arrangements were made to send to Fort Laramie for reinforcements, two hundred and thirty-six miles to the southeast. The mail carrier, a man named "Portugee" Phillips, volunteered to make the attempt. We never expected to see him again, but still, there was some hope. Nobody in the fort slept that night. We expected the Indians to attack us every moment. But our anxiety was lost, as they failed to make any demonstration against the post.

The next morning, Colonel Carrington went with men and wagons out to gather the remaining dead soldiers which Ten Eyck had not found the day before. We did not know but the colonel and his command would meet the same fate as had their comrades on the previous day. We were overjoyed, therefore, when they came back, but sadness overcame us when, nearing the fort, we saw seven wagons loaded with naked bodies – arms and legs in all shapes, divulging the horrible manner in which our brave comrades had died. It was a horrible and a sickening sight, and brought tears to every eye, to see those men, many of whom had served four years in the War of the Rebellion, meeting such an awful death on the western plains. Some of these men had but ten days more to serve, when their enlistment would have expired, and they could have returned to their far eastern homes.

I do not know as anyone has ever given out any information as regards the number of Indians killed and wounded in the Fetterman disaster, but I will give you the figures that were told to me. In the spring of 1867, before I was discharged, a small band of Crow Indians, mostly squaws, came from the Little Big Horn. Some of these squaws were in my quarters at the fort, and I asked them to tell me all they could about the fight, and how many were killed. They said that about one hundred and fifty were killed and about three hundred wounded, of which one-half would die. I do not know if these figures are correct, or if anyone really does know the extent of the Indian loss, but this is what was told me by these squaws.

We had a large frame building which was built for quartermaster's supplies, and which had not yet been put to use. Our massacred and mutilated comrades were there made ready for burial. A long trench was dug and they were laid side by side out in that lonely wilderness.

I had a narrow escape from the same fate myself. Before the Fetterman disaster I had made arrangements for a horse to ride out on the next raid against the Indians. I was on guard mount when the call came, and that is the reason I am alive today, instead of sleeping with my comrades out there in Wyoming. As soon as the cavalry started, I ran for my horse, and upon meeting Captain Brown's orderly, I said, "Where is that horse for me?" To my query he replied, "You are too late; they have all gone." If I had secured that horse I would not be writing this.

Winter was now on in full force, and we looked with anxious hearts for some tidings from Fort Laramie. We had no telegraph, of course, so we had to wait for news by courier. At last word came that reinforcements had started our way. How our drooped spirits revived at this joyous news! Red Cloud could easily have wiped out every vestige of this fort, had he ever attacked us in full force, and why he did not attempt this is an unanswered question.

When the reinforcements started from Fort Laramie, under Colonel Wessels, the snow was two feet deep, and more, in some places, and the mercury was from twenty-five to forty degrees below zero. Marching was necessarily slow. Sometimes the reinforcements encountered blizzards. They had to shovel snow, often waist deep, and sleep in tents, with the thermometer down at an awful degree of frigidity. They were suffering almost death in their efforts to reach us. They encountered untold hardships without a murmur. Some of them did not get beyond Fort

Reno, on account of frozen limbs, which there had to be amputated. Washington's troops at Valley Forge did not suffer more than did these brave men.

About this time feed for our stock was getting woefully scarce. We had to send teams up the river for fuel, and haul in limbs of cottonwood trees for feed for our stock. The weather had become so cold and the snow so deep we could no longer go to the timber cuttings. With our regiment was a troop of the Second U.S. Cavalry. Their horses became so nearly starved that we had to stretch a chain, in place of a rope, from post to post, and tie the animals so far apart that they could not reach each other, for they would gnaw the hair from each other's manes and tails. The posts had to be covered with hides, flesh side out, or the horses would have eaten the posts. They would gnaw anything in the shape of wood. It was pitiful to witness the suffering of these poor patient animals; and at night, especially, we could hear them fairly moan and groan like a human being in their agony of hunger. I have seen six mules hitched to a wagon and sent out after wood and brush – the brush to feed the stock – and often but four animals would bring back the two wagons; the remainder were left dead on the way, where they had dropped from exhaustion and hunger. This was one of the most terrible experiences at the fort, and strongly impressed me.

The winter was so severe that we could not get through to Fort Laramie for provisions. Rations for the men were now very scarce. We had to cut down on allowances. It began to look like starvation for men and animals both, and we were finally reduced to nothing but a little hardtack and condemned sow-belly. Food became so scarce and of such poor quality that scurvy broke out, and nearly every man had it, which placed us in sore straits, and made our sufferings doubly hard to bear.

There was one company of our regiment up at Fort C. F. Smith on the Big Horn River. We had heard nothing from them since before the Fetterman disaster. We did not know but they had met the same fate. An offer was made to two soldiers to go over the mountains and get some tidings of them. A sergeant and private volunteered to go. They went as far as the pinery on mules, accompanied by two men who were to bring back the mules. They carried rifles and well-filled haversacks, of such provisions as we had, and started from the pinery on foot on that perilous journey over an utterly strange country.

With hard struggling through deep snow, they missed running into any Indians, and landed safely at Fort C. F. Smith, where they found all was well. Here they remained for a few days, resting from their perilous trip, and then started back on their hazardous return. A guide was sent back with them, and they had horses from Fort Smith to ride, so their starting was a comfortable one, but their troubles were not all over. One day when they stopped to rest and eat their dinner, the guide being on the lookout for Indians, he soon came running to the men saying that a band of Indians was coming. They all mounted and made haste for the mountains near at hand. The savages finally pressed them so hard that they abandoned their animals. One of the men dropped his rifle and they also lost what provisions they had, together with their blankets.

Here they were, in a howling wilderness, without food or blankets, and several days' journey before them. Their sufferings were indescribable. They evaded the

Indians, but, without food, their lot was indeed a hard one. They managed to kill one rabbit, and this they ate raw. Their shoes gave out and they were obliged to take their coats and wrap them about their feet. Their indomitable pluck saved them however, for about eleven o'clock one night they reached the fort, but they were in a frightful condition. Their feet were frozen and they were nearly starved. They were obliged to go into the hospital, and were still there when I left the fort.

I was a member of the Eighteenth U.S. Infantry band, and was promoted the last six months of my service to Principal Musician, with the rank of sergeant, therefore belonging to the non-commissioned staff, and being placed in command of all the musicians at the fort.

It seems beyond comprehension, at this late day, to look back and realize what we went through. The weather was so cold that winter of '66 and '67, that men could not remain on guard but a few minutes at a time, for fear of being frozen. The relief would make the rounds, and another relief would start. Think of men on a platform four feet above the ground and only six feet long – which was where the sentries were stationed – and this space all the room they had in which to exercise enough to keep themselves from freezing, with the thermometer at forty degrees below zero! I can remember one time when it reached that point and remained there for ten days. Our food was such that it was impossible to get enough men for guards who did not have the scurvy. Sick men, poor food, shortage of fuel, zero weather and surrounded by thousands of bloodthirsty savages, eager to lift our scalps!

I was discharged March 28, 1867. On the 9th of April I started for my home in Ohio, accompanied by

my wife and baby girl, who had been born at Fort
Sedgwick the previous year. There were about a
dozen of us who left that morning, with only a few wagons. The day before we started was fairly warm, and
the snow was melting fast. By night it had turned
cold and was snowing, and so fierce was the storm that
night that in the morning we found ourselves confronted by two feet of snow. We had a three days' journey
to reach Fort Reno. It was a terrible journey, but we
finally pulled through in safety. When we arrived we
found the Powder River so high from the melting
snow that we had to remain there for some time. It
was time for Van Volzah, the mail carrier, to arrive
with mail from Fort Laramie. He did not show up.
Day after day we were detained, but still Van Volzah
did not come. Then it came time for John Phillips,
who was carrying mail from Phil Kearney south, to
arrive. He did not appear until two days overtime.
Then in the night he came in. The other mail carrier,
Van Volzah, never did get to Reno, for he was waylaid,
killed and scalped on his way in. His mail bag was
found, but it had been ransacked and the letters and
papers scattered around in the sagebrush. "Van" had
two other men with him and two pack mules. The
latter were loaded with onions, which he was taking
through to Fort Phil Kearney, for the men who were
suffering with scurvy. I was surprised to learn, several
years afterward, that Phillips was then alive. How he
ever got through on those trips without losing his
scalp, I cannot imagine. However, he was a very brave
frontiersman, and his pluck and nerve carried him
through many a tight place.

When we finally did leave Fort Reno, the weather
had moderated, and we had a nice trip all the rest of

the way in. As much as I wanted to get back to civilization, among friends, and away from such a hard life, I disliked to part with the many friends I had made at Fort Phil Kearney.

After we left Fort Reno and crossed the Powder River, we pitched our tents, cooked our meal and acted as though we were going to camp there for the night. When our fires were out, about ten o'clock that night, we started ahead so as to get through a deep canyon and give the Indians that might be prowling around, the slip. As we were discharged soldiers, we had but a few wagons. It seems so strange to me to realize that I traveled from Julesburg through to Fort Phil Kearney and back again, with so few comrades as an escort, through a hostile Indian country, and still have my scalp.

There was a man by the name of A. B. Ostrander who was a member of my regiment, though he was only eighteen years old. He left Fort Phil Kearney in April, 1867, with Major Van Voast and about forty men—discharged soldiers and a few civilians, one of the latter being an old trapper whom we called "Big Sam," by reason of his size. He and Ostrander slept under the same blankets on the way down. Major Van Voast had the only tent in the outfit; he also had two horses. One night they made camp on a ridge right in a thick clump of sagebrush. After the Major's tent was put up, his two horses were lariated and the picket pins driven down on the inside of his tent. The major said he did not intend to have the savages steal *his* horses. During the night a little bunch of savages crawled up through the brush, pulled up those picket pins and got away with both of the major's horses. He never heard the last of that joke the savages played on him. As the Indians were making their get-away the sentry fired a shot, which, of course, created a commotion. Ostrander started to get up, when Big Sam grabbed him by the back of the neck and pushed his face down into the dirt, exclaiming: "Don't you get on your feet in a mix-up like this, boy!" It so happened that there was a bunch of prickly-pear in the very spot where Ostrander's face was pushed, and his features were so badly scratched and disfigured that it took several weeks for the sores to heal.

Early in the morning six Indians rode around the outfit, just out of rifle range, yelling in a tantalizing manner—but they did not return the major's horses! Ostrander had a fine sorrel horse which he had purchased from Lieutenant Harrison of the Second Cavalry, and this horse was loaned to the major for the balance of the trip, while Ostrander rode in the ambulance.

My party had left the fort some time in advance of Ostrander's, but as we stopped at Fort Sedgwick he and his party overtook us. I recall that Ostrander put his head out of the ambulance, and it was all tied up in a handkerchief, and the report was circulated that he had been scalped.

When I look back to those wild days on the frontier, and take into consideraton the many friends I made among the soldiers; the beautiful scenery of that vast mountain region, the snow-capped peaks, our staunch, well-made fort and its surroundings—when I look back to it all, it is a pleasure to recall those thrilling days.

FORT C. F. SMITH, MONTANA TERRITORY, 1867

From a sketch by Capt. I. D'Isay, after drawing by Anton Schonborn. Reproduced from the original owned by Captain John A. Perry.

Route of the Bozeman Trail; Description of Forts Reno, C. F. Smith, and Fetterman

No two persons seem to exactly agree upon the absolute route of the Bozeman Trail throughout its entire length. There are as many different roads traced on maps as there are draughtsmen. True, in the main, the roads agree as to essentials, but the variations are numerous. The Bozeman Trail or Road, as here set forth, is worked out from several reports: From Fort Sedgwick to Fort Laramie by Colonel Carrington; from that fort to Fort Reno, from a drawing made by F. G. Burnett;[104] from Fort Reno to Fort C. F. Smith, from the orginal field notes of Mrs. A. L. Garber;[105] from Fort Smith to the gold-fields and Virginia City, by Arthur L. Stone[106] and Colonel Carrington's map made from Jim Bridger's surveys; from the Platte to Virginia City by David B. Weaver.[107]

Technically the Bozeman Trail commenced at Fort Kearney, Nebraska, where all the soldiers from the east and south, who were to fight Indians, were assembled, from here being sent into all parts of the western country infested by Indians – and that practically

[104] F. G. Burnett, Fort Washakie, Wyoming.

[105] Mrs. Garber, Big Horn, Wyoming, was Miss Vie Willits when she made the survey in 1909 and 1910, making the journey with her father, walking a greater part over the trail, sometimes riding in a wagon, often on horseback.

[106] *Following Old Trails.*

[107] Montana Historical Society *Collections,* vol. viii.

included all of the West at that time. Fort Kearney was located on the south side of the Platte River, along the Oregon Trail, Fort McPherson being the next station to the west; the next post, Fort Sedgwick, was one hundred and ten miles up the South Platte. Fort Sedgwick was considered by Colonel Carrington as the real starting point of the Bozeman Trail, which from this post, went to the northwest, crossing the South Platte toward the North Platte, following for many miles Lodge Pole Creek. Near Courthouse Rock, on the Oregon Trail, the trail went directly west, keeping on the south side of the North Platte, passing Chimney Rock, Scotts Bluffs and Fort Mitchell. Northwest from here the route was very direct until the Laramie River was crossed, and where Fort Laramie was located. The Bozeman Trail did not cross the North Platte at the fort, but continued on the south side of the stream until a natural ford was built or a ferry had been constructed.

Mr Burnett locates the Bozeman Trail from Fort Laramie on the south side of the Platte, running very close to the river, and following the Oregon Trail to the northwest, crossing Horseshoe and Elkhorn Creeks, until reaching Bridger's Ferry, about two miles east of the present day railroad town of Orin Junction. Following the North Platte on its north side, after the Platte had been crossed, the trail continued to the northwest, until just west of the mouth of La Prele Creek, opposite what is now the site of old Fort Fetterman. From here, the trail broke away from the beaten path to the west, and departed almost to the north, where it shortly turned to the west. From here the entire trail was in a generally northwest direction, until Fort Smith was reached. Sage, Willow and Brown's Spring

Creeks were crossed near their beginnings, when the Dry Fork of the Cheyenne River, made from the three creeks, was passed, bringing the trail to Bear and Sand Creeks. On the north side of Wind River there is a postoffice called Ross, the trail going by its site on its west. Then the road crossed Nine-mile Creek, going directly north to the Dry Fork of the Powder River, down which the trail went until it reached the main Powder River, by a ford over which wagons passed, and reached the first fort in the Sioux country, Fort Reno (Connor).

Mrs. Garber describes in minute and accurate detail the rest of the route of the Bozeman Trail to Fort C. F. Smith, Montana. "From Fort Laramie the Bozeman Trail took a general northwesterly course, and upon nearing the Powder River, followed down the long ravine known as the Dry Fork of the Powder River. This Dry Fork crossing on the Powder is still well known and used, although it has never been successfully bridged, and has varied almost a mile in location, owing to the ever-shifting and sliding banks of that stream.

"From Powder River the trail still used much of the distance to Crazy Woman's Fork, although the crossing of the latter was a mile below the present bridge at the Trabing postoffice (eighteen miles southeast of Buffalo, Wyoming). As Fort Reno was located about four miles below the Dry Fork ford, from 1865 there was a much used road leading down the northwest side of Powder River to the fort and again back from the fort to the trail toward Crazy Woman. This distance of almost thirty miles from Powder River to Crazy Woman, has remained practically unfenced, and the Bozeman Trail, along with various recent roads, is used today. From Crazy Woman to Clear Creek, the present road almost follows the course of the trail past the 'wallows' for sixteen miles to the 'Big Spring' at the 'Cross H' ranch. At this point, where the lane now runs directly north into Buffalo, the trail passed off to the northeast, and followed along low ridges, through what are now the 'Cross H' and Foote ranches, coming down to a crossing of Clear Creek a mile below Buffalo. Through these ranches, although much of the trail has been plowed and under cultivation for twenty-eight[108] years, wherever the native sod is unbroken, the grass grown tracks are readily traced. Across one ravine, where a large irrigating canal has absolutely obstructed the use of the road since 1883, the tracks are plainly indented in the sod. The Clear Creek ford is still in use by the ranchers, and is known as the 'Hamilton' ford, because a man bearing that name lived on the west side of the ford. From this ford, the trail runs toward the northeast, past the Frank Grouard house and over French Creek; and then up the hills, just northeast of the Johnson County fair grounds, and down into Rock Creek valley; thence up the valley for about half a mile to a ford now in use just below the Mather's and Monker's house, and on past that house through the gap in the divide below.

"From Shell Creek to Piney few traces can be found, but it is well known that the trail followed the general course of the present county road, varying but little, except where the lanes are now twined out around corners of fields. The Piney crossing was a little more than a quarter of a mile up stream from the present iron and cement bridge. The road up onto the Prairie Dog (Massacre Hill) divide, ran through the same

---

[108] Thirty-eight years (1920).

gap as at present. Along the summit of Massacre Hill the trail ran northward and down that natural hogback, to a point on Prairie Dog Creek below the present bridge, and back of the building on the Banner ranch; thence to the north of the present lane and between the big butte and the pond on the Terrill ranch; then to Pomp Creek in practically the same course at present traveled. Here the trail crossed to the southwest of the present road, and through a gap in the hills to the south of the Payne ranch; thence along the western divide down to a ford on the west fork of Mead Creek, a quarter of a mile south of the present lane. This stream, though small, has a very muddy, swampy bed, difficult to ford or bridge. This old original crossing is found to be inlaid with rocks.

"Through gaps in the hills, the trail passed on down to Cruse Creek, running off to the northeast of the present 'upper' road. Cruse Creek was crossed near the 'Westgate' house, and then, to avoid the abrupt hills west of the valley, the trail ran down the valley north for over a mile to the low gaps in the hills one mile east of Big Horn, where the present county road runs. Thence, the trail crossed into the Little Goose valley, to a ford west of the Sackett barns. This ford has been fenced up for thirty years, and so little used that no proofs are left for newcomers, but fortunately a few old-time freighters remember and agree. Thence, the trail ran up to Jackson Creek valley and passed over the Beaver Creek divide, through the gap to the 'William Meanor' ranch on Beaver Creek, near the county bridge. To the northwest the trail then ran as directly as possible for a point on Big Goose, long known as Beckton, from the fact that Honorable George T. Beck, Cody, Wyoming, was the pioneer rancher of that section.

"The next stream, Soldier Creek, was crossed just above the present 'P K' ranch. Wolf Creek was crossed near the present county road and Tongue River at the 'Upper crossing,' where Dayton is now situated. Five-mile Creek and crossed near the present Five-mile schoolhouse, and Pass Creek near the buildings on the Peter Reynolds ranch, the north line of which is the Montana state boundary. Thence, just northeast, Twin Creek was crossed on the Zachary ranch. Then the old trail unfenced, and, but little changed, runs on through the Crow Indian reservation to the Big Horn River, and is used occasionally by Indians and round-up wagons. The fords on the Little Big Horn, Lodge Grass, Rotten Grass, Soap Creeks and War Man's are all distinct. Across the valley of the Little Horn the trail is visible for many miles, as it winds up the divide on either side. In the Rotten Grass valley, west of the crossing, and again on the first Soap Creek divide, are rifle pits that mark the battlegrounds of the Bozeman Expedition of 1874. It is interesting, that here in the reservation, where the trail is most distinct, there are invariably two or three equally worn grass grown tracks up the slopes, where Indians might have been expected. Thus, the tradition of trains traveling abreast for safety is proven.

"War Man Hill is a very long, steep descent, and here the road has been worked and graded in recent years. Tradition places the trail on the first long hog-back north of the present road, and as all loaded wagons would have been pulled down grade, this is very probable. Fort C. F. Smith, after it was built, overlooked and guarded the Big Horn crossing."

James Bridger,[109] as chief guide, and guide Williams,

---

[109] General W. F. Raynolds, on the Yellowstone Expedition of 1859-1860,

examined the entire route of the Bozeman Trail, from Fort Kearney, Nebraska, to Virginia City, Montana, with a view to an exact report on its condition, resources and the possibility of numerous cut-offs to shorten it. The distances were tabulated as follows:[110]

THE BOZEMAN TRAIL surveyed by James Bridger for Henry B. Carrington in 1866

	Miles
From Fort Kearney to Fort McPherson (Nebraska)	88
From Fort McPherson to Fort Sedgwick (Colorado)	110
From Fort Sedgwick to Fort Laramie (Dakota) Wyoming	161
From Fort Laramie to Fort Reno (Dakota) Wyoming	169
From Fort Reno to Fort Phil Kearney (Dakota) Wyoming	67
Crazy Woman's Fork and Clear Creek, two important stops. Lake DeSmet on right, six miles from Fort Phil Kearney.	
From Fort Phil Kearney to Peno Creek Branch .	5
To North bank of Peno	7
To second crossing of Peno Creek . . .	6
To crossing of Goose Creek	4

had Major Bridger with him as a guide. The expedition was sent into the West by the government to establish wagon roads to and in Montana from the North Platte and Sweetwater Rivers. It was at this time that Bridger found a wagon way on the west side of the Big Horn Mountains from the Yellowstone to the Sweetwater. A large part of this route was used by Bridger in the Bridger-Bozeman race to Virginia City in 1864. This expedition also surveyed up and down the Yellowstone over that part of the country through which the Bozeman Trail passed from the Big Horn River to the sources of the Madison just west of Virginia City; moreover, Bridger guided the expedition from the North Platte along the east side of the Big Horn Mountains to the Big Horn River, where in 1866 Fort C. F. Smith was established. The trail made by the expedition along the east side of the mountain was not exactly that used for the Bozeman Trail; it was nearer to the mountain and, hence, more difficult of travel. It was doubtless for this reason that the knowing Bridger, in 1864 condemned Bozeman's proposed road which in reality did not run close to the Big Horn Mountains, but many miles to the east toward Pumpkin Buttes where travel was not difficult.

[110] A condensed tabulation taken from Carrington's *Some Phases of the Indian Question*, p. 29.

To Brown's Fork of Tongue River 13
    Between Tongue and Little Big Horn eight forks
    are crossed. Between Little Big Horn and Big Horn
    are nine small streams.

To East Fork of Little Big Horn 17

To Grass Lodge Creek 15

To Rotten Grass Creek 16

To Fort C. F. Smith (Montana) 8

To Dubois Creek (N.W. by W.), seven miles from
    the mountain 10

To North Fork of Dubois (N.W. by N.), seven miles
    from mountain 10

To South Fork of Prior's River (N.W.) . . 15

To Ice Water Springs (N.W. by N.) . . . 15
    Nine miles from here to Millard's Spring.

To Spring Creek (W.N.W.) 8
    Summit between Prior's and Clark's Fork on road

To Clark's Fork, nearly west 12

To Rocky Fork, 45 ft. wide, 3 ft. deep with a good ford 7

To Berdan's Creek, branch of Rocky Fork, crossed twice 12

To South Fork of Rosebud, up Berdan's Creek for
    three miles 10

To Rosebud River camp, about twenty miles from the
    mountains 8

To Stillwater, W.S.W., road crosses the main Rose-
    bud and follows up Stillman Fork of Rosebud . 6

To Emmil's Fork W.S.W., one divide is reached be-
    fore reaching this stream 18

To Big Boulder Creek, eight miles up Yellowstone val-
    ley road over level prairie for nine miles level . 17

To Yellowstone Ferry, ferry diagonally across the river 12

Yellowstone Ferry to Warm Springs, S.W. . . 4½

To Twenty-five yard River 10½
    S.W. 5 miles across ridge of Yellowstone.

To Beaver or Pass Creek, road runs S.W. by S. . 17

To Cold Spring Creek, up Beaver Creek . . . 10

To Head-waters, cross divide to east branch Gallatin
    River 5

To Bozeman City, down east Gallatin River . . 4

To Madison River, S.W. to W. Gallatin River 13
   miles, road runs across the valley for twelve miles . 33
To Meadow Creek, road crosses Madison River, then
   up stream five miles, westward up canyon four miles
   to main divide of Hot Springs Valley, thence south
   across the divide to Meadow Creek, twelve miles . 21
To Virginia City – by cut-off, usual road is 22 miles . 16

Total distance from Fort Sedgwick 967

Distances between the established Forts on the Bozeman Trail in 1866:

Fort Kearney to Fort McPherson (Nebraska) .	. 88
Fort McPherson to Fort Sedgwick (Colorado)	. 110
Fort Sedgwick to Fort Laramie . . .	. 161
Fort Laramie to Fort Reno	. 169
From Fort Reno to Fort Phil Kearney	67
From Fort Phil Kearney to Fort C. F. Smith	91
From Fort C. F. Smith to Virginia City	281

The Bozeman Trail (an account in Frank Harmon Garver, *Early Emigrant roads and trails in Montana*). This route left the Oregon Trail at Red Buttes on the Platte River and ran northwestward through Fort Laramie, Fort Reno, Fort Phil Kearny (all in Wyoming) to Montana. It entered the present Big Horn country near the source of the Little Big Horn and followed down the valley of that stream until it turned west to the Big Horn, which it reached at Fort C. F. Smith. From there it ran westward to the vicinity of Bridger, Carbon County, where it joined Bridger's Trail, the two routes proceeding together northwestward to the Yellowstone and down the same to the mouth of Shields River. Here they separated, the Bozeman Road continuing in a westward direction, via Bozeman Pass, to Bozeman. This trail was laid out by J. M. Bozeman and was named in his honor. It was also called the Bonanza Trail. Because of the route taken through Wyoming it was shorter than Bridger's Trail.

At first the Bozeman Road crossed the Yellowstone as indicated by Bridger's survey just west of the mouth of the Boulder, but latterly there was established the Yellowstone ferry up the river just east of the mouth of the Shields.

Fort Reno

As before stated, Fort Connor was established and the construction of the buildings commenced August, 14, 1865, when General Patrick E. Connor arrived at Powder River while on the Powder River Indian Expedition. Captain Palmer described the commencement of this fortification as follows: "August 14, 1865 – The first timber was cut today for building a stockade, the general having decided to erect a fort on the opposite bank of the river at this point. The Powder River is, at this point, a very rapid stream, water muddy, like the Missouri; timber very plenty, ranging back from the river from one-half to a mile; grass not very good; no chance to cut any hay anywhere on the river."

When Colonel Carrington came to Fort Connor on June 28, 1866, after surveying for other places for the possible erection of a fort, he decided that there was no better place in that neighborhood than the old site, and accordingly commenced to reconstruct the post, naming it Fort Reno. All of the work of construction was the roughest kind, "the only tool used in any of the buildings was doubtless an axe." All buildings at this post were of logs, excepting the commanding officer's quarters, which were built of adobe, the adobe being dark as the color of dirt, while the adobe used in Fort C. F. Smith on the Big Horn was of a light buff color; the roofs were all of dirt.

A. B. Ostrander, formerly a private of Company B, Twenty-seventh U.S. Infantry, and who was stationed both at Forts Reno and Phil Kearney during the Indian troubles of 1866 and 1867, has given the authors a description of Fort Reno, from which, combined with that of Edward A. Parmelee[112] and Mrs. Garber, it has

[112] Clerk under Quartermaster H. H. Link at Fort Reno, 1866-1868.

been possible to reconstruct the ground plan of the fortification. Mr. Ostrander writes: "Powder River, coming from the southwest, wound and turned until just south of the fort. Then it ran due east for a short way and turned abruptly north. The Bozeman Trail, just south of the fort, ran northwest, until it reached the ford in the Powder River, when, by a sharp turn, it went its way almost due north, though slightly to the east, passing along the entire length of the east side of Fort Reno. Just west of the ford was a deep hole, from which all the drinking water came. After crossing the ford, the trail climbed a steep hill, fifty to sixty yards high, and then struck level land at the southeast corner of the post, running between it and the lower corral. When the trail reached the northeast bastion of the fort, it abruptly curved to the west, passing between the post and the sutler's store, owned and operated by A. C. Leighton, running from here in a general northwest direction until reaching Fort Phil Kearney. North of the Fort, and about two hundred yards from the sutler's quarters, was a ravine—a drop in the ground common on all prairies. This drop or ravine was from ten to twenty feet deep, and could not be seen until one came very close to it, thus making an excellent hiding place. The bends in the ravine turned from northeast to southwest, until at a point some two hundred yards from the northwest corner of Reno, where there was a gully (marked 'Indians' on fort plan) leading up and out of the ravine. Out of this depression in the ground, Indians would ride up to the Fort, make faces at the building or the soldiers and then dash back to safety again. We often heard the hoofbeats of their ponies in this ravine, but seldom saw the savages.

"One morning, however, we had an exciting time.

One of the teamsters had killed a coyote, and Captain Freeman[113] had the doctor at the post load the carcass with strychnine and other poison, and then scattered the meat at different places on the prairie, in the hope of attracting some timber wolves that had been prowling around the fort, the skins being very valuable and much sought after. We were successful, but it was at an awful cost. Early in the morning there were seen three or four wolf carcasses, and a private named Blair, having but four months more to serve before his discharge, volunteered to go out and get the skins. At a place where I have marked 'Blair' on the map, the process of skinning the wolves commenced, when, in less time than it takes to write this, six Indians rode right up and out of that hidden gully, filled Blair with arrows, took his scalp and then tomahawked him right before our eyes! We did everything possible to go to his relief, but of course it was too late.

"The sutler's store was, as indicated, located nearly opposite the double gate on the north side of the fort. The lower corral, just east of the southeast bastion, contained the quartermaster's and commissary supplies, as well as the employees' quarters. This building was right on the edge of the timber bordering on Powder River.

"Jim Kelly, a former member of my company of the Twenty-seventh Infantry, says that when the fort was first built in 1866, it was just one square with a timber stockade dividing it into two parts, indicated by the line in the drawing. After the lower corral was built and put into use, the upper part of the stockade was removed, while the lower part, back of the hospital and laundress' quarters was left. The flag-pole was situated

---

[113] General Henry B. Freeman.

in the center of the western half of the stockade, south of which were the two buildings for quarters for Companies B and F. In the north part of the enclosure, commencing about fifty feet from the northwest bastion, and about six feet from the stockade, was a long one-story adobe and log building with a dirt roof, this long building being divided into quarters by thin partitions, as follows: commanding officer's quarters, single officers' quarters, quartermaster's office and adjutant's offices. About fifteen or twenty feet east of the adjutant's office was a double gate in the stockade, which was kept open from guard mount until retreat. It was closed at other times, as was the gate on the east side. These two gates were the only openings in the stockade. The building north of the east gate was divided into non-commissioned officers' mess quarters, barber shop and bakery, the vacant place east of the building being used for firewood. To the south, and along the side of the old stockade, were the hospital and laundress buildings, the southeast part of the stockade being used for wagons."

John F. Finerty, war correspondent for the Chicago Times during the Sioux campaign of 1876, accompanied General George Crook's column on his campaign into the Powder River country. The results of his observations are embodied in his *Warpath and Bivouac*. His observations of Fort Reno are illuminating. "On June 2, 1876, we marched for old Fort Reno. It is one of the three forts abandoned by the government under treaty with the Sioux in 1868-'69 . . . On the left bank of the Powder River we observed the ruins, nothing left but bare walls, scorched timbers and rusty pieces of iron. . . The fort is beautifully located, commanding a view of the country far and near, and to surprise it would have been impossible, with even ordinary vigilance. The lowlands along the river were plentifully wooded, a circumstance that caused the death of many a brave fellow of the former garrison, as the Indians used to lie in wait for the small parties sent out to cut timber, and massacre them in detail. The entire mountain barrier of the Big Horn, softened and beautified by distance, is visible to the westward. Fort Reno had been the main defense of the old Montana Road, and since its abandonment, up to within a few years, few white people, even in large parties, were venturesome enough to travel that route. The fort had a strong stockade, and must have been quite a fortress. Loads of old metal, wheels, stoves, parts of gun carriages, axles and other iron debris, sufficient to make a Chicago junk dealer rich, were lying there, uncared for.

"Two hundred yards north of the abandoned site is the cemetery where thirty-five soldiers and one officer, all victims of the Sioux Indians, sleep their last sleep. A small monument of brick and stone had been erected above their resting place, but this the Indians did not respect. The moment that the garrison that had erected the fort had crossed the river (on the way to Fort Laramie after Reno was abandoned in 1868) it had been set upon by the Indians and almost razed to the ground. The slab upon which were distinguishable the words: 'Erected as a memorial of respect to our comrades in arms, killed in defense,' was broken. The stones placed to mark the graves were uprooted by the vengeful savages, and many of the mounds were either leveled or scooped out. Even the rough head boards, which proclaimed the names of the gallant dead were shivered into fragments, but the patronymics of Privates Murphy, Holt, Slagle, Riley and Laggin,

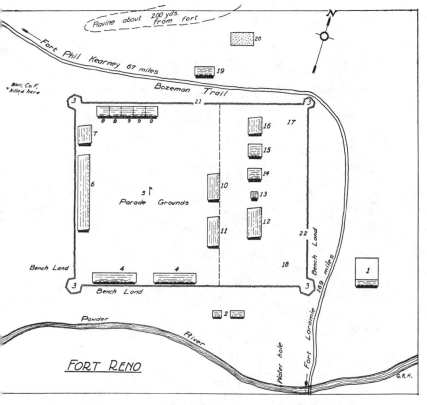

FORT RENO [114]

Prepared from information furnished by A. B. Ostrander, Vie Willits Garber, F. G. Burnett, and Edward Parmelee.

1) Corral and teamsters' quarters; (2) Sawmill; (3) Blockhouses; (4) Barracks; (5) Flagstaff; (6) Storehouse; (7) Commanding officer's quarters; (8) Officers' quarters; (Eastern 9) Post headquarters and Adjutant's office; (Middle 9) Post headquarters, (Master's headquarters; (Western 9) Officers' quarters; (10) Hospital; (11) Laundry; (12) Storehouse; (13) Guardhouse; (14) Barber shop; (15) Bakery; (16) Mess room; (17) Wood storage; (18) Place for wagons; (19) Sutler's store; (20) Cemetery; (21, 22) Gates.

nearly all of the Eighteenth Infantry, killed May 27, 1867, could be distinguished by putting the pieces together. The most stoic of mortals could hardly fail to look with some degree of emotion at the lonely and dishonored resting place of these hapless young men, so untimely, and even ingloriously, butchered by a lurking foe. They sleep far away from home and civilization, for even yet the place is only visited by the hardy ranchers and cowboys."

When Edward Parmelee, during July, 1910, visited old Fort Reno, accompanied by a party, two of whom lived in Buffalo, the other on a ranch adjoining the old fortification, he found only two small pieces of headboards marking the soldiers' graves. The only readable inscription was "Pri" "Co" "Kill," and the other "y S v 66." Mr. Parmelee, in September, 1910, under

[114] Mrs. Garber offers the following description of Fort Reno as obtained from her excavation of the ruins in 1909 and 1910, the distances all having been carefully measured by her and her father. The two descriptions here presented were made absolutely independent of each other:

"At Fort Reno, where a stockade of cottonwood logs enclosing the log and adobe quarters, a slightly-elevated mound indicates an enclosure about two hundred and twenty yards square. Near the southwest corner of this enclosure are the crumbled walls of a black adobe building, thirty feet square, of which part of the south wall still stands, two to four feet in height. To the east of this are heaps of burned ruins where buildings stood, and a few feet directly south is a depression, appearing to have been a large cellar for ammunition and other supplies. Further to the southwest, and outside of the main enclosure, are heaps and mounds that probably mark the location of the stables. Still further south, the ever varying course of the Powder River has washed away the low-lying bottom-land where the sawmill stood. About three hundred yards to the north of the old stockade was the cemetery."

In addition to these two descriptions of Fort Reno, there have been obtained diagrams and information from E. A. Parmelee of Omaha, who served in the capacity of clerk to Quartermaster Lieutenant H. H. Link at Reno, from its commencement in 1866 to its abandonment in 1868, and from F. G. Burnett. From the information obtained from these four individuals, three of whom were at Fort Reno when it guarded the Bozeman Trail, the diagram of the fort here presented has been drawn, all information substantiating each other in the essential details.

directions of the government, had the bodies removed to the National Cemetery at Crow Agency, Montana. There were only found the graves of thirteen soldiers, twelve from Fort Reno and one from a nearby ranch, all thirteen being interred side by side on the battlefield where Custer made his last stand.

Mr. Parmelee states, in regard to Fort Reno and the depredations surrounding the post: "The Indians did not annoy Fort Reno as much as they did Fort Phil Kearney. About August 2d, 1867, when the Indians attacked the wagon box corral, six miles west of Fort Phil Kearney, and Lieutenant Jenness was killed, there were many Indians on all side of Fort Reno, but there was no attack. I have never been at Fort C. F. Smith, but I understand that there was concert of action on the part of the Indians at the three posts, and I think there was some fighting at Fort Smith on or about August 2d, 1867. The Indians were on all of the hilltops around Reno for two days, and were busy with signals, but there was no shooting.

"Fort Reno was not often annoyed by raids. Once in 1867, Bair or Blair was killed by a small party of Indians while gathering pelts from wolves. On another occasion there was an alarm at the corral at night but no real danger was done. There was a ravine just north of the fort, where a company of cavalry could pass without being seen from the fort. I know of but one instance where emigrants sought refuge at the post, and that was in the summer of 1867, when an elderly man with his daughter of about twenty-three years, in a light wagon, hauled by a poor team, came into the post on his way to Montana. He stated that he had come from Sioux City, Iowa, and had seen no indications of Indians. He further stated that he proposed to resume his

Ruins at Fort C. F. Smith, 1920

journey the next morning. The commanding officer of the post told him that he had had all of the luck that was due him, and that he would not be allowed to leave the post until a detachment of troops was going north. The old man was quite indignant, but he waited until Major Van Voast permitted him to leave."

Fort C. F. Smith

Colonel Henry B. Carrington, on the morning of August 3, 1866, sent Lieutenant-Colonel N. C. Kinney with his company and that of Captain Brown, toward the Big Horn River, on which, or near its banks, was to be established a post which was to bear the name of Fort C. F. Smith,[115] the command taking with it three hundred tons of hay and a year's supply of provisions. This isolated, lonely post was established August 12, 1866, just south of the Big Horn River, between Spring Gulch on the northwest and Warrior Creek on the southeast. No official plan, design or drawing of this post seems to be in existence, and no government plans have come to the observation of the authors, hence, the plans as presented were drawn from descriptions of those who were there when the fort was protecting the emigrant on the Bozeman Trail, and those who have visited the old site and taken measurements. From Mr. Burnett and Mrs. Garber the most instructive information has been obtained.

Mr. Burnett states that Fort C. F. Smith was about one hundred and twenty-five yards square, built partly of logs and partly of light buff adobe, the soil thereabout being of that color. On the southeast corner of the fort there was located a lookout or guard house.

---

[115] Named for Gen. Charles Ferguson Smith, who received three brevets for distinguished service in the Mexican War. General Smith died April 25, 1862.

The south wall was of adobe, as was the west wall, while the north and east walls were, in part, at least, of logs, the fortification being erected on a benchland. Along the north wall, inside, were the adobe quarters of the officers, while the barracks were along the south wall, three buildings in number, as were the officers' buildings. The storehouse was along the east wall, about in its middle, and directly north of it was a log building used for offices; the quartermaster's department of logs being near the center of the parade ground, which occupied the center of the enclosure, the flagpole being just south of the middle barracks near the north wall. The gate was on the east side of the stockade, just outside of which was the sutler's store owned by A. C. Leighton. This building was also built of logs. Near the northwest corner of the fort was a sawmill, very close to Spring Gulch. North and east of the mill were four log buildings, used by the teamsters and employees, while east of these buildings was one large building, the north half being used for the stables and the south part utilized as a corral.

Mrs. Garber draws the following conclusions from her survey of Fort C. F. Smith in 1909 and 1910:

"At Fort C. F. Smith are the most extensive ruins of the three Bozeman Trail forts, owing to the fact that the surrounding country has remained unpeopled. C. F. Smith, a two-company post, was substantially constructed of light colored adobe. The site was indeed well chosen, at the border of a broad plain overlooking the Big Horn River. If guards were on duty, it was impossible for anyone to come within three miles of the post without detection. The stockade, one hundred and twenty-five yards square, was built in such a way as to form the outer wall of the soldier's barracks along

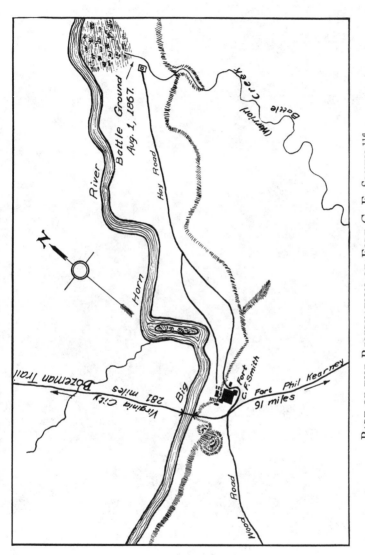

PART OF THE RESERVATION OF FORT C. F. SMITH [116]

Scale, 2 inches to the mile. Redrawn from a map made January 27, 1881, by Capt. Edward L. Hartz, Twenty-seventh U. S. Infantry.

the south. Through these barracks two driveways entered. This double south wall, facing the mountains, nearly all remains today in a jagged line, from two to ten feet high. At the southeast corner of the stockade was a boulder tower, which served as a lookout and guard house, and now lies in a dilapidated heap. The east wall, which is now only a mass of broken mounds, was an adobe structure, supplied with port holes, as were the north and west walls. Behind the stockade, to the north, the bank of the Big Horn slopes abruptly toward the river; here are two large, deep depressions marking the dugout stables that were guarded from above by a row of rifle pits. A similar row of rifle pits is well defined outside the western wall, which has crumbled to mere mounds of earth. The central portion of the enclosure of the stockade served as a parade and drill ground, with three large officers' quarters at the rear, facing the south. The corners of the middle one are standing in tall columns, and a few feet in front is a hole in the ground where the flag-staff stood. A few pieces of charred window casings remain in the south wall, and in several places on the inner corners a sort of whitewashed clay plaster can be chipped off. Many pieces of broken stoves and door knobs are to be found among the rubbish, and here and there a rusty can or bit of broken bottle."[117]

---

[116] The reproduction of the "Fort C. F. Smith Reservation," here presented, is the only official map that has been found locating the Bozeman Trail around Fort C. F. Smith and the Hayfield battle ground. Obtained through the courtesy of U. S. Senator F. E. Warren.

[117] "We found (1874) the adobe walls of Fort Smith still standing, the neatly walled and well arranged cemetery nearly as left, except that the Indians had wrenched the gates from the hinges, and the boards at the head of the gates are displaced, and some of these hacked and otherwise defaced; but the names on all of them are yet legible. The beautiful monument in the center of the enclosure with the names of all buried – twenty-three in number – engraved on it, is but little defaced. Nineteen of those buried in this

But scant information can be obtained of the hardships and dangers surrounding Fort C. F. Smith, which, by the fact of its distance from help (being ninety-one miles from Fort Phil Kearney and two hundred and eighty-one miles from Virginia City, and with no telegraphic communication) made the officers and soldiers often work out their own salvation in the method of protecting their lives. A. B. Ostrander, who was at Fort Phil Kearney, as well as at Fort Reno, writes the authors: "From the day I landed at Reno and Phil Kearney, Fort C. F. Smith was an unknown quantity. From February 20, 1867, until April 26, 1868, not a word came from there except once, when a party of Crows came to our fort, about forty of them, with pelts and skins to trade. The Indians reported all quiet at Fort C. F. Smith."

Jim Bridger was often sent to Fort Smith to interview with the Crow Indians, who always were willing to join the whites to fight the common foe, the Sioux. Colonel Carrington states, in his official report, relative to these visits of Bridger: "Messenger from Fort C. F. Smith brings message that at request of Mr. Bridger, a party of Crows visited the post, reporting five hundred lodges of Sioux in Tongue River valley, all hostile. Cheyenne chiefs, viz: Black Horse, Red Arm, Little Wolf, Dull Knife and others, with whom I had council in July (1866), and who went beyond the mountains south, as they promised, brought me the same report." Sep-

little enclosure were killed by Indians." – Montana Historical Society *Collections*, vol. i, p. 274.

Quively (A. M.) *The Yellowstone Expedition of 1874*: "The ruins of Fort C. F. Smith are (1876) in a good state of preservation, though they were abandoned eight years ago. Its adobe walls do not yield to the incendiary's torch, or the Sioux would have long since got rid of them." – Montana Historical Society *Collections*, vol. ii, p. 183, Journal of Lieutenant James H. Bradley.

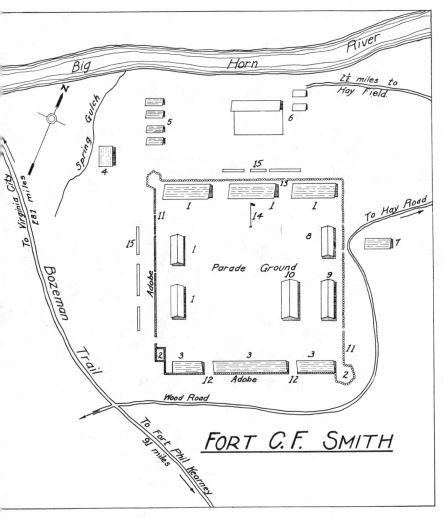

FORT C. F. SMITH

Drawn from information furnished by Vie Willits Garber and F. G. Burnett.

(1) Officers' quarters; (2) Block and guardhouse; diagonal corner also a blockhouse; (3) Barracks; (4) Sawmill; (5) Teamsters' and employes' log cabins; (6) Stable and corral; (7) Sutler's store; (8) Office; (9) Storehouse; (10) Quartermaster's department; (11) Port holes situated at several points in the four walls of the stockade; (12) Wagon gates; (13) Small gate; (14) Flag staff; (15) Rifle pits.

tember 25th another report makes the statement that "at Fort C. F. Smith a force guided by Jim Beck-wourth[118] (also spelled Beckwith) who went to see them, said that they were Crows, but changed their minds and declared themselves to be Sioux. They pretended friendship, but getting no presents, and not being admitted near the fort, they scalped a white man within sight of the garrison. They pretended that they, with the Arapahoes, had made peace with the Crows. I do not believe it."

Constant attempts were made by the Indians to capture the supply wagons, and heroism was constantly alert on the part of the soldiers and teamsters. A trustworthy example of the hardships encountered by these troops is given by Dennis Driscoll of Monarch, Wyoming. Mr. Driscoll was a corporal under Captain C. F. Thompson, of the Twenty-seventh Infantry. This company was one that guarded supplies en route from Fort Phil Kearney to C. F. Smith. On July 3, 1867, a company was returning to Phil Kearney, and had reached a point forty miles from Fort Smith when the Indians surrounded them and stampeded their stock,

---

[118] There were four companies at the Big Horn building, C. F. Smith. Captain John W. Smith of Bozeman, was the post trader at this place, and with him was Jim Beckwith, a mulatto, who had been sub-chief among the Crow many years before. In a quarrel he had killed another chief and had to leave the tribe. After several years spent on the Pacific coast he came back, and had regained his influence in the tribe. As soon as the troops came to the Big Horn, Smith sent him to the mouth of that river to bring up the Crows who were camping there. Beckwith was taken sick at the camp and died while being brought back in a travois. The Crows came to the new post, and by order of the commandant were allowed to trade for large quantities of powder and lead. Several times during the fall the Crows and Sioux would make peace for a day, during which time the former tribe would trade this ammunition to the latter, receiving in exchange five times its value in buffalo robes. Soon afterward the Sioux would burn the powder, but the lead came back to the whites in the form of bullets. – Leeson (M. A.) *History of Montana*, p. 199.

with the single exception of a blind white mule. The only chance of safety was to get word back to Fort Smith and thus obtain aid. Corporal Driscoll volunteered to carry the message, and, riding the mule, made his way, under cover of night, along the foothills at some distance from the trail. The following morning, after numerous perilous escapes, when his mule had been killed, and he himself wounded in one foot, he crawled to the ridge of Backbone Mountain (the hogback between War Man and Black Canyon Creek) and on to the wood road leading to the fort. Here he lost consciousness, but was soon discovered and taken to the fort. The messages were found in his pocket and aid sent to Captain Thompson's relief long before Mr. Driscoll rallied enough to speak.

Major E. R. P. Shurly was sent to Fort C. F. Smith, being attached to the column of General John E Smith, who left Fort Sedgwick with three hundred and fifty men on May 2, 1867, for Fort Phil Kearney, from there being commanded further north to Fort C. F. Smith, having arrived at Phil Kearney July 2d. He writes: "When General Smith's column, as it was called, reached Fort Phil Kearney, it was suggested to the general that an old boiler and engine, then at the post, could be used toward building a sawmill at Fort Smith. These were parts of a mill burned by the Indians. Accordingly the quartermaster, General Dandy, caused a six wheeled truck to be made for transporting the engine. Drawn by twelve yoke of oxen, it was, after much trouble, hauled to Smith. Then it took all the expert mechanics in the ranks to get the thing into shape.

"It was a wonderful mill when completed. All of the running gear was made of wood. An original sawmill surely; but by its aid the question of lumber for the new barracks was settled.

"Old Fort C. F. Smith was situated on one of the most pleasing sites in Wyoming (then a part of Montana). It was built on a bluff, five hundred yards from the Big Horn River, and a mile above the great canyon that extends westward one hundred miles to the Shoshone River. Fort Smith was one of the three posts built to hold the Indians in check. It was a stockade post, and once stood an assault against a force of Indians twenty times the strength of the garrison. After our arrival, the old wooden barracks were replaced by buildings of adobe, the bricks being made by the men, the lumber sawed at the mill.

"The Indians were bad. The government did not mean war, but the Sioux, Arapahoes and Kiowas did. They lost no opportunity to let us know it. We were then considered out of the world, and were, so far as getting news from the east was concerned. Months intervened between mails. Wagon trails were closely guarded, and even then there was constant fighting with the large bands of Indians, who took advantage of any inattention of the escort to 'jump the train.'

"The garrison at the fort was most of the time in a state of siege. A man going from the stockade to the river took chances. Occasionally our friends, the Crows (Absarakas) to the number of three or four hundred would camp near us. Then we had lively times. Their old enemies, the Sioux, would come in to give them a fight, and the garrison would look on.

"Old Fort Smith was a monotonous post. The sun would rise out of the plains and disappear over the mountains. Slowly the days passed. Game was abundant. From the top of the stockade could be seen buffalo, elk, antelope, and sometimes bear. Small game was equally plenty, but it was risking one's life to hunt. Many took chances, however, so we were usually provided with game. The country was fruitful in season, with wild plums, grapes, and berries, and the streams were alive with trout. During the winter of 1866, however, the garrison lived mainly on corn. No trains came through, while the Indians, numbering thousands, had their winter quarters on the Little Big Horn.

"That this post was an isolated and desolate one is best shown by the following story: Our colonel was after a 'soft snap' in the east, but he was not in the best graces of Secretary of War Stanton. The Eighteenth Infantry at that time was stationed at Louisville enjoying peace. Apparently our colonel had been pestering Stanton to be sent further east than St. Louis, for, upon opening another letter from the Colonel, Stanton turned to his clerk and demanded:

"'Which is the next place, to hell, to send a regiment?'

"'To the Powder River country,' was the prompt reply.

"'Then order the Eighteenth Infantry there at once,' commanded Stanton.

"And so we were sent to Fort C. F. Smith!"

Fort Fetterman

In time there was built a fort near where the Bozeman Trail along the North Platte turned from its direction directly to the west and went its way to the northwest. Opposite this bend in the river there was established, July 19, 1867, Fort Fetterman,[119] named in honor

---

[119] Coutant (George) *History of Wyoming*, vol. i, p. 594: "The logs

of Captain William J. Fetterman, who lost his life in the Fetterman disaster near Fort Phil Kearney, December 21, 1866. The buildings were erected at the mouth of La Prele Creek, where it empties into the North Platte. This fort took the place of Marshal Station, which was located also on the south side of the Platte, but a few miles up the creek. Under the command of Major William McE. Dye, four companies were placed at this new fort, A, C, H, and I, of the Fourth Infantry, assisting in the construction of the fortification, which was a substantial structure, becoming extensively used as a supply station for the soldiers fighting the Indians, when Forts Reno, Phil Kearney, and C. F. Smith were abandoned. The fort on the south bank of the Platte was about eight hundred yards from the Platte and one hundred and thirty feet above it, being built on a plateau. By 1872 the fort had been enlarged, and was one of the best equipped military establishments in Wyoming, which, by this time, had become a territory. The garrison was maintained until 1878, when, the Indians having been driven on their reservations, it was abandoned, the large wood reservation and the fort site being sold by the government to private parties.[120]

John F. Finerty, the "fighting pencil pusher" of the

for the fort were cut by enlisted men, and these were converted into lumber at the two sawmills located at the post. This fort played a conspicuous part in the Indian wars for the next few years. It was a substantial structure, with all of the appointments to make of it a first class post, and when Fort Caspar was abandoned and the three forts north of it, Reno, Phil Kearney, and C. F. Smith it became of necessity an important supply point for the army operating against the Indians in the Northwest.

[120] At this fort General George Crook on May 28, 1876, assumed command of the expedition that went northwest to help subdue the Indians, the command consisting of fifteen troops of cavalry, about nine hundred men, and three companies of Infantry, three hundred men. The road traveled was over the Bozeman Trail, to the site of Forts Reno and Phil Kearney.

Chicago Times, who accompanied Crook's column through the Sioux campaign of 1876, into the Powder River country, wrote thus of Fort Fetterman in his *Warpath and Bivouac*: "Fort Fetterman is now abandoned. It was a hateful post, in summer, hell, and in winter, Spitzbergen. The whole army dreaded being quartered there, but all had to take their turn. Its abandonment was a wise procedure on the part of the government."

A Private's Reminiscences of Fort Reno[121]

HANDLING THE MAIL AT FORT RENO, D.T., IN 1866-67. The arrival, overhauling and distribution of mail at Fort Reno, D.T., in those days was an important event. It was anxiously awaited and longingly looked for. Its arrival and "coming in" was an "episode." The day and date of its arrival was an "epoch," for incidents and circumstances were remembered among the men as happenings from and after that point of time.

The following "epitome" will give an account of methods used in handling it: We generally had from an hour and a half to three hours' notice of its approach and arrival. About five miles to the south and across the Powder River valley, was high land, which, at its western extremity, ended at a sharp point and a bluff. The trail from Fort Laramie wound around this point, and watchful eyes were scrutinizing that point every second during daylight, hoping, longing, or dreading to see who or what might appear.

After turning this point, the trail descended gradually in a northeasterly direction, until it struck the timber in the river bottom-land, and then turned sharply to the west until it reached a point between the fort proper and the lower corral.

According to conditions of the weather and of the

121 By A. B. Ostrander, former private Company B, Twenty-seventh U. S. Infantry.

trail itself, the time made between the point of first observation and arrival at the fort, would vary; but it was always long enough, when a mail party had been sighted, to keep everybody on the anxious seat with longing anticipations.

On arrival at post headquarters, the mail carrier would bring in his bag and turn it over to the post adjutant, Lieutenant T. S. Kirtland. The only key to it was in the possession of the lieutenant, and he kept it under lock and key in a drawer of his table. The lieutenant would unlock the padlock, remove it, and then place the lock and key back in the drawer. All this carefulness did seem ridiculous to me, in view of the fact that we two headquarters clerks (Clarke and myself) did all of the separating, sorting, and some of the final distributing of the mail matter.

A blanket was spread out on the floor, and after the lock and key had been provided with such proper protection, the bag was taken by Clarke, who dumped the contents in a pile on the blanket. The bag would then be replaced so that its mouth would be open and in a position so that we could throw into it all matter destined to points beyond Fort Reno.

Then Clarke and myself, on our knees, and opposite each other, with the pile between, and with both hands, would begin operations. Every article addressed "Fort Reno" was thrown off in a pile by itself, and each one for points up the trail was thrown back into the bag at once, so that when the last piece was handled, the separating was completed. Clarke would restrap it; the lieutenant would relock it and the mail carrier could then proceed on his way. All this before our own mail could receive any attention.

The first time I tackled this work, I had only been

at the post less than one week, and was green at it, and guess I was inclined to talk too much in the way of criticisms of the methods, "modus operandi," etc., and it is a wonder to me now that I didn't get a more serious calling down than was given me in the way of explanations at the time.

On my knees, leaning forward, my back twisting from side to side, and both hands busy, I got tired, and straightening up for a few seconds' rest, I remarked: "This is a nice thing for us to be doing—handling everybody else's private letters." Clarke merely gave a grunt and said, "What's th' matter with you?" I replied, "Well, this mail ought to be put up separate at Fort Laramie. They could make one big bundle for us and for each post up the trail; then all we'd have to do would be to take out our own bunch and let the rest go on."

Clarke gave another grunt and said, "Shut up and go to work." Lieutenant Kirtland and Van Volzah (the mail carrier) were seated near by watching us. The lieutenant remarked in a pleasant tone of voice, "That would make four separate bundles to leave Laramie with—one for Bridger's Ferry and one for each of us at Reno, Phil Kearney and C. F. Smith, and as they would vary so much in bulk and weight, Van Volzah would find it hard work to balance the sack on back of his horse."

I kept right on working and talking, for I retorted, "They could put 'em in separate sacks then—one sack labeled for each post. There'd be no delay here then, only long enough to put our own up above mail in its proper sack." The lieutenant, still in a pleasant mood said, "I guess Van would find some trouble handling four sacks on one horse."

I still thought I had the best of the argument when I said, "He always has three or four soldiers for an escort, and I guess each one of them could carry one sack to help him out."

I looked up at "Van" and he was smiling, but the lieutenant continued in a more sober tone, "The mail carrier is sworn in by the government and is responsible. He gets ten dollars a day for it while on the trip, and no one else is allowed to handle the bags."

Clarke was growing impatient and let out a grunt, so I subsided, but was not convinced. Then, as now, it was a mooted question in my mind if a soldier could not carry or handle a locked bag of mail while en route, how was it that we two enlisted men were allowed to handle every individual article of its contents? I give it up.

Just before the conversation recorded above, I had picked up two letters addressed to myself, and in my delight I exclaimed, "Glory!" and started to stuff them in my pocket. A quick exclamation from Clarke caused me to look up. He said, "Throw 'em out," and nodded in the direction of our own mail pile. "But they are for me," I exclaimed, handing them to him so that he could read the addresses. He took them and without even looking at the addresses, threw them in the Reno pile, but looking me straight in the eyes, gave a wink, and nodded toward the officer. I was afraid to enter into any discussion with him in the presence of the lieutenant, but made up my mind to have it out with him later, but before the mail was finally disposed of I found it was unnecessary, and that Clarke had really done me a kindness by his action.

Having disposed of the mail carrier, our own mail was all placed on the adjutant's table. We put it there, addresses up, and the lieutenant himself saw to its distribution. Mail for officers and their families was laid one side and delivered to them or their representatives at once. Mail for enlisted men was separated by companies and handed to the orderly-sergeants, who were always on hand and waiting for it, and lastly, the headquarters mail was disposed of, and I got mine.

When the lieutenant handed me a bunch of six letters there was a smile on his face, and I knew he must have "got onto" that by-play during the separating.

Once the mail arrived in the night – long after taps, and the procedure differed in a slight degree. The blanket was spread on the dirt floor of our bunk room in rear of the office. Candles were lighted and stuck around in niches, and blankets were hung before the window. When separation by posts was completed, and after the mail carrier had received his sack and departed, our mail, as usual, was placed on the adjutant's table, blankets hung before door and windows, and the lieutenant "did his little bit." If there were any officers present they could, of course, get their mail at once, no matter what hour it was, but the enlisted men had to wait until after reveille the next morning. Generally it would be sent over to company quarters at "breakfast call," and sometimes some poor devil would become so interested in his news from home, or elsewhere, that he forgot, and neglected to put in the time after breakfast in brushing up and polishing his accoutrements, preparatory to inspection at guard mount, with the result that he was ordered to "fall out," and received a reprimand and got "police," or some other unpleasant duty, instead of an assignment as "orderly" for the day to the commanding officer and post headquarters – a job eagerly striven for by every soldier coming on guard.

A NIGHT ALARM AT FORT RENO. About 8:30 one evening in the early part of December, 1866, I was sitting on a stool in one corner of the adjutant's office at Fort Reno, enjoying my pipe.

Clarke, the headquarters chief clerk, was seated at his table folding and addressing little three-cornered "billet doux," which contained the countersign for the twenty-four hours succeeding guard mount the next morning. These would be distributed to the officers and others entitled to them after the new guard had been posted and instructed. Lieutenant Kirtland, the post adjutant, was seated on a chair tilted back against the wall, his heels resting on a rung of the chair, reading a book by the light of a solitary candle on the table at his left. In the quartermaster's office, which adjoined ours, with only a thin board partition between, Ed Parmelee, the quartermaster's clerk, was playing on his flute. In soft, low tones he was giving us a delightful concert, consisting of Sunday-school tunes and popular airs of the day. Everything was peaceful and serene.

Suddenly we heard a shot fired, followed by a series of unearthly yells. In less than one second Lieutenant Kirtland's chair legs struck the floor, his book fell from his hands, he blew out his candle and sprang out of the door. Clarke was equally as quick in blowing out his candle. He and I quickly got our caps, each grasped his Sharpe's carbine and followed after the lieutenant.

He was standing about ten paces away, looking in the direction from which the alarm had come. Clarke and I stepped to his side and just as we reached him we heard five or six rifle shots, followed by derisive yells. I also heard "bees" buzz and hum in the air. You know you never hear the bullet from a rifle until it has passed beyond its power to do harm to the hearer.

The lieutenant remarked: "Those shots came from the lower corral. What the devil are they aiming at the fort and our quarters for?"

The moon was shining brightly, and we could see the men pouring out of "B" and "F" company quarters, and hear the orderly-sergeants forming their details into line, awaiting orders.

Soon they started for the east gate on the double-quick, and we three started for the same spot and at the same gait. Arriving there it was unlocked and thrown open by the sergeant of the guard, assisted by others, and a picket line was formed, extending from this gate down to the main gate of the lower corral. The distance was considerable, and the men were stationed about six or eight feet apart, facing toward the river, ford, and trail from the south.

I took a place near the center of the line, about half-way between the gates, and very soon began to have an uneasy feeling in the back part of my head, so I turned and faced the other way, toward the north.

In a few moments Lieutenant Kirtland passed down along the rear of the line, and stopping in front of me said, "What are you facing this way for? Turn around!" I started to return, but remarked, "Lieutenant, I don't like that ravine about two hundred yards over there. You know it was from a gully coming out of that ravine that Indians got Blair this morning."

The lieutenant wheeled around on his heel, gazed to the north and west a few seconds, and then said to me, "All right; as you are," and passed along down the line. In a few minutes I happened to cast my eyes sideways each way and found that every second man in line was facing north.

We stood there "at ease," but at mighty good "attention" for about twenty minutes or half an hour. Finally Captains Proctor and Freeman came along the line, coming out from the main gate of the lower corral. I heard Captain Proctor, the commanding officer, give the order, "Sergeants, take your men back to quarters."

I heard the sergeants give orders to "fall in" but as I was on detail and not subject to company discipline, I proceeded to "fall out," and started on a dog trot for the fort gate, so as to get in before the push.

I got there first and proceeded to the adjutant's office, where I relighted the candles, put away my gun and cap just as the lieutenant and Clarke both came in together. I wanted to talk and ask Clarke some questions, but was afraid to speak up in the presence of the officer. In a few minutes, however, Lieutenant Davis, who was "officer of the day," came in to write out his report, and from his conversation with Lieutenant Kirtland, we got the particulars.

It seems that just at dusk, a few minutes before darkness obscured the trail, four horsemen had been seen rounding the bluff point where the trail from Fort Laramie could first be seen from the fort. We had been eagerly expecting mail from the east every hour for nearly four days. These horsemen were supposed to be Van Volzah, the mail carrier, and his escort, but they could not be positively identified, owing to the dim and fading light.

All hands were delighted at prospects of "news from home." As it took from an hour and a half to two hours and a half for an outfit to reach the fort from that point where they were first observed, Clarke and I had made all arrangements for overhauling the mail that night after taps. We had a blanket spread on the dirt floor of our bunk room; secured an extra supply of candles and everything had favored a quick dispatch.

One of the sentries on post in the lower corral had a long beat. It took in the whole south side of the corral from corner to corner. There was no opening or gate on that side, so it was not an important post; more of a "police beat" and situated inside the stockade.

Shortly after he had been posted, at eight o'clock, the sentry heard hoof beats on the trail on the other side of the river, and soon he could hear the water splash as the parties were crossing the ford, and then, coming up through the timber and brush, they rode right up to the stockade, where four heads appeared over the top, looking in. In the dark it was not possible to distinguish either form or features.

As there was no opening gate or regular approaches right there, the sentry did not think it necessary to give the usual challenge. "Halt! Who goes there?" and feeling sure it was the mail carrier, he merely called out "Hello, Van, got a big mail?" Evidently the advancing parties had not expected to find a sentinel there, as the only response he received was "Ugh! Ugh! Ugh! Ugh!" In an instant his rifle was cocked, and doubtless the riders heard the click of the weapon, for before he fired they had wheeled and dashed into the dark timbers.

As the peal of his rifle was ringing through the woods and on the cold night air, the riders – Indians, of course – let out their warwhoops with a vengeance. It is a lovely sound. Open your mouth as wide as you can and yell as loud as you can, and while you are yelling, just slap your mouth rapidly with the palm of your hand, and you will have a beautiful illustration of the dulcet tones of an Indian yell.

The excitement was over for the time being, but some of the boys didn't sleep very soundly that night. The possibilities of what "might have been" kept them nervous and wakeful.

Van Volzah did not show up with the mail until nearly forty-eight hours later, and he was quite indignant to learn that a parcel of measly Indians should be taken for him.

Poor "Van" was killed in less than six weeks afterward, by the Indians, and I helped gather up the remnants of his mail in the sagebrush, one day's travel out of Fort Reno.

I was at Reno the night "Portugee" Phillips went through with Colonel Carrington's dispatches from Fort Phil Kearney, following the Fetterman slaughter. I did not see him, but I was in my bunk in the adjutant's office and heard the sentry challenge him, and heard his reply, "Scout with message." They took him down to the corral for a brief rest. I knew him well afterward, but did not learn the particulars of his ride.

Fort C. F. Smith and the Hayfield Fight[122]

I will try and explain as near as possible about the Hayfield fight two and a half or three miles east of Fort C. F. Smith, this fort being situated on the Big Horn River. This fight occurred on the 1st day of August, 1867. I will also state the events which precipitated both that fight and the battle at the Wagon Box corral six miles west of Fort Phil Kearney, about ninety miles south of Fort Smith. The Wagon Box fight was on the 2d day of August of that same year.

In the summer of 1867 the Sioux, Cheyennes and Arapahoes had gathered all their fighting warriors together on a stream about fifteen miles east of Fort Smith. There were several thousand of the hostiles, and they had combined for the purpose of wiping out all the forts on the Bozeman Trail which had been erected in 1866 by Colonel Henry B. Carrington of the Eighteenth U.S. Infantry.

At that time the Crow Indians were at peace with the hostiles – something very unusual, especially as regards the Sioux. With the whites the Crows were always friendly, but with the Sioux they generally were bitter enemies.

I was in the employ of A. C. Leighton, the post sutler at Fort Smith, who also operated stores at Forts Phil Kearney and Reno. I served Leighton in the

[122] By F. G. Burnett, civilian employe at Fort Smith.

capacity of general utility man, being wagon master, clerk, or anything at which he desired me to turn my hand. In July and August, 1867, I was working in the hayfield, where we had a camp established northeast of Fort C. F. Smith, as it was too far from the fort to go to and from daily.

It seems that bands of Crow Indians had been visiting the camp of the hostiles every few days. Several of them came to the hayfield where we were at work and told us of the great strength of the Sioux and their allies, giving such outlandish reports (so we thought at the time) of the multitudes of fighting men they had seen, and the immense number of lodges, that we thought they were trying to frighten us, and we paid little attention to their talk and did not believe their stories.

On the 31st of July, another party of these Crows stopped at our camp where we were hard at work cutting and curing hay, and begged us to leave at once and return to the fort. They told us the hostiles were coming to attack the fort the next day, and that they had seen more warriors than they could count. It was the intention of the allied tribes, so the Crows said, to destroy all the forts, from the Big Horn to the Platte, and drive the white men out of their country. We merely laughed at their fears. We considered that it was some sort of a joke that they were trying to play on us. We had been fighting small parties of Indians almost daily, and had confidence in our ability to take care of ourselves and drive off any hostiles who attacked us in force.

The Crows told us that the Sioux and Cheyennes had had a disagreement about which of the three forts to attack first. One faction wanted to wipe out Fort

Smith first and then go down and clean out Fort Phil Kearney, following that with a combined attack upon Fort Reno. Others wanted to destroy Phil Kearney first, as it was the most detested of the three forts. Not being able to come to any definite agreement, the hostiles decided to take a vote on the proposition. The Crows told us the question was settled by the Indians lining up in two squads. After this had been done, it was found that the fighting force was about equally divided on the matter, so it was decided to divide the force and attack both forts at the same time, as the hostiles considered themselves sufficiently powerful in numbers to capture and destroy both Forts Smith and Phil Kearney. Such was the report brought to us by these Crows who had seen the matter decided. The band which was to attack Fort Phil Kearney left at once, as they had about ninety-five miles to travel, and did not reach the Wagon Box corral until two days later, August 2d. The balance of the hostiles waited until the following day and then started to try and capture Fort Smith. They encountered us at the hay field, and there we gave them such a drubbing that they made no attempt against the fort itself.

Right here I want to give a little description of the corral which we had constructed at the hayfield. It had been built about a week before the Indians descended upon us. Good sized logs were first laid on the ground around a space about one hundred feet square. Upright posts were set in the earth at certain distances apart, and to these posts stringers were nailed. In between the stringers were tightly woven masses of willow boughs with the leaves and twigs attached, and so thickly interlaced as to form a good place for our stock at night and for defensive purposes, should we be attacked. The barricade was so constructed that it was impossible to see through the willows. There was a picket line strung across the corral north to south, and about fifteen feet west of the center. We had the wagon beds set off the wagons on the west side of our little improvised fort with about three feet of space between them, and about four feet back from the fence. They were covered with canvas in the usual manner, and we used them to sleep in. There were also three tents in the northwest corner of the corral. This arrangement prevented anyone from seeing across the corral from the outside. I believe the fact that we were thus pretty effectually hidden is the only thing that saved us that day.

On the morning of August 1st there were ninteen of us at work in the hayfield as usual. It was about nine-thirty when a fusillade of shots, accompanied by the warwhoop and yells of the Indians, warned us that the story told by the Crows had pretty much of an element of truth to it. We all got back to the corral without losing a man, and here we began preparations for a most determined resistance. The soldiers had just received fifty-caliber breech-loading rifles, and each man had fifty rounds of ammunition. We citizen employes were all armed with repeating rifles – Henry and Spencer guns, save one man, Zeke Colvin, who was using an Enfield musket which he had carried through the Civil War.

Of course the only chance we had was to keep down out of sight. However, Lieutenant Sternberg and another soldier were both killed at the beginning of the fight through their own carelessness. They insisted on standing up, and called on us to do the same, and to "fight like men." The rest of us knew that the only

HAY FIELD FIGHT

AUG. 1, 1867.

FROM DATA FURNISHED BY F. G. BURNETT

Figures indicate positions of fighters.

(1) Capt. Colvin; (2) Lieut. Sternberg killed; (3) Al Stephens; (4) F. G. Burnett; (5) George Duncan; (6) Man located here who lost his nerve and never fired a shot during the battle; (7) Bob Little; (8) Holister, wounded; died next day; (9, 10, 11) Soldiers; (12) Soldier killed; (13) Soldier stationed here who lost his nerve and threatened to commit suicide; (14) Soldier wounded with arrow; (15) Zeke Colvin; (16) A sergeant; wounded in shoulder; fought bravely throughout battle; (17) Billy Hanes; (18) Soldier; (19) Sioux chief killed here by Capt. Colvin; (20) Soldier known as "Scotty," wounded; fought desperately through engagement; (21) Cook tent at lower left, outside corral.

chance we had was to lie down and keep out of sight—and we did it!

After the death of the lieutenant, Captain D. A. Colvin took charge of our party. He had won his straps in the Civil War, and was a seasoned veteran—cool, absolutely fearless, yet discreet. He ordered every man of us to do our fighting from over the top of the lower log which formed the corral, and behind which we were pretty well screened by the willows. Everything that was a foot or eighteen inches above ground was simply shot to pieces by the Indians.

I don't believe there is another man living, or that ever lived, who has killed as many Indians in a day as Colvin did on the occasion of the hayfield fight. He was armed with a sixteen-shot repeating rifle, and had a thousand rounds of ammunition. He was a dead shot, and if he missed an Indian in that fight none of us ever knew it. He fired about three hundred shots that day, and after the fight the ground out a little way from where he was lying was simply covered with dead Indians. He killed one of their chiefs as the savage was leading a charge against the corral on foot, and this chief was the first Indian to cross Warrior Creek, only a few yards distant from the corral. The others attempted several times to recover his body, but we made it so hot for them that they were obliged to abandon the attempt.

Captain Colvin's brother, Zeke, killed the first Indian of the fight. The warrior was riding toward the corral with a fire-brand, with which he apparently hoped to set our barricade on fire. Colvin shot the Indian's horse, as the latter was almost against the corral. The animal fell, pinning its rider down, and while the Indian was just crawling out from beneath the horse and starting to run, Colvin brought him down with another quick shot.

Several times the Indians fired burning arrows into the willow lattice work of our barricade, hoping to smoke us out. They also set fire to the grass on three sides of it, but they never succeeded in getting a fire started where it damaged us any. We were all ready to grab our wounded and take to Warrior Creek, only twenty-five or thirty feet south of the corral, but we managed to extinguish every fire they started, even though the willows were dry enough to burn.

There were thirty-one head of mules and one horse in the corral picketed to the cable stretched across from north to south. All this stock was either killed or wounded, except one mule and the horse.

Among our crowd there was a big bully of whom we had all been afraid. We had expected great things of this man when it came to a show down, but at the critical moment—when the fighting started, the coward hid himself and never fired a shot all through the battle. Another man—a soldier, kept threatening to commit suicide, for fear the Indians would get him alive and hold him for torture. Zeke Colvin finally took the fellow's gun away from him, and the fellow hid himself in a hole which the dogs had dug near the fence. He kept so quiet that we thought he was dead, until after the fighting was over.

All the while we were fighting for our lives, from 9 a.m. to 5 p.m., we wondered why no reinforcements came from the fort to our relief. We knew they must have heard the sound of our guns. We also knew there were plenty of soldiers at the fort, who, aided by the citizens, could have easily held the fort against the Indi-

123 "The commander of the post, being aware of the fighting all that time

ans.[123]   But there was no attempt made to send us reinforcements until the fighting was all over and the Indians had withdrawn, having come to the conclusion that
we were impregnable, and that they could neither drive
us out into the open nor smoke us out.

It appears that Captain Hartz, with his company of
soldiers, was escorting a wood train from the mountains
to the fort, and when he reached a point where he could
overlook the valley where the hayfield was situated,
he heard and saw the battle in progress.   He had a pair
of powerful field glasses with which he looked the valley over and saw what a desperate situation we were in.
He hastened to the fort as quickly as possible, where he
reported to the commander that the men at the hayfield
were surrounded by at least two thousand five hundred
Indians, and asked for three or four companies of soldiers to go to our relief.   And now comes the almost
unbelievable part of my story:

Instead of granting Captain Hartz's request, the
commander immediately ordered the gates of the fort
to be locked, and refused to allow a man to leave while
the battle was in progress!   We were thus left to fight
it out as best we could.   The commander of Fort C. F.
Smith disgraced himself that day, and that is the reason
there never has been any official report made by the
military authorities of the hayfield fight near the fort.
It is a tabooed topic, and of course no military writer
would dare take up the subject.[124]

As to the Indian loss in this fight, it would be impossible for me to make a correct estimate, but I would

refused to allow a relief party to go out, although officers were eager to go,
all day long; and, finally, as the shades of the evening approached, he con-
sented to their urgent appeal." – William Camp.

[124] The authors have also been thus advised by a competent military
authority.

swear to the best of my knowledge and belief that Captain Colvin himself killed and wounded more than one hundred and fifty of the Indians. He was armed, as I have previously stated, with a sixteen-shot Henry rifle, had over a thousand rounds of ammunition for it, and was one of the best rifle shots I ever saw, being absolutely steady under fire. As he did most of his shooting at distances of from twenty to seventy-five yards, it was almost impossible for him to miss a target as big as a man at such short range. He was shooting steadily from nine-thirty in the morning until five o'clock in the afternoon, and the ground around where he was stationed was literally covered with empty shells from his rifle.

The soldiers were all armed with "needle" guns, and each had plenty of ammunition. Bob Little and George Duncan, two of the citizens, used Model of 1866 Winchester rifles. Each had plenty of cartridges and were brave, steady men, doing splendid execution all day. I was armed with a Spencer carbine, and had, in addition, a double-barreled shotgun. We all had revolvers as well, which we reserved for close quarters.

The loss on our side was Lieutenant Sternberg, a citizen named Hollister, and a sergeant whose name I have forgotten, killed. In addition, we had four men wounded, all soldiers but one. One of these wounded men was a sergeant. He was shot through the shoulder and most painfully injured. He and two of the other wounded men never failed to assist us in every charge made by the Indians. We had placed them in a tent where they would be out of the intense heat of the day, but whenever the Indians pressed us too closely these men would stagger out and stay with us until we had driven the Indians back to cover. The sergeant's wound was such that he could not use a rifle, but we kept two revolvers loaded for his use, and right well did he use them in every attack.

Two days after the hayfield fight, Colonel Greene arrived at the fort with two companies of cavalry. The fight was, of course, the sole topic, and it was regarded as a miracle that our loss was so slight in comparison with the immense number of Indians opposed to us. The Crow Indians, of whom I have made mention, and who were going back and forth to the village of the Sioux, reported after the fight that the Sioux loss was terrible, and that we had killed and wounded hundreds of their warriors. They reported to us that the village was filled with wounded, who were dying rapidly from their wounds, and that the Sioux were carrying their dead out of the village and caching them on some ledges in the adjacent hills.

Colonel Greene asked these Crows if they would guide him to the place, in order to get a more correct estimate of the Indian loss. They agreed to do this, and the colonel, accompanied by his two troops of cavalry and several citizens, including Captain Colvin, A. C. Leighton, the sutler at Fort Smith, myself and others, all went to the first ledge, which was situated about two miles south of the hayfield. Here we found over fifty bodies. The Crows requested that the colonel and his detachment accompany them to the next ledge, which was about two miles east of the first burial site. They said there were many more bodies there than on the first ledge. However, Colonel Greene refused to go further, knowing that the Sioux had yet plenty of fighting warriors left, and not caring to bring on another engagement with them. We therefore returned to the fort, satisfied that the Crows were telling the truth.

It is my opinion that the hayfield fight was the fiercest engagement with hostile Indians in all the Indian battles of the West, considering the small number of whites and the fact that we were outnumbered more than a hundred to one.

After the fighting was practically all over, the commander of the fort allowed three companies of soldiers to come to our "relief"—when we had no need of any! The commander of Fort Smith never was known to send out a relief party to aid besieged soldiers or civilians, and I will further state that all the time I was employed there I have no recollection of the commander ever going outside the stockade! I will let the veil of charity be drawn and not mention this commander's name, but I will say, however, that there were plenty of officers, from lieutenants up, who were better qualified to command that post than was the general in charge.

The second or third day after the fight we returned and built a new corral, using cottonwood logs this time, with plenty of sod. It was constructed out in the open valley, about half a mile northeast of the old one, and about the same distance from the Big Horn River. We had the protection of a company of infantry at the new corral, but were never again attacked in force. There were raiding parties bothering us considerably—sometimes two or three times a day, trying to run off our stock or burn what hay we had cut and cured. They certainly made things lively for us.

After finishing the hay contract, another one was made to furnish wood to the fort at twenty-seven dollars and fifty cents per cord. We hauled this wood principally from the mountains, five or six miles away. I do not recall that the Indians ever attacked any of our wood parties. We hired two men to guard our camp, scout around and keep us in meat. They were Baptiste Pourier, better known as "Big Bat," and Frank Berthune. They were both splendid men. "Big Bat" was the bravest scout and the best hunter I ever knew. He did wonderful work for General Crook in the Sioux campaign of 1876. He is yet living at Manderson, South Dakota – or was, as late as July, 1920.

The quartermaster's citizen employes at Fort C. F. Smith all lived in dirt roofed log cabins outside the fort. I do not remember that any of them ever were compelled to leave their cabins and get inside the fort for protection from prowling Indians. It is my opinion that none of the three forts along the Bozeman Trail would have been in any great danger if they had been attacked. The post of Fort Phil Kearney was surrounded by the best stockade I ever saw. It was absolutely invulnerable against Indians. As for Forts Reno and Smith, although they were not so well protected, I do not believe the Indians could ever have taken them as long as ammunition and provisions held out.

There were several adobe buildings at Fort Smith, and the stockade also was partly of the same material. Fort Phil Kearney had no adobe buildings.

At Fort Reno the stockade was built of cottonwood logs. The quarters and all other buildings had dirt roofs. There was no timber but cottonwood available, to my knowledge. There were never more than two companies quartered at this post. Kemp Caldwell, an old schoolmate of mine, was in charge of the sutler store there from the time the fort was established until it was abandoned. The store was outside the stockade, but Caldwell never was obliged to seek the protection of the fort, that I can recollect.

The Indians never made any direct attack against any of the three forts on the Bozeman Trail. Fort Reno was not an ideal location for water or grass, but strategically it was an important location. The old post was an open, rude affair, with a stockade surrounding the warehouse and stables, leaving the quarters for soldiers and horses without protection. The water was alkali and muddy. The fort was situated one hundred and fifty feet above the river, and all the water had to be hauled for the command, though upon the arrival of Colonel Carrington a fine spring was found near the fort. After the post was placed under the command of Colonel Proctor it was entirely surrounded by a stockade within which were blockhouses with bastions having loop holes, so that all four sides of the fort could be protected. There was a strong stone magazine in addition.

Down at Fort Phil Kearney, in 1867, a man named Washington built a log cabin with a dirt roof, about one hundred and fifty yards from the fort on the Little Piney. Here he started a garden of vegetables and also served meals to those who desired them. He was driven inside his cabin many times by the Indians, but never abandoned the house to seek the protection of the fort. He had a wife, but no children. Both he and Mrs. Washington were crack rifle shots, and after the Indians had made two or three attempts to clean the pair out, they discovered it was too costly a proposition, and gave them a wide berth thereafter.

I was well acquainted with "Portugee" Phillips who made the ride for help from Fort Phil Kearney to Fort Laramie on the night of the Fetterman disaster. I do not, at this late day, remember what he told me about where he kept himself hidden through the daytime on that trip, but I do recall that he had many narrow escapes. He never failed to take a chance when it seemed necessary. He was clear grit, and others less deserving than he have received greater honor and praise.

In the spring of 1867 I was attached to a wagon train which was crossing the Platte River at the Bridger Crossing. Phillips and a small squad of cavalry, who were scouting at the head of the train, came back and reported that the Indians were about to attack a wagon train several miles ahead of us. Our captain left a squad of soldiers to guard our train, and took the balance of the company, with several volunteer citizens, and started to the relief of the besieged train. I accompanied this party. On our approach we discovered that the Indians were trying to surprise the train by sneaking through a gulch that ran into the river just below where the train was corraled. We had been careful of our approach and the Indians had not discovered us. They were so intent on their scheme that we managed to get to the foot of the ridge near the gulch which they were cautiously descending. Just as they started to charge the train, we ourselves charged right among them, and you never saw such a surprised bunch of redskins. We knocked over several of them. A lieutenant, a private and myself found that we had cut off one Indian, and some one of us got in a lucky shot that killed his horse. We chased him into a hollow where the warrior put up a stubborn fight. He shot the horse ridden by the soldier and wounded the lieutenant in the knee. We then managed to kill the Indian. We took from him the first Winchester rifle I had ever seen. The lieutenant and the private had to ride one horse to camp and the officer suffered agony with his wounded knee. He had been shot with an arrow and we were unable to pull the barb from the wound. We found on getting back to camp that several of the others had done good work in the fight.

[In the reprinting of this work in 1960, is added the following portion of a letter from Mr. Brininstool to the publisher, written just prior to the publication of this work in 1922. It adds an interesting note to the accounts of the Wagon Box and Hayfield fights.]

There has never been anything printed regarding life at these forts at any time, nor has there but very little – and that of no value historically – regarding either the Wagon Box fight or the Hayfield fight. Naturally the Carrington books would say nothing detrimental to his time of service at Phil Kearney. There is no mention made of the Wagon Box fight in either *Absaraka* or *Army Life on the Plains* – probably because it occurred after Carrington had left, but if he were giving historical data with accuracy, it seems queer that this important affair should be passed right over.

No true account of the Wagon Box fight has ever been made until it was written by the three men whose stories we have secured. If for no other reason they should be printed to refute the false statements which have been printed heretofore. Therefore let these men tell their stories and give the public the truth.

Of the Hayfield fight, there never was ANY account of it printed at any time. General King told me personally that it was a forbidden topic in army circles (for the plain reason that the commander, Gen. Bradley, played the coward in refusing to allow a relief party to leave the fort to aid the 19 men in the hayfield). I was asked by Gen. King to please not mention Bradley's name, as they had always been close friends. So I withheld it. Burnett insisted that I flay Bradley good and hard and give the public his name, but we both (Dr. Hebard and myself) decided not to do it.*

---

* David (Robert B.) *Finn Burnett, Frontiersman*, 1937, pp. 189-195, also discusses this matter.

Red Cloud; the Great Ogallala Sioux War Chief

"The Red Napoleon of the Plains," is a most fitting title for Red Cloud, the famous Ogallala Sioux war chief, whose warriors were the scourge of the plains in the '60's, and whose depredations in the immediate vicinity of Fort Phil Kearney, culminating in the tragic Fetterman disaster, December 21, 1866, and, the following 2d of August, in that most extraordinary engagement, known to history as the "Wagon Box" fight, are among the most important happenings in the history of our Indian wars in the West.

Red Cloud (Makh-pi-ya-luta) is supposed to have been born at the forks of the Platte River in Nebraska, in 1822, although the chief himself did not know the exact year of his birth.[125]   He died at Pine Ridge reservation, South Dakota, December 10, 1909. Like Sitting Bull, he ever refused to become reconciled to the white man's way, but, unlike the former, he was not, in his later years, the crafty, cunning and treacherous savage that Sitting Bull ever was.   Red Cloud had many fine and noble qualities, possessed by no other Indian of his time, unless it was Chief Joseph, of the Nez Perces. After the "Wagon Box" fight of 1867, Red Cloud went no more on the warpath in person, and, although it has been charged by incompetent authorities that he was a "persistent instigator of outbreaks and massacres, pro-

---

[125] On Red Cloud's monument, at Pine Ridge reservation, it is recorded that the chief was born in 1824.

fessing deep piety, while really plotting deviltry," there is no foundation whatever for the untruths which have been printed about him by nine-tenths of the writers of Western history, who never had the opportunity of learning the finer and stronger side of Red Cloud's character. It is true that in the '60's he was an enemy to be feared by the whites, and that he left many a bloody trail along both the North and South Platte and the overland trails to the far west; but when it is considered that Red Cloud was merely fighting for his land, his home and the hunting grounds of his people — and what white man could not have done this? — when it is considered that the United States government broke faith with the Sioux, time and again, as with nearly all other tribes; that at that time nearly every white man on the plains "had no use for Injuns, only dead ones;" that there were many unscrupulous and dishonest Indian agents on the reservations, ever ready to feather their own nests at the expense of Uncle Sam's red wards, and that the Indian was robbed, cheated, tricked and most outrageously treated by nearly every white man with whom he came in contact, it is not to be marveled at that Red Cloud's hatred for the despoiler of his hunting country and the usurper of his lands vented itself in such a manner.

Of Red Cloud's boyhood there is but little record. His parents were not prominent in any way among the tribe, and it is probable that the future great Sioux chieftain was brought up like any other Indian lad. About the time Red Cloud attained his sixteenth year he began to attract attention, and gave promise of developing into a warrior of no small prominence, becoming to be looked upon as a sort of leader among the other younger Indians because of his ability in skirmishes with the Crows and Pawnees, both of whom were hereditary enemies of the Sioux.

A sister of Red Cloud once stated that when he was but three years old he was stolen from his parents, who were at that time living on a reservation in Wisconsin, and that some eighteen years later his people located him and desired him to return to them. He came and stayed a few weeks but the story goes that he preferred the tepees of his adopted tribe, deserting his relatives for his foster-parents very shortly.

It was in the '60's that Red Cloud's fame and notoriety as a great war chief and leader reached its zenith. In 1865 the United States government wanted to build a wagon road into the Montana gold region by way of Powder River – right through the heart of the finest hunting grounds possessed by the Sioux. Very naturally Red Cloud entered a most emphatic objection to such a proposition. He declared it would drive away the game, which was the chief sustenance and support of his tribe. That country was then the very cream of the buffalo range – and the buffalo furnished everything required by the Indian in the way of food, clothing and skins for lodges – which was all he desired for his welfare and happiness. During the fall of 1865 a council was proposed to Red Cloud, to effect, if possible, some peaceable settlement whereby the proposed road might be constructed, but he grimly forbade any such negotiations, utterly refusing to attend the council.

Thus matters continued until the following June, when another council was proposed to him, and this time Red Cloud decided to be present. It was held at Fort Laramie, and there was a great gathering of Indians at this conference. When negotiations were opened, Red Cloud arose, and repeated his objections to endangering the principal hunting grounds of his people. He made no secret of his opposition, but fiercely denounced the proposed plan, which was favored by Spotted Tail, Big Mouth, and other chiefs of lesser fame. In the midst of the palaver, Red Cloud again sprang to his feet, and pointing a finger at Colonel Henry B. Carrington, of the Eighteenth U.S. Infantry, who was in attendance, on his way, even then, to the Big Horn and Powder River country with a government expedition, the chief exclaimed, in ringing tones:

"You are the white eagle who has come to steal the road. The Great Father sends us presents, and wants us to sell him the road, *but the white chief comes with soldiers to steal it, before the Indian says yes or no!* I will talk with you no more! I and my people will go now, and we will fight you! As long as I live, I will fight for the last hunting grounds of my people!" And drawing his blanket across his shoulders, Red Cloud stalked majestically from the council, refusing to accept any of the presents sent him by the government, and threatening to massacre every white man who crossed Crazy Woman's Fork of the Powder River.

Although Red Cloud had "shied his castor into the ring," so to speak, the government, decided, nevertheless, to go ahead and build the necessary forts along the proposed route of travel, in which soldiers were to be maintained to safeguard the road. Colonel Carrington was given charge of the details, which included the rebuilding and garrisoning of Fort Reno on Powder River, and the erection of two more forts further northwest – one at the forks of the Big and Little Piney, later known as Fort Phil Kearney, and the other on the Big Horn River, known as Fort C. F. Smith.

But hardly had Carrington laid out the lines of Fort

Phil Kearney and begun to cut the logs for the stockade, before Red Cloud descended indeed like a "red cloud" upon him. So closely did the wily Sioux chief draw his lines about the little garrison, with a force of warriors numbering upward of three thousand, that not a stick of timber could be cut, nor even a load of hay hauled from the flats close by the fort, without a heavy guard being detailed to accompany the woodchoppers and hay cutters. Fights and skirmishes were of almost daily occurrence, and Red Cloud exhibited considerable generalship in the signal system used by his forces. General Carrington states that in one skirmish the chief's signals "covered a line of seven miles, and were displayed with wonderful rapidity and accuracy." It was impossible to think of venturing out after game, which was abundant in the neighborhood, without fear of an ambush. To sum the disturbances all up, Red Cloud's warriors, from the first of August, 1866, until the close of that year, murdered one hundred and fifty-four persons, comprising soldiers and citizens, wounded twenty more, and captured and drove away three hundred and six oxen and cows, three hundred and four mules and one hundred and sixty-one horses, making hostile demonstrations in front of the fort and committing hostile acts fifty-one different times, as well as attacking nearly every wagon train and person attempting to pass over the Bozeman Road. And yet Congress had reported that "all was at peace in the Big Horn country!"

But Red Cloud's greatest "coup" was counted on December 21, 1866, when a small decoy party of his warriors attacked one of the wood trains en route from the fort to the pinery for timber. Colonel Carrington dispatched Captain William J. Fetterman, with eighty men, to disperse the Indians, warning and instructing him to positively not go beyond a certain point known as Lodge Trail Ridge, lest he be drawn into an ambush. So great was Carrington's apprehension that Fetterman's enthusiasm and recklessness would lead him to throw caution to the winds, that, as the little command left the fort, the colonel sprang upon the banquette, or sentry platform, inside the stockade and repeated his warning to Fetterman: "*Under no circumstances whatever must you cross Lodge Trail Ridge.*" Fetterman promised obedience, but as soon as he was out of sight of his commander, he disregarded his orders and crossed the fatal ridge. Here the main body of Indians, numbering upward of three thousand, were secreted, and they arose from their hiding places in hordes, surrounded the soldiers and killed every man, most of them – in fact, Carrington's report says all but six – being dispatched with spears and clubs. The fight did not last to exceed twenty minutes. All the bodies were most shockingly mutilated in a fiendish manner by the exasperated and infuriated Sioux.

Red Cloud's fame now spread like magic, and he was heralded as the greatest leader of all the hostile Indians on the plains, being regarded as "big medicine" by his tribesmen because of his success in all his operations against "the hated fort on the Little Piney." His notoriety, however, was short-lived. The following August he again planned and made an attack on some wood choppers in the pinery, about six miles west of Fort Phil Kearney. This time, however, Red Cloud's "big medicine" failed. Unknown to the Indians, the troops, but two weeks previously, had been armed with a new breech-loading rifle – the first ever used against Indians by Uncle Sam's army on the plains. The celebrated "Wagon Box" fight was the result of this attack. The Indian loss, while never definitely known, has been given by some writers and historians as one thousand one hundred and thirty-seven. Others place the figures at from two hundred to five hundred, which is probably nearer correct, although Red Cloud himself, many years later, when questioned, is said to have stated that he "went into the fight with three thousand braves and came out with but half of them." When asked if he really meant that his loss was so enormous, the old chief is alleged to have replied: "It was a big fight. The long swords fought as I had never seen them fight before. My warriors were as numerous as blades of grass. I went in with many. I lost over half. The long swords shot true to the mark. My warriors never fought again."

This was Red Cloud's last great fight with the whites, although he continued for some time to harrass all small parties passing over the Bozeman Road.

In 1868 it was thought expedient by the government to again try to effect a treaty with the now famous war chief of the Sioux. His only ultimatum was that all the forts which had been erected through his hunting country should be abandoned, as well as all further attempts to open a wagon road into Montana. Red Cloud would accept no other conditions whatsoever, and the government at once accepted the terms as dictated by himself. The entire region was once more given over to the Sioux nation, which had thus won a complete victory. Red Cloud even refused to sign the treaty until all the troops had been entirely withdrawn and the forts completely abandoned, after which the Indians immediately burned them to the ground.

From that date Red Cloud kept his word with the

government, so far as again taking to the warpath in person was concerned. He took no part himself in the great Sioux war of 1876, although it has been stated that he "secretly aided and encouraged the hostile element," just as it has also been alleged he espoused their cause during the Ghost Dance war of 1890-1891 in South Dakota; but there is no foundation whatever for such reports.

And now for the other – and better – side of Red Cloud's character, from a strictly authentic source:

Captain James H. Cook, of Agate, Sioux County, Nebraska, is unquestionably better able to give to the public the real truth about Red Cloud than any other living person. He knew the great chief intimately for thirty-five years, and was the one white man in whom Red Cloud placed implicit confidence. Captain Cook is an extensive cattle rancher, with large holdings and interests along the Niobrara River, where he has been located for more than thirty years. Red Cloud was a guest at Captain Cook's ranch for weeks at a time, on numerous occasions, for years after he had forsaken the warpath. Captain Cook served with distinction as a scout, guide and trailer through the Apache campaign in Arizona in 1866, and has numerous documents from high army officials, testifying to his ability, energy and efficiency while serving the government during its Indian troubles. He also rendered most valuable aid during the Ghost Dance war at Pine Ridge reservation, South Dakota, having a personal acquaintance with all the leading chiefs among the Sioux, particularly with Red Cloud, Little Wound, American Horse, and Young-Man-Afraid-of-His-Horses. He is an adept in the sign language, and also speaks the Sioux tongue fluently. During all those

CAPTAIN JAMES H. COOK, IN SCOUTING RIG, 1879
For more than 35 years Captain Cook was Chief Red Cloud's most
intimate white friend

years, as now Captain Cook was highly respected by the Pine Ridge Sioux, and considered a warm friend and personal adviser on all matters pertaining to their interests. At one time he was slated for agent at Pine Ridge reservation, but the Indian Department was taken over by the Interior Department before his case was acted upon.

Captain Cook has given to the authors of this work insights into the life of Chief Red Cloud which could not possibly be obtained from any other living source, for the reason that he was the only white man in whom Red Cloud had implicit confidence and was ever considered as a close, intimate friend – a man brought up in the open, like himself, and a plainsman in every sense of the word. Captain Cook first met the chief in 1875, when on a friendly visit to the Red Cloud agency during the autumn of that year. He was accompanied by Baptiste Gangnier,[126] better known as "Little Bat," one of the most noted frontier characters of the '70's – a wonderful scout and trailer, and so-called to distinguish him from Baptiste Pourier, known as "Big Bat," another remarkable frontiersman.

On the occasion of this first trip to the lodge of Red Cloud, Captain Cook was warmly welcomed, on the statement of "Little Bat" that he had brought his friend, the white hunter, to pay his respects to the chief. Many of Red Cloud's sub-chiefs were sent for on this occasion, and a friendship was there begun with these Sioux leaders which continued without a break as long as they lived.

It was during this trip that Professor Marsh, of Yale College and the Smithsonian Institute, called upon Red Cloud with a government escort. He wanted permis-

[126] Also spelled "Gaunier" and "Garnier."

sion to hunt in the Sioux country for fossils and petrified objects, or "stone bones," as the Indians called them. The professor was not accorded a very enthusiastic reception by the red men.   They looked at him askance and with suspicion when he told them the object of his trip, thinking that his real mission was to prospect for gold in their lands. Captain Cook interceded for Professor Marsh, telling Red Cloud the real purport of his visit, whereupon the desired permission was at once given.   The professor and his party were in no manner molested nor disturbed by the Indians during their bone-hunting expeditions, in the interests of science. Red Cloud's word was as good as his bond.   In fact, the noted scientist and the great Sioux chief became warm friends, and the chief paid Professor Marsh a visit at his home in New Haven, Conn., some time after.

Red Cloud had promised Captain Cook to some time give him his life story.   Many white men had heretofore tried to get the chief's consent to be "written up," but he had steadfastly refused.   He said that he did not want anything to do with any white man who desired his life story to be printed in a book, with the object of making money.   Captain Cook, however, never found himself in a position where a competent interpreter and stenographer were available during any of the chief's visits to the Cook ranch.   Years passed by; Red Cloud grew old and infirm; his mind became somewhat clouded and the promised story never developed in the form Captain Cook intended.

According to Captain Cook, Red Cloud was a marvelous student of Nature, acquiring a wonderful knowledge of the plant and animal life throughout the vast region over which his tribe migrated.   He deplored beyond measure, and with sorrow in his heart, the destruction by the white men of the vast buffalo herds, which meant food, clothing and shelter to his people; and his heart was filled with hatred against the whites for their wanton, wasteful killing of the noble game animals with which the country teemed. Meeting Red Cloud—not as an Eastern man, but as a fellow hunter, a dweller of the plains, gave Captain Cook an opportunity to study the character of this noted Indian in a manner never gained by any other white man. Therefore, the friendship between them was far more enduring and stronger than it otherwise would have been. Red Cloud noted, with mingled sorrow and rage, that the oncoming hordes of white despoilers of his land must be stopped, or the game would all be killed or driven away, and his people reduced to beggars, dependent entirely on the government for support and sustenance. In vain did the chief seek to impress this fact upon them. The question was a vexed one to settle. His people were not deep thinkers, nor had they the keen insight into the future possessed by himself. The baubles passed out by white traders lured the chief's supposedly faithful followers from his side. Dissatisfaction broke out and bad feeling was engendered over the treaties made with the Sioux, which was destined to end in disaster.

In his book, *The Fighting Cheyennes*, George Bird Grinnell, the well known writer of Indian life, has stated that Red Cloud took no part personally in the Fetterman fight near Fort Phil Kearney, and that he was not present on that occasion. Red Cloud has often told Captain Cook that he not only was very much in evidence in that disastrous affair, but that he led the warriors in person when they overwhelmed Fetterman's command, after passing the fatal Lodge Trail Ridge.

Captain Cook had many talks with Red Cloud on the fight—for it was a fight and not a "massacre." The troops attacked the Indians, and were simply overwhelmed by a vastly superior force. Red Cloud said that only about eleven Indians were killed outright, but that great numbers were wounded and died later. Captain Fetterman himself was killed by Chief American Horse, declared Red Cloud. American Horse has also admitted this to Captain Cook.[127] Most historians have agreed that Captains Fetterman and Brown committed suicide when they saw that all hope of escape was gone. It is not at all unlikely that the death of Fetterman was just as described by American Horse. All but six of the soldiers were killed with clubs, spears and arrows. Many of the old chiefs who took part in this fight have told Captain Cook that the soldiers seemed paralyzed with fear when they saw how they were outnumbered, and that they offered no resistance at all, being simply knocked in the head like so many dumb animals. Some of the officers, however, put up a most determined resistance, but were quickly and easily overpowered.

While a great many of the warriors from the Red Cloud agency assisted the hostiles in the Sioux war of 1876, Captain Cook declares that Red Cloud took no active part in that campaign, nor secretly aided the unreconcilables, knowing full that resistance would mean nothing but much suffering and bloodshed to numbers of his people. He was also by this time getting well along in years, and did not have the strong influence over his young men which he had exerted ten years before. They would not heed his advice

---

[127] American Horse's version of this killing was that he knocked Fetterman off his horse with a war club and stabbed him to death with a knife.

when he pleaded with them to remain peaceable.   The younger element, backed by such a youthful, fiery leader as Crazy Horse, clamored for battle against the white invaders.   The Custer fight followed, with Crazy Horse, Gaul, Crow King, and Two Moons leading the hostiles; but Red Cloud's fighting spirit was broken. It has been contended that his awful defeat in the "Wagon Box" fight of August, 1867, was responsible for his thus refusing to again take to the warpath in person.   Be that as it may, he did everything possible to keep peace, although, during the Fort Robinson trouble in 1879, he was importuned to join the hostiles and make one last determined stand against the common enemy; but to Red Cloud's credit it can be truthfully said that he refused to depart from the position of peace which he had assumed.

At the time of the Messiah Craze on Pine Ridge reservation, in December, 1890, Captain Cook was sent for, because of his special and intimate acquaintance with the leading Sioux chiefs.   He went to the scene of trouble, and sought out his old friend, "Little Bat," and together they went over the situation.   They decided that no great harm could arise from the dancing, provided the Indians did not over exert themselves; but the warriors were cautioned that under no circumstances must they resort to bloodshed among the whites, unless they desired the government to step in and make trouble for them.   The general incompetency of Agent Royer, coupled with his fear and alarm, was well known to the Indians, and he was openly ridiculed and belittled by them.   He was by no means a student of Indian nature, and daily bombarded Washington with telegrams for "more troops," keeping the wires hot with his feverish and ridiculous demands.

Red Cloud was, at this time, being charged with secretly aiding the hostile element by some of the brainless "war correspondents" who were sent to Pine Ridge for "Indian stories." Pen pictures were daily drawn of the "deviltry" which the old chief was alleged to be plotting in the nice house which the government had built for him. These rumors came to Captain Cook. He was making his headquarters day and night with the Indian scouts attached to the troops, and was daily around the agency with such well known scouts as "Little Bat," "Woman's Dress," "Yankton Charlie," "Big Bat"* and others, who were all thoroughly conversant with what was transpiring at the camp of the hostiles, as well as at government headquarters, and Captain Cook asserts that nothing was ever discovered which could, in any way, reflect against Red Cloud's good reputation and peaceful attitude which he had for years been maintaining. Not the least sign of a hostile move, nor any evidence of secretly aiding the warlike element could be found against the old chieftain. There is no foundation at all for the stories which have circulated in books, and the newspaper accounts of the last Indian war of the west, that Red Cloud was the crafty, cunning, blood-thirsty villain which he was at that time painted. Coming, as this refutation does, from a man who had known Red Cloud intimately, and as man to man, for fifteen years previous to the Ghost Dance war, and had been closely associated with him in so many different ways, it can be asserted without contradiction that the aged chief remained faithful to his word—that he had forsaken his old Indian ways for the white man's road of peace.

Many times after the Pine Ridge trouble was Red

*Baptiste Pourier, now (1921) living at Manderson, S. D.

Cloud a guest at the Cook ranch on the Niobrara, his last visit occurring in 1908, the year previous to his death, and it was during this trip that an incident happened which well illustrates the warm-hearted friendship which had sprung up between Red Cloud, his people, and members of Captain Cook's family. It exhibits a tenderness of feeling which the average white man had felt never existed in an Indian's breast.

Captain Cook's eldest son was leaving home to enter Nebraska University, many miles distant in the eastern part of the state. It was the young man's first departure from the home of his parents for a prolonged stay. There were about seventy Indians in Red Cloud's party who were camped about a hundred yards from the ranch house on their accustomed visit. They knew that the young white man was going away, and what was the surprise of the Cook household, when the carriage drove up to the door, to note that all the Indian women stood lined up in respectful attitude on each side of the driveway. As young Cook passed down to the carriage, each woman gave him a hearty hand-shake, and then they began, in chorus, to chant a farewell song in the Sioux tongue. As the young man passed the Indian camp, all the warriors filed out, bedecked in their savage finery, with Red Cloud heading the procession. Young Cook was deeply touched by this farewell reception of his Indian friends; but the tears coursed down, not only his own cheeks, but those of his parents, when Red Cloud folded the boy in his arms, and fondly patting him on the back, he placed his face against that of the youth, and with deep emotion said: "I am an old man. Your father is my friend. I and my people will give you his name, and we will think of you with good hearts." Then, in turn, each Indian man embraced the youth, all exhibiting the most genuine affection in this demonstration of farewell.

Red Cloud died, as he lived, declared Captain Cook – an Indian who never pretended to be reconstructed. He further emphasizes that the old Indian people, who knew and loved the wild, free life of the plains, should not be too harshly judged by those whose modern residences now span the places once dotted by the lodges of the Sioux.

Another man whose writings and personal acquaintance with Red Cloud further bear out the statements of Captain Cook, is Professor W. K. Moorehead of Andover, Massachusetts, well known as the author of many books on Indian life. Professor Moorehead was at Pine Ridge during the Ghost Dance war, and his opinion of the noted chief is given in one of his books, *The American Indian*, in which he says:

> Red Cloud was nearly blind, and aged rapidly after 1890. Eighty-seven years is a long time for an Indian to live. Continual exposure, uncertain food supply and frail habitation break down the constitution, and one rarely sees an Indian more than sixty years of age. During the last years of his life, Red Cloud enjoyed the comforts of a two-story frame house. It was given him by the government as a special mark of honor. During the presence of the troops he kept a little American flag and a white peace flag constantly floating above it. He bemoaned the fate of his race, and from his conversation one could easily discern that he had done his duty and defended the claims of the Dakotas in adversity as in prosperity. Over twenty years ago I had several conversations with him through an interpreter. He dwelt upon the happy 'buffalo days,' and the free life of the plains of sixty years ago. We stepped outside the house, and he told me to look about the valley, for his eyes were dim; but he knew its character. I cannot give the exact words of his speech, but it was about as follows:

> "You see this barren waste. We have a little land along

the creek which affords good grazing, but we must have some of it for corn and wheat. There are other creeks which have bottoms like this, but most of the land is poor and worthless. Think of it! I, who used to own rich soil in a well watered country so extensive that I could not ride through it in a week on my fastest pony, am put down here! Why, I have to go five miles for wood for my fire! Washington took our lands, and promised to feed and support us. Now I, who used to control five thousand warriors, must tell Washington when I am hungry! I must beg for that which I own. If I beg hard, they put me in the guard-house. We have trouble. Our girls are getting bad. Coughing sickness (consumption) every winter carries away our best people. My heart is heavy. I am old. I cannot do much more. Young man, I wish there was someone to help my poor people when I am gone!"

Red Cloud felt, and felt rightly, that he had good cause for grievance and hatred because of the treatment which he and his people had been subjected to at the hands of the government. In this respect, Professor Moorehead further says:

The graft of the agencies was notoriously well known on the frontier, and many an agent became actually rich from the spoils of his office. The Indians realized the state of affairs and they resented it, and added it as another brand to the fire of their hostility against the whites. The big old chief, Red Cloud once said:

"I don't see why the government changes our agents. When one agent gets rich at his trade of looking after us, and has about all he wants, he may stop his stealing and leave us the property which belongs to us, if he keeps his place. But when one man grows fat at our expense he is removed, and a lean one sent to take his place, and we must fill his belly also, and give away to another lean one."

With but few exceptions, nearly every white man who went out on the frontier as a scout, miner, trader, hunter or explorer, exhibited the worst side of his character when among Indians. . . The Indian became acquainted with all that was bad, and saw but little of the real good of civilization. He heard more oaths than prayers; saw more saloons than churches or schools. The men whom he met were not calculated, by their acts, to inspire him with any confidence or respect for the white race. If the plains' tribes had associated with a better class of citizens before they learned the vices of civilization, I am satisfied that the historian would not be compelled to write so dark and tragic a narrative; nor would he feel constrained to hold them up as fit subjects for pity and compassion.

Considering that Red Cloud came in contact with a class of white men whose presence would not be tolerated in a respectable community; his high character, his submission to the unjust acts of his conquerors, places him, in my opinion, among the great men of America, regardless of color, birth or ancestry. His career exhibits a degree of mental capacity, a knowledge of human nature and an acquaintance with the affairs of men which we would not expect in a savage's mind. Red Cloud's bearing toward the government in the Leavenworth and Fort Robinson treaties, in having secured his end in both instances, indicates a knowledge of diplomacy of no mean order. . . Red Cloud possessed more human kindness than any of his red contemporaries. It has been affirmed that after the Fetterman fight he assisted the young men in scalping and mutilating the dead. There is no direct evidence of this. Red Cloud himself says that he never tortured a living person nor mutilated a dead body, and that those under his control were no more cruel than the Colorado citizens at the Sand Creek Massacre,[128] the soldiers in the battle of the Washita or the Seventh Cavalry at Wounded Knee. He cites the murder of Crazy Horse and several sub-chiefs after they had surrendered and were held as hostages in one of the forts. He claims that in all his fights and raids he never perpetrated cruelties like these; that he was either a staunch friend or a bitter enemy.

[128] The Sand Creek Massacre or the "Chivington massacre," as it is probably better known, was unquestionably one of the grossest outrages ever perpetrated against Indians by United States troops. This is not the time nor place to discuss that affair, but those interested may read a full account in Mrs. H. H. Jackson's *Century of Dishonor*. Further accounts may be read in Article Six of the Treaty of October 14, 1865, between the United States and the chiefs and headmen representing the confederated tribes of the Arapahoe and Cheyenne Indians. In the battle of the Washita, also at Wounded Knee, women and children were indiscriminately shot down.

In his later years he rather inclined toward the faith of the Catholics, but when younger he was reported to have said that he believed in no white man's God, but held to the Great Spirit (Waukantanka), and propitiated the evil spirits also; that if he tried to do his duty, help his people and was a good man, he should not fear to meet the Great Spirit in the hereafter. That so far he agreed with the missionaries of different denominations, but because they were in discord among themselves as to just how the Great Spirit should be worshipped, he considered that not one of them was better than another; that his religion was as good as theirs, and that he would do as his heart prompted him.

After his removal to Pine Ridge, a petty agent arrested this great man on a trivial charge, and confined him in the guard house. Immediately his warriors armed, and a great number of Indians prepared to attack the agency.

When some of the sub-chiefs, after his release, said, 'Let us kill our women and children and fight until we are gone — that is preferable to starvation here on the reservation,' he is reported to have made a dignified and manly speech, in which he maintained that the Almighty had decreed that they should continue on the reservation, virtually as prisoners of their conquerors, and resistance would only result in suffering and bloodshed, and could accomplish no good.

An intelligent savage, reared upon the plains amidst surroundings calculated to develop other than the lowest desires, and possessing a primitive idea of the truest type of manhood, he has presented us with a career which shall endure in history long after the frontiersmen shall have been forgotten.

In 1890 Red Cloud was appealed to by Father Jule, a noted Catholic missionary, to express his opinion on the causes which led up to the Ghost Dance war. The aged chieftain at that time made a most scathing arraignment of the government and the manner in which the red man was treated by the Indian Department, in the following language:

When we first made treaties with the government this was our position: Our old life and our customs were about to end; the game upon which we lived was disappearing; the whites were closing around us, and nothing remained for us to do but to adopt their ways and have the same rights with them if we wished to save ourselves. The government promised us all the means necessary to make our living out of the land, and to instruct us how to do it, and abundant food to support us until we could take care of ourselves. We looked forward with hope to the time when we would be as independent as the whites and have a voice in the government.

The officers of the army could have helped us better than any others, but we were not left to them. An Indian Department was made, with a large number of agents and other officials drawing large salaries, and these men were supposed to teach us the way of the whites. Then came the beginning of trouble. These men took care of themselves, but not of us. It was made very hard for us to deal with the government except through them. It seems to me that they thought they could make more by keeping us back than by helping us forward. We did not get the means to work our land. The few things given were given in such a way as to do us little or no good. Our rations began to be reduced. Some said that we were lazy and wanted to live on rations, and not to work. That is false. How does any man of sense suppose that so great a number of people could get to work at once, unless they were at once supplied with means to work, and instructors enough to teach them how to use them?

Remember, that even our little ponies were taken away, under the promise that they would be replaced by oxen and large horses, and that it was long before we saw any, and then we got very few. We tried, even with the means we had, but by one pretext or another we were shifted from place to place, or told that such a transfer was coming. Great effort was made to break up our customs, but nothing was done to introduce the custom of the whites. Everything was done to break the power of the real chiefs, who really wished their people to improve, and little men, so-called chiefs, were made to act as disturbers and agitators. Spotted Tail wanted the ways of the whites, and a cowardly assassin was found to remove him. This was charged upon the Indians because an Indian did it. But who set on the Indian?

I was abused and slandered, to weaken my influence for good and make me seem like one who did not want to advance. This was done by the men paid by the government to teach us the ways of the whites. I have visited many other tribes, and find that the same things were done among them. All was done to discourage, and nothing to encourage. I saw the men, paid by the government to help us, all making money for themselves and very busy, but doing nothing for us.

Now, don't you suppose we saw all this? Of course we did, but what could we do? We were prisoners – not in the hands of the army, but in the hands of robbers. Where was the army? Set by the government to watch us, but having no voice in setting things right, so that they would not need to watch us. They could not speak for us, though we wished it very much. Those who held us, pretended to be very anxious about our welfare, and said our condition was a great mystery. We tried to speak and clear up this mystery, but we were laughed at and treated as children. So things went on from year to year. Other treaties were made, but it was all the same. Rations were further reduced, and we were starving. Sufficient food was not given us, and no means to get food from the land were provided. Rations were further reduced. A family got for two weeks what was not enough for one week.

What did we eat when that was gone? The people were desperate from starvation – they had no hope. They did not think of fighting. What good would it do? They might die like men, but what would the women and children do? Some say they saw the Son of God; others did not see Him. I did not see Him. If He had come He would do some great things as He had done before. We doubted it because we saw neither Him nor His works. Then General Crook came. His words sounded well; but how could we know that a new treaty would be kept any better than the old one? For that reason we did not care to sign. He promised to see that his promise would be kept. He, at least, has never lied to us. His words gave the people hope. They signed. They hoped. He died. Their hope died with him. Despair came again. The people were counted and wrongly counted. Our rations were again reduced. The white men seized on the land we sold them through General Crook, but our pay was as distant as ever. The man who counted us said we were feasting and wasting food. Where did he see this?

How can we eat or waste what we have not? We felt that we were mocked in our misery. We had no newspapers, and no one to speak for us. We had no redress. Our rations were again reduced. You, who eat three times a day, and see your children well and happy around you, can't understand what starving Indians feel. We were faint with hunger and maddened by despair. We held our dying children and felt their little bodies tremble as their souls went out and left only a dead weight in our hands. They were not very heavy, but we ourselves were very faint, and the dead weighed us down. There was no hope on earth, and God seemed to have forgotten us. Someone had again been talking of the Son of God, and said He would come. The people did not know; they did not care. They snatched at the hope. They screamed like crazy men to Him for mercy. They caught at the promise they heard He had made.

The white men were frightened and called for soldiers. We had begged for life, and the white men thought we wanted theirs. We heard that soldiers were coming. We did not fear. We hoped that we could tell them our troubles and get help. A white man said the soldiers meant to kill us. We did not believe it, but some were frightened and ran away to the bad lands. The soldiers came. They said: 'Don't be afraid; we come to make peace and not war.' It was true. They brought us food and did not threaten us. If the Messiah has really come, it must be this way. The people prayed for life and the army brought it. The Black Robe (Father Jule) went into the bad lands and brought in some Indians to talk with General Brooke. The general was very kind to them, and quieted their fears, and was a real friend. He sent out Indians to call in other Indians from the bad lands. I sent all my horses and all my young men to help General Brooke save the Indians. Am I not right when I say that he will know how to settle this trouble? He has settled it.

The Indian Department called for soldiers to shoot down the Indians whom it had starved into despair. General Brooke said: 'No. What have they done? They are dying. They must live.' He brought us food. He gave us hope. I trust to him now to see that we will be well treated. I hope that the despair that he has driven away will never return again. If the army had been with us from the first there never would have been any trouble. The army will, I hope, keep us safe and help us become as independent as the whites. No Indian wants to fight; they want to eat and work and live. The Indian Department has almost destroyed us. Save us from it! Let the sun shine on us again.

As further evidence that Red Cloud was not entirely without spiritual thought and communion, the following is printed from *The Council Fire and Arbitrator*, a periodical printed in Washington, D.C., under date of June, 1883:

On the 5th of October, 1870, a council was held between Chief Red Cloud and a commission sent out to the Sioux country by the Secretary of the Interior. Honorable Felix Burnot was chairman of the Commission. When the Indians were assembled at Fort Laramie, Mr. Burnot said:

"Nothing we may do can prosper without the blessing of the Great Spirit. I therefore propose asking the blessing of the Great Spirit on our council."

He then delivered an eloquent and quite long prayer. When he closed, Chief Red Cloud arose, and first raising his hands toward the skies, he bowed till he touched the earth with his fingers. He then stood erect, and again lifted his hands toward the heavens. Then all the Indians arose and stood in reverent attitude, while the chief uttered the following prayer:

"O, Great Spirit, I pray you to look upon us. We are your children and you placed us first in this land. We pray you to look down on us, so that nothing but truth shall be spoken in this council. We don't ask for anything but what is right and just. When you made your red children, O, Great Spirit, you made them to have mercy upon them. Now we are before you today, praying you to look down on us and have pity on your poor red children. We pray you to let nothing but truth be spoken here. We hope that these things may be settled right. You are the protector of those who use the bow and arrow, as well as those people who wear hats, and I hope we don't pray to you in vain. We are poor and ignorant, but

our fathers have told us that we would not be in distress if we
asked for your assistance. O, Great Spirit, look down on your
children and take pity on them!"

Chief Red Cloud died at Pine Ridge agency, South
Dakota, December 10, 1909, and the following day
was buried in the cemetery of the Holy Rosary Mission. In his latter years, the old chief was inclined
toward the Catholic faith, and it is stated to the authors
of this work by Father Grotegeers, superintendent of
Holy Rosary Mission, that it was largely through the
influence of Chief Red Cloud himself that the mission
was established, and that he was more instrumental in
bringing this about than any other one person.

Five children were born to Red Cloud and his wife.
They were: Jack Red Cloud (dead), Mrs. Louisa
Richard (dead), Mrs. Libbie Slow Bear, Mrs. Fannie
Chase Alone, Mrs. Charges-At-or-Kills-Above. The
three latter yet live on Pine Ridge reservation. All of
Red Cloud's children raised large families, and the
grandchildren number a score or more. There are also
many great grandchildren of the noted war chief of
the Sioux.

At the time of Red Cloud's death, his intimate white
friend, Captain Cook, suggested to Jack Red Cloud,
the old chief's son, that his father should be buried on
what is known as "Red Cloud Buttes," which form a
part of the former Red Cloud agency. It is a most
commanding site, and a fitting place for the remains
of this noted old warrior to lie at rest, overlooking a
vast section of territory, where his warriors, in days
past, roamed by thousands in perfect freedom. Captain Cook's idea was that a tomb should be hewn from
the solid rock, and the remains of the great chief properly interred therein, while a heavy iron door should

CHIEF RED CLOUD AT THE AGE OF 75

bar all vandals and curiosity seekers from disturbing the bones of this noted Indian chieftain and statesman. The Catholics, however, demurred, giving as their reason that the Buttes were not "consecrated ground." It is not unlikely, however, that this may be done at no distant day. Jack Red Cloud was in favor of the plan, as were the old people of the tribe.

Many of the old Ogalalla Sioux, who have been making annual visits to Captain Cook's ranch since the death of Red Cloud, have made highly complimentary remarks regarding an oil painting of the aged warrior which was made in the Cook home in 1902, when Red Cloud was a guest there. The painting was executed by a friend of the Cook family, and Red Cloud posed for some time, in order that the likeness might be as perfect as possible. That it is a work of art is emphasized by an incident in connection with their visit to the ranch of several aged members of the tribe some time after the death of their chief. An old Indian woman, nearly ninety years of age, who was brought into the room where the painting was being exhibited, upon catching her first glimpse of it, dropped the staff upon which she had been leaning, and tottered over to the painting, resting on an easel, wailing as she went. Placing both her bony hands on the face in the canvas she peered about and behind the canvas, in astonishment, as though she felt that she must be gazing upon the spirit of Makh-pi-ya-luta, her departed chief and brother, whose name she kept repeating, mingling it with shrill wails, until she was led from the room. This compliment paid the artist was certainly "from the heart."

On another occasion a younger woman, a relative of the chief, after being shown the portrait, left the room, wailing, and went to the top of a high, rocky butte, about a quarter of a mile distant, where she remained for three days, mourning and fasting. At the end of that time several of the Indian women took food and water to her and persuaded her to return to the camp with them. This tribute to the skill of the artist in bringing back to these Indians so realistically the face and form of their beloved chieftain, was certainly genuine, even though it might be classed as "hysterical" by some philosophical people who have been trained to control their emotions – sometimes to the freezing point.

Jack Red Cloud died July 2, 1918, at Pine Ridge reservation, and his remains also rest in the Holy Rosary Mission cemetery. He was about sixty years of age, but never arose to the high position attained by his noted father, although Captain Cook says he was buried with unusual honors.

Jim Bridger-"The Grand Old Man of the Rockies"

The western plains and mountains brought forth thousands of men noted for their valor, bravery, daring, sagacity, woodcraft, frontiersmanship and skill in guiding wagon trains and military expeditions across the trackless prairie and barren desert and through snow capped mountain fastnesses on the way to the land of gold beyond the setting sun, or in trailing and bringing to bay the savage hordes that sternly fought the advances of civilization; but among those dauntless spirits there was one who stood head and shoulders above all others as the greatest scout, trapper and guide, the most skilled frontiersman, and the quietest, most modest and unassuming prairie man in all the west. That person was James Bridger, Major Bridger, or, as he was more commonly and familiarly known, "old Jim Bridger," the "grand old man of the Rockies." No history of the American western frontier would be complete without a sketch of the life of this remarkable man.

Richmond, Virginia, and March 17, 1804, was the place and date of birth of this greatest of plainsmen. His father and mother were James and Chloe Bridger, of whom history records but little. At one time they conducted a hotel in Richmond, and it would appear that Bridger, senior, was in fairly comfortable circumstances, since he also owned a good sized farm in the state of Virginia. Apparently, however, neither the

Virginia farm nor the hotel business served to hold him in that section of the country, since he removed to St. Louis in 1812. Four years later his wife died and three children were left motherless. Bridger's sister then came and acted as mother to the children until the autumn of 1817, when the father died, and James Bridger Jr., and his young sister were left orphans, another brother having died shortly before.

Thus at the tender age of thirteen, young Jim Bridger was forced out into the world to make a living for himself and sister, and although it was a rather difficult undertaking for one so young, he operated a flatboat ferry near St. Louis for a time; but apparently this was too strenuous for a boy of his age, for soon he became apprenticed to a blacksmith named Phil Cromer or Creamer, to learn that trade. Here he worked steadily until eighteen years of age, when the desire to see something of the great West, together with a spirit for adventure, induced him to join a band of William Ashley's trappers who were starting for the Rocky Mountains under the command of Andrew Henry, one of the original incorporators of the old Missouri Fur Company and later a partner of Ashley. The expedition left St. Louis in April, 1822.

The party met with great misfortune on its way up the Missouri River. One of their boats, which was loaded with merchandise valued at ten thousand dollars, was upset. To add to the trouble, Indians stole several horses belonging to the party while some of the trappers were marching up the river after the accident to the boat. Thus, it was found necessary to winter at the mouth of the Yellowstone River. Here the party hunted and trapped until the following spring.

The summer of 1823 found young Jim Bridger with

JIM BRIDGER, "THE GRAND OLD MAN OF THE ROCKIES"

Greatest of all plainsmen, scouts, and guides. Born in Richmond, Virginia, March 17, 1804; died near Westport, Mo., July 16, 1881.

a party of Henry's men fighting the Indians in the Yellowstone country. The fort which Henry had erected near the mouth of the Yellowstone, was abandoned after twenty-two of his horses had been stolen. The entire party then moved over near the mouth of the Big Horn River, following it toward its source. It was on this expedition that South Pass was discovered (1824). Through this pass the Oregon Trail later took its course to the Pacific slope.

Doubtless on the expedition of 1823 Bridger was a trapper companion of Hugh Glass, among others. The story of Glass's terrific combat with a huge grizzly bear is a well known western classic. While en route up Grand River, Glass, who was accounted one of the best rifle shots in the command, was often detailed to go out after game. While forcing his way through a heavy thicket one day he stumbled upon a she bear with two cubs. Before Glass could make a move to defend himself, the bear sprang upon him, bore him to the ground and tore off a huge chunk of flesh from his body, which she offered to her cubs. The trapper endeavored to escape from the animal, but was again pounced upon and mauled and mangled in a shocking manner. His cries for help were heard by some of his companions who hastened to the spot and dispatched the bear as she was standing over Glass's supposedly dead body. However, the trapper was yet alive, but was so horribly torn and disfigured that it was not thought possible that he could live. It was further feared that if the entire party were delayed to determine whether Glass would live or die, they might be attacked by Indians any moment. Finally Major Henry offered eighty dollars to any two of the men who would remain behind until Glass either died or recovered sufficiently to be removed to the nearest trading post. A trapper named Fitzgerald and one other – a much younger man, whom tradition says was Jim Bridger – agreed to remain with their injured companion. Five days they watched, but Glass clung to life with a tenacity that was marvelous. At last, seeing no prospects of the immediate death of their companion, the two watchers deserted him to his fate, even taking his rifle and accoutrements, and leaving Glass without means of protection. Overtaking the main body of trappers the two men stated that Glass had died and they had buried him as well as was possible. They showed the rifle in confirmation and the story was believed. Glass, however, did not die, but gradually recovered his strength, and in a miraculous manner contrived to reach Fort Kiowa, a post on the Missouri River, a hundred miles away.

History has not been able to prove that Jim Bridger was one of these two wretches who deserted Glass in his unfortunate condition; and taking into consideration Bridger's well known courage and the fact that he was a man to be depended upon in times of great danger, it is not at all likely that the story is true. However, the facts are given as recorded in various publications, and the reader must form his own conclusions.

There is no proof to dispute the claim that Jim Bridger was the first white man to see Great Salt Lake. This was in 1824. Bridger concluded that he had discovered an arm of the Pacific Ocean, inasmuch as the water was salty. He so reported to his companions upon his return from following Bear River to the lake.

In 1830 the Rocky Mountain Fur Company was formed by Thomas Fitzpatrick, Milton Sublette, Henry Fraeb, Jean Baptiste Gervais and Jim Bridger, they having bought out the firm of Smith, Jackson and Sublette (the latter being William Sublette, a brother of Milton) who had come to the conclusion that younger men were elbowing their way to the front, and that it was a good time to sell out. However, the Rocky Mountain Fur Company existed, not legally to be true, but four years, and its business was carried on in a rather haphazard manner.

During the summer of 1830, Bridger, with a large company of trappers, entered the Big Horn Basin. The party crossed the Yellowstone and marched to the Great Falls of the Missouri. They then turned southward and ascended the Missouri to the Three Forks, following the Jefferson Forks to the divide. Great quantities of furs were trapped, after which the party continued south several hundred miles, finally reaching Ogden's Hole on the northeast shore of Great Salt Lake. On this trip it is supposed that Bridger first saw the wonders of Yellowstone Park. His description of what he had seen seemed so greatly exaggerated that he was not believed. He repeated the grandeurs of that magic spot to everyone he met; but was greatly disgusted because nobody would put any faith in his stories regarding the new wonderland.

[129]"Prior to 1860 Bridger had related these accounts to military and scientific men, as well as to others, and although he seems to have convinced these gentlemen that there was something in his stories, they still attributed less to fact than to fancy.

"In his efforts to spread a knowledge of this region, Bridger was as determined as John Colter had been before him and with little better success. He tried to have his narratives published but no periodical would lend itself to his service. The editor of the Kansas

[129] Chittenden (H. M.) *The Yellowstone Park.*

City Journal stated editorially in 1879 that Bridger had told him of these wonders fully thirty years before. He had prepared an article in 1856 from Bridger's descriptions, in which the latter told about the mud springs and other wonders of that part of the country, or, to use his own expression, 'it was a place where hell bubbled up.'

"The editor of the Journal was much interested in the matter at that time, but did not print it because a man who claimed to know Bridger told him he would be laughed out of town if he printed 'any of old Jim Bridger's lies.'

"The persistent incredulity of his countrymen and their ill concealed ideas of his honesty, to say nothing of his mental soundness, were long a cloud upon Bridger's life, but, more fortunate than Colter, he lived to see himself triumphantly vindicated. The editor of the Journal later publicly apologized to Bridger, who was then living at Westport, Mo.

"Whether from disgust at this unmerited treatment, or because of his love for a good story, Bridger seems finally to have resolved that distrust of his word – if it must exist – should at least have some justification. He was, in fact, noted for 'drawing a long bow' to an unparallelled tension, and for never permitting troublesome scruples of conscience to interfere with the proper embellishment of his yarns. These were generally based on fact, and diligent search will discover in them the 'soul of truth.' These anecdotes are yet current along the Yellowstone, and the tourist who remains long in the Park will not fail to hear them.

"When Bridger found that he could not make his hearers believe in the existence of a vast mass of volcanic glass, now known to all tourists as the interesting

'Obsidian Cliff,' he supplied them with another glass mountain of a truly original sort. Its discovery was the result of one of his hunting trips, and it happened in this wise:

"Coming one day in sight of a magnificent elk, he took careful aim and fired. To his great amazement the elk not only was not wounded, but seemed not to have even heard the report of his rifle. Bridger drew considerably nearer and took more careful aim than before, but with the same result. A third and fourth shot proved similar. Utterly exasperated, he seized his rifle by the barrel and resolved to use it as a club. He rushed madly at the elk, but suddenly crashed into an immovable vertical wall, which proved to be a mountain of perfectly transparent glass, on the further side of which, still in peaceful security, the elk quietly grazed! Stranger still, the mountain was not only of pure glass, but was a perfect telescope lens and whereas, the elk seemed but a few hundred yards away, it was, in reality, twenty miles distant!

"Another of Bridger's 'discoveries' was an ice cold spring near the summit of a lofty mountain, the water of which flowed down over a long, smooth slope, where it acquired such a velocity that it was boiling hot when it reached the bottom! Bridger reasoned that as two sticks rubbed together produce heat by friction, so the water rubbing over the rock became hot!

"To those who have visited the west shore of Yellowstone Lake and know how simple a matter it is to catch the lake trout and cook them in the boiling pools without taking them from the line, the groundwork of the following description will be obvious enough: Somewhere along the shore an immense boiling spring discharged its overflow directly into the lake. The specific gravity of the water is less than that of the lake, owing probably to the expansive action of heat, and it floats in a stratum three or four feet thick upon the cold water underneath. When Bridger was in need of fish, it was to this place that he went. Through the hot upper stratum he let fall his bait to the sub-jacent habitable zone, and having hooked his victim, cooked it on the way out!

"In like manner the visitor to the region of petrifactions on Specimen Ridge, in the northeast corner of the park, and to various points in the hot springs district, will have no difficulty in discovering the base material out of which Bridger contrived the following picturesque yarn:

"According to his account, there existed in the Park country a mountain which was once cursed by a great medicine man of the Crow nation. Everything upon the mountain, at the time of this dire event became instantly petrified and has remained so ever since! All forms of life were standing about in stone, where they were suddenly caught by the petrifying influences. Sagebrush, grass, prairie fowl, antelope, elk and bears may be seen as perfect as in actual life. Even flowers are blooming in colors of crystal, and birds soar with wings spread in motionless flight, while the air floats with music and perfumes siliceous and the sun and the moon shine with petrified light!

"In this way, Bridger avenged himself for the spirit of distrust shown for what he related. The time presently came, however, when the public learned not only how large a measure of truth there was in his stories, but also how ingenious a tale he could weave from very inadequate material."

In the early days of the West, people who went over

the Oregon Trail continuously commented upon the wonderful healthy climate, but insisted that nothing would grow in the country along the trail. One day driven to exasperation, Bridger, who was with a party of unbelievers as to the productivity of the soil along the Sweetwater, said as he was arranging his camp near the base of Independence Rock which is one mile in circumference,–"Grow? Anything will grow here. See that ere rock? When I first came to this section I threw a pebble across the Sweetwater. Well, that ere rock was once my pebble."

"Two Ocean Pass," the most remarkable pass, it is said, in the world, was discovered by Bridger also in the '30's. It is eight thousand one hundred and fifty feet above sea level, and about a mile in length and the same in width. From the north a stream comes from the canyon. In the pass this stream divides, the waters on one side flowing into the Atlantic by way of Yellowstone River, while the Pacific is fed from the same stream by way of Snake River. Fish from these streams pass from one water to the other. Bridger used to tell about this river and of the fish passing through it, but the story was simply called "one of old Jim's lies," and not taken seriously. Years later the truth was discovered, and this is now one of the greatest curiosities of Yellowstone Park. A small lake near the headwaters of the Yellowstone River has been named Bridger Lake in honor of the noted frontiersman.

Bridger attended the summer rendezvous of the trappers in Pierre's Hole in 1832. This meeting of the mountain men was one of the most important ever held, marking as it did a turning point in the Rocky Mountain fur trade. Much opposition was breaking out, and it became evident, at this annual rendezvous that war to the knife was to be the watchword henceforth.

When the rendezvous finally broke up, Bridger, with Thomas Fitzpatrick and a company of boon companions hied themselves to the Jefferson Fork of the Missouri, a favorite trapping ground. Rival trappers led by Andrew Drips and Henry Vanderburgh, of the American Fur Company, followed on their trail. This was evidently done with a view of letting the more experienced trappers seek out the richest trapping territory and then boldly and brazenly, by underhanded methods, break in on the ground and try to beat Bridger and Fitzpatrick out of their valuable fur territory. Rather than have any words or trouble with their rivals, both Bridger and his companion sought other sections; but their tormentors promptly followed them. Bridger thereupon determined to teach them a lesson, and boldly invaded the Blackfoot Indian country, hoping that Vanderburgh and Drips would follow. The expected happened. The rivals were attacked on a stream which was one of the sources of the Jefferson, and Vanderburgh was killed, the Indians stripping his flesh from the bones and throwing the skeleton into the river. Bridger himself did not escape unscathed, for soon after he was attacked by Indians of the same tribe. In the fight which followed, Bridger and the chief met in a desperate hand-to-hand encounter, during which the trapper received two severe arrow wounds in the back, and was also felled to earth by a blow from his own gun, which the chief wrenched from his grasp. One of these arrow points remained embedded in his back for nearly three years, when it was removed by Dr. Marcus Whitman, the noted missionary, at that time en route to Oregon, and who met the Bridger trapping party at the rendezvous of 1835.

Interesting mention of the extraction of this arrow point from the back of Jim Bridger is made by Reverend Samuel Parker, A.M., a missionary who had received an appointment through the American Board of Commissioners for Foreign Missions "to ascertain by personal observation the condition and character of the Indian nations and tribes and the facilities for introducing the gospel and civilization among them." The caravan with which Dr. Parker traveled reached the Green River rendezvous of the trappers in August, 1835, where his journal[130] records the following:

> In the afternoon we came to the Green River, a branch of the Colorado, in latitude forty-two degrees, where the caravan held their rendezvous. This is in a widely extended valley, which is pleasant. . . The American Fur Company have between two and three hundred men constantly in and about the mountains, engaged in trading, hunting and trapping. These all assemble at rendezvous and bring in their furs, and take new supplies, for the coming year, of clothing, ammunition, and goods for trade with the Indians. But few of them ever return to their country and friends. Most of them are constantly in debt to the company, and are unwilling to return without a fortune; and year after year passes while they are hoping for better success. Here were assembled many Indians belonging to four different nations; the Utaws, Shoshones, Nez Perces and Flatheads, who were waiting for the caravan to exchange furs, horses and dressed skins for various articles of merchandise.

> While we continued in this place, Doctor Whitman [131] was called to perform some very important surgical operations. He extracted an iron arrow, three inches long, from the back of Captain Bridger, which he had received three years before in a skirmish with the Blackfoot Indians. It was a difficult opera-

---

[130] Parker (Samuel) *Journal of an Exploring Tour Beyond the Rocky Mountains.*

[131] Dr. Marcus Whitman, treacherously murdered by the Cayuse Indians while engaged in missionary work in Oregon. Dr. Whitman and his entire family were slain November 29, 1847.

tion in consequence of the arrow being hooked at the point by striking a large bone, and a cartilaginous substance had grown around it. The doctor pursued the operation with great self-possession and perseverance; and Captain Bridger manifested equal firmness. The Indians looked on, while the operation was proceeding, with countenances indicating wonder, and when they saw the arrow, expressed their astonishment in a manner peculiar to themselves. The skill of Doctor Whitman undoubtedly made upon them a favorable impression. He also took another arrow from under the shoulder of one of the hunters, which had been there two years and a half. After these operations, calls for surgical and medical aid were constant every hour of the day.

In 1835 Bridger, with Thomas Fitzpatrick and Milton Sublette, bought out the post which William Sublette and Robert Campbell had erected in the autumn of 1834 on the Laramie. The famous trio, after the passing of the Rocky Mountain Fur Company, entered the service of the American Fur Company, which had heretofore been the detested rival of the former company. Bridger was associated with this company for about eight years. He also conducted various hunting enterprises with a trapper named Vasquez during that time.

The winter of 1836 Bridger passed upon the Yellowstone with a large body of trappers, among them being Kit Carson. Early in January of that season, while busily engaged with their traps, signs of a large war party of the Blackfeet were discovered, and as the presence of this enemy would seriously interfere with their work, the trappers determined to give the savages battle. Forty of the best shots set out to find the Indian camp. It was discovered to be upon an island in the Yellowstone, where the Indians had intrenched themselves. A fierce battle ensued. When morning came it was discovered that the Blackfeet had left. The trappers thereupon returned to their camp, but Bridger expressed the opinion that the Indians would return with reinforcements to renew the attack. Sentries were posted and a sharp watch maintained throughout the day, during which time the trappers strengthened their fortifications. When the Blackfeet finally appeared it was discovered that there were upward of one thousand in the band.

Within sight of the waiting trappers a great war dance was indulged in to stimulate the warriors to fierce action. While the American Indian is not, as a rule, given to making charges against barricaded bodies of their foes, on this occasion they did charge with a fury which none of the gallant little party of defenders had ever before experienced in Indian warfare. They were greeted by a galling fire from the deadly rifles of the trappers. This proved too much for the red men, and they broke and fled out of range. Although the fighting continued for two days, there appears to have been but little loss on either side, and the Blackfeet finally withdrew. Bridger and his brave little band were not again molested during that season.

In the spring of 1837 the Bridger party, while on the Upper Yellowstone and in the heart of the Blackfoot territory, encountered another war party of their implacable foes. Another fierce battle ensued, in which both Bridger and Kit Carson experienced hairbreadth escapes. The trappers were the better armed, and finally drove their opponents from the field.

The next few years were spent by Bridger in the employ of the American Fur Company trapping throughout that section of territory west of the Big Horn River. Numerous thrilling escapes from hostile savages were encountered.

As a trapper, Bridger's work seems to have ceased about 1843, or at the time when the historic Fort Bridger was built. This point became a noted one on the line of overland travel for many years; Bridger selecting the spot because it would bring him in much revenue from the emigrants. The Mormon Trail also was close at hand, and the North and South Platte routes met near Fort Bridger, thus making the place an important one to all travelers. Here Bridger established a blacksmith shop, supply store and trading post, and as most of the emigrants were well supplied with money, and were, moreover, generally obliged to purchase provisions and supplies about the time Fort Bridger was reached, a considerable business was transacted. Of this post Bridger says, in a letter to Pierre Chouteau in December, 1843: (doubtless written by someone else, as Bridger never learned to write).

> I have established a small fort, with a blacksmith shop and a supply of iron, in the road of the emigrants, on Black Fork of Green River, which promises fairly well. They, in coming out, are generally well supplied with money, but by the time they get here, are in want of all kinds of supplies. Horses, provisions, smith-work, etc., bring ready cash from them, and should I receive the goods ordered hereby, will do a considerable business that way with them. The same establishment trades with the Indians in the neighborhood, who have mostly a good number of beaver among them.

It is quite apparent, however, that Bridger did not spend all his time at his fort, but made frequent trapping expeditions into the mountains, as in the fall of 1844 he led a trapping party to Milk River, having received reports that beaver were plentiful along that stream. His party consisted of thirty picked men. The trapping was a failure, and in November the party arrived at Fort Union, where they spent the winter.

Bridger was well known to Laidlaw, who was in charge of the fort at that time, and made his camp about a half mile distant from the post. Bridger was greatly disappointed over the failure of his trapping expedition, but the inmates of the fort were relieved at the appearance of his outfit, concluding now that with such a formidable party encamped close at hand, the danger of an Indian attack was greatly lessened. Bridger appears to have regaled the fort officials with wonderful tales of his prowess. "The main substance of Bridger's conversation was his brave men, his fast horses and his fights with the Blackfeet, till we were induced to believe that . . . there would be no danger for us in case of an attack by the Sioux."[132]

However, for once, Bridger appears to have relaxed his vigilance. Shortly before the latter part of December, Indians stampeded the horse herd belonging to the fort. Six animals were stolen and one of the herders wounded in the leg. Bridger's party was called upon to recapture the stolen animals and punish the thieves. The Indians were pursued to the base of a high hill, upon which they made a stand. Here they taunted their pursuers and dared them to come up and fight. Bridger's men, however, concluded that discretion was the better part of valor, and refused to attack the Indians, greatly to the disgust and mortification of Bridger, who was unable to account for their cowardice. In vain did he attempt to rally them to the charging point. Not a man would attempt to scale the hill. After jeering the trappers and daring them to come up the hill and give battle, the savages leisurely took their departure, having killed one man, and decamping with all the stolen stock. So chagrined was Bridger over the outcome of this affair that he dispersed his men and returned alone to the mountains.

Bridger's fort has well been characterized as a veritable oasis in the desert, and most excellent judgment was shown on the part of the founder in establishing his headquarters in such a favored spot. Bridger obtained the land from the Mexican government before it became a part of the United States. Here he lived (spasmodically, it is true) until 1857, when he leased the property to the United States for the sum of six hundred dollars per year – which rental, by the way, never was paid; and thirty years passed before the government finally paid Bridger six thousand dollars for the improvements he had made to the property – but not a cent for the land itself. Indeed, his rights were totally ignored.

A description of Fort Bridger is interesting here:

[133] SUNDAY, June 17 (1849) – An hour or so before noon we came to Fort Bridger, situated on Black's Fork, at the foot of the Utah Mountains, which loom up grandly above the beautiful fertile valley surrounding this trading post, one of the most attractive spots thus far seen. Jogging on in advance of the train, by the time the wagons came up I had made an inspection of the fort, besides taking a rest. There are several log buildings, surrounded by a high picket fence, and having a heavy wooden entrance gate. The owners of the fort are Major James Bridger, an old mountaineer, who for the past thirty years has been engaged in trading with the Indians about the headwaters of the Missouri and Columbia Rivers, and Colonel Vasquez, whom we met beyond the South Pass, as already related. In company with Mr. Scully I visited several of the apartments of the fort, among others the rooms occupied by the families of the proprietors, through which we were conducted by Mrs. Vasquez, who entertained us in an agreeable and hospitable manner, notably, by inviting us to

[133] Johnson (W. G.) *Experiences of a '49er.*

'sit upon chairs,' a situation somewhat novel – one to which, for some time past, we had been unaccustomed.

Opening upon a court where the rooms occupied by the Bridger family. Mr. Bridger, with a taste differing from that of his partner (who has a white wife from the states) made his selection from among the ladies of the wilderness – a stolid, fleshy, round headed woman, not oppressed with lines of beauty. Her hair was intensely black, and straight, and so cut that it hung in a thick mass upon her broad shoulders. In a corner of Mrs. Bridger's room was a churn filled with buttermilk, and dipping from it with a ladle formed from a gourd, Mrs. Vasquez filled and refilled our cups, which we drank until completely satisfied.

It chanced that we were enabled to repay the kindness shown by this lady without the least sacrifice on our part – a fact to be regretted. In the course of conversation, when speaking of the comforts of which she was deprived by living so far from the haunts of civilization, Mrs. Bridger mentioned the loss of a skillet lid, and her inability thus far to replace it. It was curious that it should be so, but such was the fact that we were the owners of the identical article coveted. Our skillet had been fractured and thrown away, but with that peculiar inclination which many possess of clinging to articles that have become wholly useless, we had treasured that skillet lid, and now, in the briefest possible time, even before one could say 'Jack Robinson,' it was transferred to Mrs. Bridger's kitchen. Fifty skillet lids would not have been worth the smile which greeted us when making our presentation speech; and it was plain that it was altogether useless to attempt to get out of debt. As we turned to leave, a still further burden was placed upon us when we were given a roll of freshly churned butter of a rich, golden yellow, and glistening, as it were, with drops of dew.

In a storeroom of the fort was a considerable stock of buffalo robes, one of which I purchased for the sum of five dollars. It was an exceptionally large, fine robe, with long, silky hair, and its equal I have rarely seen. It was, moreover, greatly needed, as I had suffered much from exposure when sleeping on cold, and often wet ground. Other storerooms were nearly bare of goods. In one was a keg of whisky, a jar of tobacco, a box of clay pipes and but little else. I should mention, however, some large pipes made of a red stone called 'Saint Peter's rock,' said to have been brought from the upper Mississippi, and highly esteemed by the Indians. The price at which they are sold, too – five dollars – would indicate that they are considered valuable, while Mr. Bridger informed me that there is a very ready sale for them. They are not even bored out, but simply shaped as pipe bowls are, and thus sold.

A famous character living at Fort Bridger was one Judge Carter, the sutler of the fort. He is reputed to have been a man of much education, great wealth and unbounded hospitality. One other feature of the Judge seems to have made a hit with the wayfarer, and that was his discriminating taste in the selection of wines and cigars. When Bridger and the Judge would get together for a congenial glass, the former was wont to remark that he "never in all his life and varied fortunes saw any bad whiskey. It was all good. True, some brands were better than others, but it was all good; there never was any bad whiskey."

But Bridger had his troubles in spite of the excellent location of his trading post. The Mormons had a grievance against him in 1856, and made threats against his life. Confiscating all his stock of merchandise and everything else of any value, they destroyed the buildings of the fort by fire, Bridger barely escaping with his life. His loss, he alleged, was one hundred thousand dollars. The Utah Expedition under General Albert Sidney Johnston, was the outcome of this affair, Bridger acting as guide to the expedition. Upon arriving at the spot where the fort had stood, Johnston was tendered the use of the site by Bridger, and the army wintered there. This was the time, as mentioned elsewhere, that the government "purchased" from the frontiersman his Mexican grant of the property, but never paid a cent for it, alleging that he did not have a clear title to the land. This was but one of the many injustices done Jim Bridger. After building up this little oasis in the desert, and seeing it made the rendezvous year after year, of trappers, Indians and emigrants, and establishing a post that had been of inestimable value to the government, it was a serious loss to the frontiersman to be thus deprived of his little possessions.

Bridger's experience with Sir George Gore, the wealthy Irish nobleman who came to America in 1854 for a grand hunt in the Rocky Mountains, is rich in the dry humor for which the famous plainsman was noted.

It is not likely that another such caravan as Sir George's ever invaded the Rockies before or since. "His retinue consisted of forty men, supplied with one hundred and twelve horses, twelve yoke of oxen, fourteen dogs, six wagons and twenty-one carts."[134]

Sir George arrived at St. Louis, where he outfitted and proceeded across the plains to Fort Laramie. Here the caravan halted and spent the winter. Sir George appears to have been a very democratic sort of person, notwithstanding his English title. He had heard of the value of Bridger as a guide, and succeeded in inducing him to accompany his party in that capacity. During the winter at Fort Laramie, Sir George devoted a good share of his time in studying the wild, motley crowd with which he was associated, and became deeply interested in the noted hunters, trappers and Indian chiefs who made the fort their headquarters and rendezvous.

With the coming of spring, Sir George's caravan, with Bridger in the van, started for the headwaters of the Powder River; thence, turning up the Yellowstone

[134] Montana Historical Society *Collections*, vol. i, p. 128.

to the mouth of Tongue River. Greatly delighted with
the beauty of the scenery and the wild, free life he was
leading, Sir George here erected a fort, where he and
a goodly number of his outfit spent the winter of 1855.
Sir George found in Bridger a most agreeable and
desirable companion, and Bridger himself was equally
impressed with the Irish nobleman. It is related that
Sir George would tarry in bed until about ten o'clock,
then arise, take a bath and go on a hunt, sometimes
staying out as late as ten o'clock at night, but would
always insist upon having supper served and Bridger
seated with him. After the meal, Sir George would
read aloud to his guide from Shakespeare, and endeavor to draw out his ideas of the author.

Bridger did not seem impressed with Falstaff, de-
claring it "wuz too hifalutin' fer him," and that "that
'ere Fullstuff wuz too fond of lager beer." To the
tales of Baron Munchausen he only shook his head,
remarking: "I'll be doggoned ef I kin swaller anything
that 'ere baron sez; derned ef I don't believe he's a
liar!" He further commented on them by remarking
that "some of his own adventures among the Blackfeet
would read jist as wonderful ef writ down in a book."

One evening Sir George entertained Bridger by reading to him Sir Walter Scott's account of the battle of
Waterloo, and asked him if he did not regard that as
the most sanguinary battle he had ever heard of; to
which Bridger replied:

"Wal, now, Mister Gore, that thar must hev been
considerabul of a skrimmage, doggone my skin ef it
musn't. Them 'ere Britishers must hev fit better than
they did down to New Horleens whar ol' Hick'ry gin
'em the forkedest sort o' chain lightnin' that perhaps
you never did see in all yer born days," and upon Sir

George expressing a little incredulity in regard to the estimation Bridger placed upon the battle, the latter added:

"You kin jest go yer pile on it, Mister Gore, you kin ez shore ez yer born."

In the spring of 1855 the Gore party left the fort on the Tongue and ascended the river, meeting with a large party of Crow Indians, where several days were pleasantly spent in their village. Later, the party returned to the mouth of the Tongue, where Sir George had a couple of flatboats built, and he, with sufficient men to handle the boats, floated down the Yellowstone to Fort Union, first sending his wagons and other paraphernalia to Fort Union overland with the rest of his command. It is not likely that Bridger accompanied Sir George, as he was back at Fort Bridger in 1856 when his troubles with the Mormons occurred.

When Sir George arrived at Fort Union he concluded to continue down the Missouri River by boat, and made an agreement with the commander of the fort for the construction of the boats, but when they were completed a wordy war ensued regarding the terms of the deal. The commander, Major Culbertson, had agreed to take Sir George's wagons and outfit, but they could arrive at no decision, which so aroused the wrath of Sir George that he piled all his stock in a huge heap in front of the fort and burned it, even going so far as to guard the fires until the property was all destroyed and then raking the ashes over to recover the iron work and tires of the wagons, which he threw into the Missouri, determined that nobody at the fort should enrich themselves a penny at his expense. He then either sold or gave away to vagabond hangers-on among the Indians his cattle and horses, and he and his party continued on down the river in the same two flatboats in which they had arrived at the fort.

At Fort Berthold the party wintered with an Indian chief. Here Sir George became a great favorite, but such a slaughter did he and his men make among the buffalo herds during the winter of 1855-56 that the attention of the United States government was drawn thereto, and steps were taken to prevent any further annihilation by the Gore party. Sir George returned to civilization and St. Louis by steamboat in the spring of 1857.

During the Indian campaign of 1865, Bridger guided General Connor's column from Fort Laramie to Tongue River, where he took part in an Indian fight. Of this expedition Captain H. E. Palmer, of the Eleventh Kansas Cavalry, says, in a daily diary he kept throughout the campaign:

> When our advance reached the top of the ridge dividing the waters of the Powder River from those of the Tongue, I was riding in the extreme advance in company with Major Bridger. As we reached the top of the hill, we halted our steeds while I raised my field glasses to my eyes and took in the grandest view I have ever seen. I could see the north end of the Big Horn range, and away beyond, the faint outline of the mountains beyond the Yellowstone. Immediately before us lay the valley of Peneau Creek, now called Prairie Dog Creek; and beyond, the Little Goose, Big Goose and Tongue River valleys and many other tributary streams. The morning was clear and bright, with not a breath of air stirring. The old major, sitting upon his horse, with his eyes shaded by his hands, had been telling me for an hour or more about his Indian life – his forty years on the plains; telling me how to tell Indian trails and distinguish the tracks of the different tribes; how every spear of grass, every tree and shrub and stone was a compass to the experienced trapper and hunter – a subject that I discussed with him nearly every day.
>
> As I lowered my glass from examining the panorama be-

fore me, the major said: 'Do you see those 'ere columns of smoke over yonder?' I replied: 'Where, Major?' to which he answered, 'Over by that 'ere saddle,' (meaning a depression in the hills not unlike the shape of a saddle) indicating a point nearly fifty miles away. I again raised my glasses and took a long and earnest look, but for the life of me could not make out any columns of smoke, even with a strong field-glass. The major was looking without any artificial help. As soon as the general and his staff arrived I called his attention to Major Bridger's discovery. The general raised his field-glasses and scanned the horizon closely. After a long look, he remarked that there were no columns of smoke to be seen. Major Bridger quietly mounted his horse and rode on. I asked the general to look again, as the major was very confident he could see columns of smoke, which, of course, indicated an Indian village. The general made another examination and again asserted that there were no columns of smoke. However, to satisfy curiosity, and to give our guides no chance to claim they had shown us an Indian village and we would not attack it, he suggested to Captain Frank North, who was riding with his staff, that he go with seven of his Pawnee scouts in the direction indicated, to reconnoiter, and report to us at Peneau Creek or Tongue River, down which we were to march. I galloped on and overtook the major, and as I came up to him overheard him remark: 'These damn paper collar soldiers telling *him* there were no columns of smoke!' The old man was very indignant at our doubting his ability to outsee us, even with the aid of field-glasses. Just after sunset on August 27th, two of North's Pawnee scouts came into camp with the information that Captain North had discovered an Indian village! It was this village which Connor captured next day, the fight being known as the battle of Tongue River.

When Colonel Henry B. Carrington's expedition left Fort Kearney, Nebraska, May 19, 1866, en route to the Powder River and Big Horn country to establish the forts which the government had determined to build, later known as Forts Phil Kearney, and C. F. Smith, and the strengthening of Fort Reno, irrespective of the wishes and warnings of Red Cloud and other leading Sioux chiefs, Jim Bridger was the man selected to act as chief guide to the expedition, because of his great knowledge of the country into which the command was going, and also because of his intimate acquaintance with all Indian wiles and subtlety.

En route, the party entered a deep gorge of the Platte River, where some of the members of the expedition desired to go ahead and examine the canyon. Bridger was consulted as to the safety of the plan, and remarked: "Better not go *too fur*. Thar's Injuns enough lyin' under wolf-skins er skulkin' on them cliffs, I'm a-tellin' ye. They foller ye allus. They've seen ye ev'ry day, an' take it frum me—when ye don't see any of 'em that's jest the time to watch out fer their devilment." The next morning it was learned that but nine miles distant, Indians had swooped down on the ranch of a man named Mills and had run off his stock. Bridger then stated that there was no doubt but that the marauders were members of Red Cloud's band, who had already begun to put into execution the threats of the great Sioux leader; and Bridger further declared that in giving presents to the Indians at the Laramie peace council in June, they had simply made gifts to positive enemies; also that the expedition "was advancing directly in the face of hostilities."

The Laramie peace conference of June, 1866, was an important one, and it had been hoped by the government that no objections would be made by the Sioux to opening the proposed wagon road into Montana, and erecting necessary forts to maintain soldiers in that part of the country. At this council Jim Bridger was an attentive spectator, and Colonel Carrington thus describes him in *Absaraka, Land of Massacre*:

In front of them all, and to the left of the table, sitting

on a low seat, with elbows on his knees and chin buried in his hands, sat the noted James Bridger, whose forty-four years upon the frontier had made him as keen and suspicious of Indians as any Indian could be of another. The old man, already somewhat bowed with age, after long residence among the Crows as a friend and favorite chief, and having incurred the bitter hatred of the Cheyennes and Sioux alike, knew full well that his scalp would be the proudest trophy they could bear to their solemn feasts; and there he sat or crouched, as watchful as though old times had come again, and he was once more to mingle in the fight, or renew the ordeal of his many hair breadth escapes and spirited adventures. . . To us he was invariably straightforward, truthful and reliable. His sagacity, knowledge of woodcraft and knowledge of the Indian was wonderful, and his heart was warm and his feelings tender whenever he was confided in or made a friend. . . He cannot read, but enjoys being read to. He was charmed with Shakespeare, but doubted the Bible story of Samson tying foxes by the tails and, with firebrands, burning the wheat of the Philistines.

After Carrington's expedition had reached the spot on which it was determined to erect the post known later as Fort Phil Kearney, and had begun the work of cutting and hauling logs from the pinery, six or seven miles distant, Bridger was ever on the alert and watchful. "He would walk about," says Carrington, "constantly scanning the opposite hills that commanded a good view of the fort, as if he suspected Indians of having scouts behind every sage clump or fallen cottonwood."

That Jim Bridger was a great comfort to the few women and children who were at Fort Phil Kearney with their husbands and fathers during those trying months of almost daily warfare and Indian savagery, is plainly evident from the mention made of the famous scout in Mrs. Carrington's *Army Life on the Plains.* She says:

There was one faithful, honest and simple minded white man at the post, the colonel's confidential guide at all times, who seemed instinctively to know the invisible as well as the visible operations of the Indians – good old Jim Bridger. His devotion to the ladies and children, and his willingness to cheer them as best he could, were as prized as were his quaint tales of experience among the Crow Indians. I learned afterward from the colonel that the department commander, Philip St. George Cooke, living at Omaha, even at the time of our greatest peril, ordered the discharge of Bridger because of the expense, and on the back of the order was endorsed by the colonel: 'Impossible of execution,' and Bridger was retained.

From 1862 until 1869 or 1870 Bridger remained on the plains in the capacity of guide and scout for various government expeditions sent against hostile Indians, and in locating the most feasible routes between the different military posts already, or about to be established in the Indian country. After the government, in 1868, had abandoned the forts along the Bozeman Trail, which Colonel Carrington had built and maintained through most trying times, Bridger was transferred from these posts to Fort Laramie, where he was a familiar figure for many years.

Honorable John Hunton, an old-time resident of Fort Laramie, yet living there, in his eighty-fifth year, has given to the authors of this work much information about Jim Bridger, as the two were very intimately acquainted. In his correspondence he says:

I became acquainted with Jim Bridger about the middle of October, 1868, when he was transferred to Fort Laramie, having been given a lay off to recuperate his enfeebled condition. Seth E. Ward was the post sutler here at that time, and Colonel W. G. Bullock was his general manager. I was one of six employes. Three of us employes, John Boyd, Hopkins Clark, and myself, occupied the bunkroom in the sutler store building, and Bridger was given a bunk in the same room. Here he remained, occupying the room with us most of the time, until about the middle of April, 1868. He made two or three trips to Cheyenne and Fort D. A. Russell during the time he was here, but I do not think he was absent at any time to exceed ten days. He seemed to prefer to be around here, and to be alone, or with some one or two persons who did not annoy him by constant questioning. Sometimes he seemed to like to talk, and always made a good listener when the subject of conversation interested or pleased him. When it did not, he always curled his upper lip with a sneer and left the audience. He told me many times he did not like to sacrifice his feelings, intelligence or personal pleasure 'when it was such an easy matter to walk away from a damn fool talking.' I have more than once seen him walk away from a group of army officers in the officers' club room (where he was always a welcome guest) because some officer would comment on something or somebody when Bridger would think the comment was made in ignorance or malice. From an educational standpoint he was ignorant, not knowing how to either read or write.

He told me he was born in Virginia, and that his parents removed to Carondalet, Mo., when he was about four years of age. He said his mother's name before marriage was Tyler, of the President Tyler family; that he left home and came to the Rocky Mountains when a boy; that he first went up the Missouri River to the mountains, and then back to where Independence now is, and then west again to the mountains. He said he was first at Fort Laramie 'in his teens,' but did not know or remember the exact year; that he spent the winter that old man Laramie was killed, 'down at the fort' and 'around here,' and was one of the party who went out to search for Laramie 'when he did not come back in the spring as he said he would;' that the party went up the Laramie valley searching it and all its tributaries; that they found an unfinished cottonwood log cabin on the north side of the river below the mouth of Sabille Creek, and one broken beaver trap near it, but 'no Laramie.' He said that he learned some two years later from the Arapahoe Indians that some of the tribe had killed Laramie and put his body under the ice in a beaver dam; that he believed he had traveled more over the Rocky Mountain region than any other white man except one, whose name I do not remember, but it was not Kit Carson. He had great respect for Carson and *some* of the other prominent mountaineers, but for others — General Fremont among them — the utmost contempt. He had many traducers among the would be great trappers, guides and scouts, but none who ever thought it prudent to court a personal verification of their accusations or insinuations. His home was near Independence, Mo. He had an Indian family, and one of his sons lived in Cheyenne in '68 or '69.

He was sent by the government from here to Fort Fetterman in the spring of 1868 to conduct the large number of freight trains then being used for the transportation of the supplies from the abandoned posts of Phil Kearney, C. F. Smith and Reno from that place through the mountains to Medicine Bow station and Fort Fred Steele on the Platte. After that job he quit the government service. I saw him in Cheyenne about the latter part of August, 1868, for the last time, and then for only a few minutes. He was at that time in rather feeble health.

Previous to his death in Denver in the summer of 1917, A. J. Shotwell, who was also a personal friend of Jim Bridger, gave, in correspondence to the authors of this work, much valuable and interesting information about the famous mountaineer and plainsman. Mr. Shotwell became acquainted with Bridger under somewhat peculiar circumstances. He had long been an ardent admirer of the frontiersman. In 1865 Shotwell was a member of the Eleventh Ohio Cavalry, and was stationed at Fort Laramie. There he became a part of General Connor's expedition through the Sioux country almost as far north as the Yellowstone. Jim Bridger was the chief guide on this occasion, and Shotwell had hopes of becoming acquainted with him some time while the expedition was out, but during all that time so prone was Bridger to hold himself aloof that there were but few chances for anyone to have any conversation with him.

"We were out on this expedition two months," writes Mr. Shotwell, "traveling during that time nearly eight hundred miles, and every night Jim Bridger made his camp alone beside our own, so as to be near the scout who was attached to our mess. He would cook his frugal meal, and as soon as darkness approached, wrap himself in his blanket for the night. But with the first peep of day he was astir, and after a hasty cup of coffee and some jerked meat, he would saddle up, and after calling on General Connor, quietly ride away again, and we would see no more of him until evening, when he would ride into camp, and after a short conference with the general, find his accustomed place for the night again. And so each day was a repetition of the day before.

"By the last of August we had arrived in the Big Horn mountain country, and one evening were making camp. The wagon train of ninety wagons had just formed their circular corral, and the various messes had started camp fires, when one of the scouts came in, reporting a large Indian camp, which he judged to be forty miles distant. Soon Bridger was all animation, and after a hasty consultation, two hundred and fifty men, having good mounts, were in the saddle, and with General Connor at the head, set off on a night's ride to reach the band of warriors before break of day. I was one of this party, and will never forget how we rode through the silent watches of the night, with naught to light our way except the brilliant stars in a cloudless sky, and how that long column of silent men wound through rocky defiles and over stretches of grassy plains until the way seemed interminable, but all confident in our guide. When the first rays of light heralded the coming of day, we suddenly halted, and there, right before us, lay the object of our search.

"In less time than it takes to tell it, the column of mounted men had formed a crescent and were charging pell-mell into, we knew not what. If ever a band of Indians were taken by surprise, it was there and then— and all the credit was due to the quiet man who had conducted us safely to our goal. During all that engagement Bridger seemed to be always in the right place at the opportune time."

Soon after the return to Fort Laramie, Shotwell's command received news that the Eleventh Ohio would be relieved by troops of the regular army, and would soon all be home again in the east. Shotwell continues his correspondence as follows:

On the morning or our starting, what was my surprise to find Jim Bridger a passenger in the same mail ambulance that would carry us over the first stage of our journey to Julesburg, one hundred and eighty miles distant, where we expected to secure passage to the Missouri River on the Overland stage coach. We had put our belongings in the mail wagon, when Bridger came up, and throwing a bundle aboard asked, 'Where are you boys going?' When told 'through to the river,' he frowned for a moment and then said, 'So am I, and if we travel together I guess it's best to be sociable.' And here came another surprise. The man who in all the previous years was so unapproachable, soon became one of the most companionable men I have ever met, and most entertainingly related incidents in a life rich in experience.

Our journey to Julesburg consumed two days and a night, and was fraught with much discomfort, owing to our crowded quarters among the mail sacks and other baggage loaded inside to the limited space of an army ambulance. At Julesburg we were told that no passage could be had on the Overland east-bound stage short of ten days, as all space was engaged that far ahead. This information was discomforting, but relief appeared in the shape of a train of twenty-five wagons returning empty from Denver, bound for the Missouri River, via Fort Kearney, Nebraska.

We quickly made terms with the wagon master to carry us to Fort Kearney, two hundred miles on our way, from which place three different stage lines ran to as many points on the river. We were assigned to a wagon having a large, deep body, with double canvas cover; and buying a lot of hay, we cushioned the floor of our wagon to the depth of about six inches, piled in our blankets and other belongings, and got aboard — and for eight days traveled in perfect comfort.

That was indeed a memorable journey. There were many roadhouses along the Overland Trail at that time, and knowing it was the custom of freighters to camp near such places, we depended on securing meals at these houses, sleeping in our wagon at night. Our plan of travel met with a surprise the first night out — a surprise most agreeable, however. Our wagon train had halted for the night about a hundred yards from one of these caravansaries, and we and our little party had no sooner alighted and were stretching our limbs, than we observed a man approaching from the house, and as he drew near he exclaimed: 'Of all men — whom have we here but old Jim Bridger!' After further exclamations and handshakings, he continued by saying: 'Come right in, Jim; the place is yours as long as you care to stay.' Bridger replied: 'Here are two soldier boys traveling with me — I stay with them.' But the man said: 'It's all the same; Bridger and his friends included.' So we all walked in, and soon were seated to a most bountiful meal of the best the place afforded, and places to sleep were provided, and a good breakfast followed, with a lunch for the noon hour, when we took leave — and not a penny to pay!

Stories of frontier life filled that night until the wee small hours. The experience of this first night was repeated every night of our eight days' journey from Julesburg to Fort Kearney. Nothing could more vividly show the esteem in which Jim Bridger was held by frontiersmen of that time.

But before proceeding further, allow me to give you an idea of the personal appearance of this remarkable man. More than fifty years have passed since the incidents here related were imparted to me. Bridger was at that time fifty-six years of age, well preserved for a man who had passed through many trials and hardships. While I myself am now well advanced in years, I still retain in memory, I believe, a very correct picture of Bridger at the time of which I speak. Of well proportioned form of slender mold, about six feet high – probably a little less, possibly a trifle more, straight as an Indian and quick in movement, but not nervous or excitable; in weight, probably one hundred and sixty pounds, with an eye as piercing as the eye of an eagle, that seemed to flash fire when narrating an experience that had called out his reserve power. There was nothing in his costume or deportment to indicate the heroic spirit that dwelt within – simply a plain, unassuming man, but made of heroic stuff, every inch!

What would I not give if I could at this time recall all that was imparted to us during those eight days of travel in our snug quarters in the wagon train, for it was here that he unfolded, day by day, the story of his life of forty-four years in the great, almost unknown, West. He related to us that as a young man he spent his winters in trapping and his summers in exploration. These excursions made him familiar with a vast region, then comparatively unknown. On these trips he chose to go alone, with no companion save his faithful horse, his trusty rifle and a small hatchet forged from the best of steel. He was always provided with an ample supply of powder and bullets – the former carried in water-proof packages. On one of these excursions he headed north into the British possessions, and with the North Star for a guide continued on his way down the valley of the McKenzie River to the Arctic Ocean. Here, at the very threshold of the Arctic night, he could go no further, and so, turning back, he made his way to his starting point, which he reached after an absence of eighteen months, during which time he had not looked into the face of a white man or tasted bread. In time he found himself on the trail over which he had traveled when a boy, and selecting a place in the mountains not far distant from Salt Lake, he settled down and became a trader with the Indians in the country round about.

Business prospered from the start, so Bridger related to us. Soon his little trading place was doing a thriving barter. The furs obtained from the Indians were dispatched on pack animals to St. Joe, Mo., and goods suitable for exchange were brought back in return. Fremont thus found Bridger on his way to California, and spent a few days with his party, resting here, before entering on the journey across the barren land west of Great Salt Lake. Brigham Young and his party were guests in 1847. I cannot recall the date, but Bridger was finally taken with a longing to see the old home, and having an extra large accumulation of pelts, concluded to take charge of them himself. The most valuable part of the cargo was five thousand beaver skins, which he expected to sell for four dollars each. What was his surprise and gratification, upon arriving at St. Joe, to find beaver skins in great demand at seven dollars per pelt. He easily disposed of his beaver at that figure, taking thirty-five thousand dollars. This was augmented five thousand dollars by the proceeds from other pelts in his possession, aside from beaver skins, thus putting into his hands, forty thousand dollars—a princely sum of money at that time for a young man born, at most, in the wilderness. Bridger was pleased with the quiet life in the east, and having abundant ready money, bought a large tract of land, married, and, as he supposed, settled down to the quiet life of a farmer. But the call of the wild was not to be hushed, and in a few years he was back among his previous familiar scenes, returning at times to visit his family, but not remaining long.

While at Fort Laramie this story was told me of Bridger: For many years before the Union Pacific Railroad penetrated the country, Fort Laramie was the terminus of transit travel, and visitors of this kind were not plentiful, as means of travel were limited to the mail wagon that made weekly trips to Julesburg, one hundred and eighty miles distant. Globe trotters and ambitious young newspaper correspondents made up the larger part of visitors. The latter were the bane of Bridger's life. He was naturally reserved, and his interviewers of this class were persistent. One youngster made himself particularly obnoxious to the old man, and finally, with a grim sense of humor, the old scout proceeded to romance with his inquisitor. In answer to the question whether any important changes had occurred in the country since he had known it, owing to earthquakes or other natural phenomena, old Jim pointed out Laramie Peak, and gravely remarked that where the mountain then stood was a yawning chasm when he first knew the locality.

And in reply to questions regarding petrifications, Bridger further stated that he had visited a place where there was a petrified mountain on which stood forests of petrified trees, and in their branches were petrified birds, while petrified songs projected from their throats. All of this was duly 'swallowed' and taken down by the knight of the pencil.

Another laughable incident was related to me by Bridger himself. Soon after he was employed as official guide by the government, he was sent with an exploring party into the Big Horn Mountains. There was quite a party of wagons, pack animals and a squad of cavalry, all under the command of a young officer fresh from West Point. All went well until the expedition reached the Big Horn River, swollen at the time from melting snows. When Bridger suggested the plan for crossing the turbulent stream, he was curtly told that he was only employed as guide. With this, the fresh young West Pointer ordered two of the mounted men to ride in and fasten a line to the opposite shore. The horses lost their footing in the swift current and one of the men was drowned. Then, in humiliation, the West Point youth appealed to Bridger, and implored him to take the crossing in hand. This Bridger agreed to do, but admonished the youngster to retire to his tent and remain there until called for. To describe in detail the provisions made for crossing the stream, while interesting, would prove a long story. First, a crude boat was constructed of poles and willows. This was covered with some heavy canvas, and made waterproof by a liberal application of pitch, prepared from gum gathered from the spruce and pine trees. The men then stripped, and on horseback, succeeded in crossing with a line, and with this, dragged the cable ashore, which was made fast to a large tree. All hands then stretched the cable, and made it fast on the side where the party awaited with the boat secured to the cable by a slip-noose, and all were safely carried across the river, the young officer being last of all.

And here comes the laughable part of the story: The first thing the youngster did on being restored to his command was to call on the chaplain to assemble the expedition and return thanks to Providence for the safe crossing. Here Bridger's eyes sparkled as he told how that chaplain fell on his knees, and in a loud voice thanked the Lord God of Hosts for bringing the troops over in safety. 'And darn his sanctimonious skin,' old Jim concluded to me in recounting the story, 'he never mentioned Bridger once, and I felt as if I had had something to do with that plan myself.'

On parting with Bridger at Fort Kearney we reluctantly had to refuse his invitation to accompany him home. And now, after the lapse of over fifty years, I often think of passages in Bridger's life as related on that memorable journey; and when I listen to these modern day scouts who have explored the Rocky Mountains in Pullman cars, and range them beside such a man as Jim Bridger, they appear as mice in the company of a lion.

That Bridger impressed everyone with whom he came in contact by his quiet deportment and utter lack of everything smacking of display or braggadocio, is further evidenced in a letter to Shotwell from an old friend close to ninety years of age, now living in the far northwest. Shotwell does not divulge the name of this friend, but gives the authors the following extract from the letter regarding Bridger:

He was the one man of the time that I never heard anything but good spoken of. I knew scores of hunters, scouts and trappers of great and less repute, none of whom were worthy to sit at the same table with Jim Bridger. To me, the simplicity, gentleness, kindliness and absolute truthfulness of his character marked him as a man above the common. And while, as an Indian trader, he doubtless availed himself of his knowledge, chances and opportunities, yet, there wasn't an Indian on the Overland Trail that doubted Bridger's word. . .

My first few weeks at Fort Laramie seemed like a dream, so strange was all around me, and you may be sure I took note of all about me. Indians in their blankets of gaudy colors; hunters and trappers in their buckskin suits, with beaded shirts and decorated headgear, were all of intense interest to me. . .

But there was another figure that soon claimed my attention — a tall, well built man in plain civilian garb, with nothing in his makeup to mark him apart from men as they appeared back east. A man who quietly went his way and seemed foreign to all about him, but I noticed that the officers at the post, as well as all scouts and hunters, paid him marked deference. So much did this come under my notice that in time my curiosity prompted me to ask who was this strange, quiet man, and imagine my surprise on being told that this was Jim Bridger, the greatest of scouts in his time – a man who, to use a trite saying, knew the Rocky Mountain country like a book; a man invaluable to the government; a man consulted on all important military movements – in fact, an oracle in all that pertained to the vast country surrounding. This was my first insight into Bridger.

An army man whose duties brought him much in personal contact with Bridger was Captain Lee Humfreville, an old cavalry officer, who, in 1899, wrote a book entitled *Twenty Years Among Our Hostile Indians*. In his mention of Bridger he says:

James Bridger, or, as he was familiarly spoken of in that country, 'old Jim Bridger,' was the most efficient guide, mountaineer, plainsman, trapper and Indian fighter that ever lived in the far West. He knew more of that country and all things within its borders than anyone who has ever lived. He could, with the aid of a stick, scratch on the ground a map of the whole western country that was more correct than those made at that time by skilled topographical engineers with all their scientific instruments. I have seen Bridger look at a printed map and point out its defects at sight. His experience in that country was not confined to a few tribes of Indians, but to all. He was a marvelous trailer – unquestionably the most expert that ever lived. Even when old and with dimmed eyesight, he could run a trail, when mounted, as fast as his horse could carry him. He noticed every feature of the country, especially its configuration, and possessing as he did, a retentive memory, he could invariably recall all landmarks with unerring accuracy, even though he had not seen them for years.

He was much respected by army officers and by the authorities at Washington, as well as by all whites with whom he came in contact. The Indians also learned to fear and respect him. Whenever an important military expedition was planned, Bridger's services were secured whenever possible.

Bridger was an old man when I last saw him – about seventy-six years of age, and a great sufferer from goiter, brought on by long use of snow water. He was also badly ruptured, and I could scarcely understand how he rode a horse at all. Yet, with all his bodily infirmities, he was cheerful and ready to do valiant service at any time. The government appreciated his services so much that he frequently received twenty-five dollars per day, with rations, horse, arms and quarters, while in its service. It was Bridger who first brought Kit Carson to the notice of General John C. Fremont. I have seen Carson take his orders from Bridger as a soldier does from his commanding officer.

Bridger was much sought after by emigrants crossing the plains, for his reputation as a guide and Indian fighter was well known. The pilgrims annoyed him with all sorts of questions, which often compelled the old man to beat a retreat; yet he had a streak of humor, and gave them a ghost story now and then. He could reel off story after story with astonishing spontaneity. He told these stories with a solemn gravity that was intensely amusing. I know that I am largely indebted to Bridger for often keeping my spirits up when they were at a low ebb. I always knew something good was coming when he began to tell a story, but never dared to smile until the climax was reached, for that would have spoiled it all.

On a visit to Washington he was introduced to the President. After staring at him in amazement for a few minutes, Bridger turned to the member of Congress who had introduced him and remarked: 'Looks jest like any other man, don't he?'

While his trading post at Fort Bridger flourished, he was supposed to have a considerable sum of money in his possession. Some desperadoes broke into his room one night for the purpose of robbing him. Bridger, awakening from his sleep, demanded, 'What air you lookin' fer?' One of the desperadoes replied, 'We are lookin' for your money.' Bridger observed, 'Jest wait a minnit an' I'll git up an' help you.' The robbers did not wait.

I occupied the same quarters with him one whole winter, where I had ample opportunity to study his character and learn his peculiar ways and manner of living. He never did anything until he felt so inclined. For instance: If he grew sleepy in the afternoon, say by three, four or five o'clock, he went to bed, and when he awoke, say in four, five or six hours, he would arise, make a fire, roast meat, eat it and 'sing Injun,' to use his own term, the rest of the night. If he had a tin pan he would beat on the bottom, making a noise like an Indian tom-tom. He never ate until he was hungry, and as he lived largely on meats, he was thin and spare, though strong and wiry. His manner of living during the winter did not coincide with my habits or ideas, by any means, so I tried to entertain him afternoons and keep him awake until nine or ten o'clock in the evening. My first effort was in reading to him. A copy of 'Hiawatha' was found among the troops, which I read to him as long as he permitted it. He would sit bent over, his long legs crossed, his gaunt hands and arms clasping his knees, and listen to the reading attentively, until a passage was reached in which Longfellow portrayed an Indian, when Bridger, after a period of uneasy wriggling on his seat, arose very wrathy, swearing that the whole story was a lie, that he would listen to no more of it, and that 'no sich Injun ever lived.' This happened over and over again. After awhile I quieted him and began reading again, but after a short time he was sure to stop me, swearing that he would not listen any longer to such an infernal lie.

During that winter, Bridger's suit of buckskin clothing (and it was all he had) became infested with vermin, and in despair he at length asked me how he could get rid of them. I told him if he would take off his buckskin jacket and breeches and wrap himself in a buffalo robe, I would undertake to rid his clothes of the pests. He thereupon took his clothing off and turned it inside out. After spreading the garments on the ground, I poured a ridge of gunpowder down the seams of the suit, and touched it off. It burned the vermin, and it also burned the buckskin clothing badly. On the seams of the leggings I had sprinkled so much powder that it burned the garments to charred leather. They were drawn up short at the seams, and after being turned, each leg curled up until it looked like a half-moon. Bridger looked at me for a moment in great disgust, and then with a big oath said: 'I am a-goin' to kill you for that.' I was afraid he would make his threat good, for he was certainly very indignant. I laughed at him, and taking hold of the leggings I stretched them into the best shape possible, but the leather was burned to brittleness and broke at the slightest touch. Bridger did not forgive me for this for two or three days, during which time he was compelled to go about in a buffalo robe until another buckskin suit could be procured.

An instance of Bridger's courage happened under my own observation. While scouting in the South Park he was our guide. We also had with us some Arapahoe Indians and a white man who had an Arapahoe wife. After a sharp engagement with a war party of Indians who greatly outnumbered us, we were compelled to withdraw to the hillside. As soon as the Indians saw our position, a number of warriors dismounted and hid themselves in the bushes and tall grasses. From this concealment they began firing upon us. I did not consider it advisable for the time being to separate the command and send a party to charge into the ambush. Bridger all this time was growing restless, and at last challenged one of the Arapahoe allies to go into the copse with him and attack the Indians hand-to-hand. The Arapahoe refused, and Bridger abused him soundly by means of the sign language. The Indian at last grasped Bridger by the hand and the two started. It was not long before I heard the report of a six-shooter, and in a few minutes Bridger returned, holding in his hand the scalp of a warrior, covered with warm blood. He had found an Indian in the brush, and before the latter had time to move had killed him. The Arapahoe not returning, I was satisfied that his earthly career was ended, or that a worse fate was in store for him. I determined to burn the tall, dry grass, and ordered the white man who had the Indian wife to send one of the Arapahoe Indians to set it on fire. They all refused, until Bridger ridiculed them so unmercifully that the whole party accompanied him, and the grass was fired. It burned rapidly, and it was not long until the fierce flames disclosed a great many Indians hidden in the underbrush. When the command opened fire upon them they ran in every direction, but soon returned with their mounted warriors, ready to resume the fight. Bridger insisted that under no circumstances must we leave our present position, as there were at least two or three Indians to one of us. In a short time they made an at-

tack, but we had the advantage of high ground and could antic-
ipate their every movement. Bridger picked off the first Indian who got within range of his deadly rifle, and the best
shots among the troopers also used their Spencer carbines with
effect. The Indians were thus prevented from getting near us,
and after a few hours of this kind of fighting they withdrew.

On no occasion would Bridger trust an Indian. He maintained that a rattlesnake was of some good, but that an Indian
was good for nothing. He prided himself on the fact that any
thing an Indian could do, he could out-do the Indian. While
Bridger had ample caution, he also had the courage of a lion.

One of the best stories related about Bridger, which
well illustrates the wonderful knowledge he possessed
of the Rocky Mountains, is told in connection with the
building of the Union Pacific Railroad. It appears
that the engineers running the survey were in consultation at Denver as to the most feasible point to build the
line across the Rockies. The consultation became a
wrangle, and no tangible agreement could be arrived at.

Finally somebody suggested to them that Jim Bridger knew more about the Rocky Mountains than any
other living man, and could easily tell them the best
point to run the line. It was thereupon decided to
consult the famous mountaineer. Bridger happened
to be in St. Louis at the time on some business matter.
Communication was at once opened with him, although
the real object under discussion was withheld from
him, but he was urged to start for Denver immediately,
as his advice was needed on some very important matters. A railway pass was forwarded, and about two
weeks later in walked the grizzled frontiersman.

Then the engineers started to talk. They told old
Jim what they wanted, and as the plans were laid out
before him and the query propounded as to where he
considered the best point to run the line across the

mountains, a look of supreme disgust began to show itself on his face. Finally he exclaimed impatiently, "Gimme a sheet o' paper."

A large sheet of clean Manila was laid before him on the table. Reaching into the stove for a dead coal, the old man remarked, as he started to make some lines:

"I could hev told you fellers jest whar' to run yer line without even leavin' St. Louis, an' saved ye the expense of bringin' me way out yere."

An outline of the Rockies was quickly traced on the sheet, showing mountain peaks in profusion. Pointing to a particular one, Bridger remarked:

"Right thar is whar' you fellers kin run yer line to git across the Rockies, an' nowhar' else—not unless you want to do a hull lot more diggin' an' blastin' than you care to tackle."

The engineers were amazed at the old man's confident assertion, but when they came to run their line across the range, the road crossed the Rockies in the exact spot Bridger had pointed out to them. It is stated that the crude map he made is yet preserved by the railroad corporation.

F. G. Burnett of Fort Washakie, Wyoming, is also among those yet living (1920) who knew Jim Bridger intimately. He writes the authors:

Jim Bridger was a remarkable old man and had a wonderful memory. He seemed never to forget a trail that he had ever traveled, or the distance between streams or watering places, whether good water or bad, and also whether there was wood, and if there was good feed for the stock. So we always knew what sort of a camp the one ahead would be, and what kind of country we would have to travel over in order to reach it. His eyesight was failing when I knew him, so that he could not shoot very good, and he would always swear at us if we got a shot at an Indian and missed him, remarking that he never missed one when he was our age.   He was devoid of fear and rarely talked of his exploits, and history has lost many a thrilling adventure by his indifference to publicity.   He was a great friend of Chief Washakie of the Shoshones.   They were about the same age, and had many hair raising experiences together.   If he was cornered and asked to talk, he would tell the most outlandish yarns and then chuckle to himself and wonder if his questioner had gotten what he wanted.

For his first wife, Bridger married the daughter of a Flathead chief.   The date of this marriage is not given, but the wife died in 1846.   There were two children by this union – Felix and Josephine, and both were educated in St. Louis.   Felix served throughout the Civil War in the Second Missouri Artillery, and was on the plains with Custer, fighting the Indians in Texas and the Indian Territory.   This son died in 1876 on his father's farm near Little Santa Fe, Missouri.

Bridger married for his second wife a Ute woman.   She died July 4, 1849, at the birth of her child.   The little one was named Virginia, and Bridger is said to have brought her up on buffalo's milk.   She married a man named Waschman, after receiving an education in the convent at St. Louis, where she attended school with her half-sister, Josephine.

Bridger married again in 1850 a woman of the Snake Tribe, and soon after that bought a small farm near Little Santa Fe, Missouri, removing thence, with his family, from Fort Bridger the same year.   There were two children by this marriage – Mary, born in 1853, and William, in 1857.   The wife died in 1858.   Bridger was out on one of his numerous trapping trips at the time of her death, but soon after he returned to his farm, where he remained until 1862, when the government again sent for him to guide troops across the plains.

For eight years he was thus employed, but about 1870 his health began to decline, and in 1871 he moved back to his farm again.

Of the last years of his life, his daughter, Mrs. Waschman, says:

In 1873 father's health began to fail him, and his eyes were very bad, so that he could not see well, and the only way he could distinguish a person was by the sound of their voice. In 1874 his eyesight was leaving him very fast, and this worried him much. At such times he would get very nervous, and wanted to be on the go all the time. I had to watch him and lead him around to please him.

Finally I got him a gentle old horse so he could ride around and have some way of passing the time. We had a dog that always accompanied him. While father could not see very well, the faithful old horse would guide him along as he rode around the farm. Sometimes the horse would go wrong, and they would get lost in the woods. Then the dog would come home and begin to bark, and then we knew something was the matter. The dog would whine around until I would go out and find father and lead him back home. Occasionally he would take the dog, and, cane in hand, would go out to the wheat field to see how the crop was growing. Father would there get down on his hands and knees and feel for the wheat. and that was the way he passed the time.

He wished so much that he could regain his eyesight so he could again see the mountains and go back to them. He would long so much to see his old companions, and have a chat with them of the old times away back in the fifties. Again, he would have a great desire to see some of his old friends connected with the army, and would say: 'I would give anything in the world if I could see some of them and have a talk of the olden times, but I know I will not be able to see any of my old-time mountain friends any more, as I know that my time is near. I feel that my health is failing me fast, and that I am not the same as I used to be.'

At the time of his death, Bridger was living in a long, two-story building. Later, the people in the neighborhood called it the "haunted house," and would not go near the place.

Colonel E. B. C. Judson, who years ago, used to write blood-and-thunder dime novels of the west, under the non de plume of "Ned Buntline," hunted Bridger up in the latter days of his life to get material for a series of western novels, with Bridger as the chief figure. Judson was given facts enough about the great plainsman to keep him busy writing for years. Bridger and Colonel Judson became fast friends, and the noted story-writer accompanied him on one of his last trips to the mountains. Soon after this, the series of Jim Bridger stories were started. They appeared once a week in a popular publication, and Bridger's companions used to save them up and read them to him. It was this same Judson who, some years later, made Buffalo Bill a popular western "hero" in much the same manner.

General Grenville M. Dodge, under whom Bridger scouted and trailed, was one of the greatest admirers of the veteran plainsman, and pays tribute to him in the following language:

Unquestionably Bridger's claims to remembrance rest upon the extraordinary part he bore in the explorations of the West. As a guide he was without an equal, and this is the testimony of everyone who ever employed him. He was a born topographer; the whole West was mapped out in his mind, and such was his instinctive sense of locality and direction, that it used to be said of him that he could smell his way where he could not see it. He was a complete master of the plains and of woodcraft, equal to any emergency, and full of resources to overcome any obstacle. In fact, in all my experience, I never saw Bridger, or any other of the voyagers of the plains and mountains, meet any obstacle which they could not overcome.

While Bridger was not an educated man, still, any country that he had ever seen, he could fully and intelligently describe, and he could make a very correct map of any country he had ever traveled over; could mark out its streams and mountains and the obstacles in it correctly, so that there was no trouble in following and understanding it. He never claimed knowledge that he did not have of the country or its history or surroundings, and he was positive in his statements in relation to it. He was a good judge of human nature. His comments upon people that he had met and been with were intelligent and seldom critical. He always spoke of their good points, and he was universally respected by the mountain men, and looked upon as a leader also by the Indians. He was careful to never give his word without fulfilling it. He understood thoroughly the Indian character, their peculiarities and superstitions. He felt very keenly the loss of any confidence in him or his judgment, especially when acting as a guide, and when he struck a country or trail that he was not familiar with, he would frankly say so, but would often say that he could take our party up to the point we wanted to reach. As a guide, I do not think he had his equal on the plains.

Bridger was seventy-seven years of age when he died. He was buried on the Stubbins Watts farm, a mile north of Dallas, not far south of Westport, Missouri. Two of his sons, Felix and William, were buried beside him.

It was not until 1902 that General Dodge learned for the first time where the celebrated plainsman was buried, and that his grave was neglected and almost forgotten. He immediately became interested, and through the efforts of himself and other admirers of Bridger, the Mount Washington Cemetery Company, of Kansas City, donated a prominent and beautiful burial site, and the remains of the noted guide were removed to it. On December 11, 1904, an imposing monument was unveiled by Bridger's great-granddaughter, Marie Louise Lightle. It bears the following inscription:

1804 – JAMES BRIDGER – 1881

Celebrated as a Hunter, Trapper, Fur Trader and Guide. Discovered Great Salt Lake, 1824; the South Pass 1827; Visited Yellowstone Lake and Geysers 1830. Founded Fort Bridger 1843. Opened Overland route by Bridger's Pass to Great Salt Lake. Was Guide for Exploring Expeditions, Albert Sidney Johnson's Army in 1857 and G. M. Dodge in U.P. Surveys and Indian Campaigns 1865-66. This monument is Erected as a Tribute to His Pioneer Work by Major-General G. M. Dodge.

Jim Bridger was a true type of the man necessary as a trail-blazer to the great unexplored regions of the mighty west. He had many imitators, but no peers. He was the uncrowned king of all the Rocky Mountain scouts, guides, trailers, trappers, and plainsmen between 1830 and 1870.

Afterword

After the Hayfield fight of August 1st, and the Wagon Box fight of August 2, 1867, the Indian demanded from our government better equipment for fighting, in response to which request, the Indian Department distributed to them modern guns with which to defend themselves and to hunt, for the white men had driven the game off the favorite hunting grounds in the Powder River country, sending it into the mountains, where the bow and arrow were not effective enough to furnish meat for the tribes. Our government found justification in meeting these demands of the Indians for modern rifles, on the ground that, though not yet restricted to their roaming they were nevertheless being confined on a reservation, and were expected to furnish themselves with meat by means of the hunt. The cross-purposes of our government are here again displayed, in that the War Department furnished guns to the whites with which to fight the red men, while the Indian Department equipped the Indians with modern rifles which they successfully used to drive back the soldiers and emigrants!

The coming of the Union Pacific Railroad through Wyoming[135] in 1867-68 drove the red men out of the country traversed by the Overland Stage Route and the Oregon Trail, thus leaving the northern part of the Bozeman Road, which was not crossed by the new railroad, a point of special attack.

---

[135] Wyoming Territory was organized in May, 1869.

A Peace Conference held at Fort Laramie in the fall of 1867, brought forth no desired results, a few friendly Crows joining in the council, but Red Cloud, defiant as ever, refused to be present, sending by messenger a statement as to what was his aim for the continued wars against the white man – to save the valley of the Powder River country, "the only hunting ground left to his nation." In April, 1868, Red Cloud agreed to confer with a Commission for Peace, meeting again at Fort Laramie, though he did not appear before the same until November of that year, with the understanding that his former protests should be recognized – non-invasion of the cherished hunting grounds east of the Big Horn Mountains. It took over six months to have this treaty signed by representatives of our government and Red Cloud and his warriors, the first signing taking place April 29, 1868, Red Cloud not affixing his signature until the sixth of November. On March 2d of that year, the President of the United States ordered the abandonment of the three forts on the Bozeman Trail, the order not being carried out until summer for lack of transportation facilities.[136] When Forts Reno, Phil Kearney, and C. F. Smith were thus abandoned and the troops withdrawn, Red Cloud had accomplished his object; his protests and his wars had yielded their specific purpose! On account of this action on the part of our government, many years had to pass before the Powder River country and the land along

---

[136] August 18, 1868, has been stated by some authorities as the date of abandonment. A letter addressed to the authors bearing date of July 30, 1919, from the United States War Department states: "With the information that the records show that Fort Phil Kearney, C. F. Smith, and Reno, were abandoned in August, 1868, the exact date of the month not shown but prior to the 7th of that month. – (Signed) P. C. Harris, The Adjutant General."

THE SUTLER'S OLD ADOBE STORE AT FORT LARAMIE, BUILT IN 1850

The front of the building is at the extreme left. In this building the Sioux Indian treaty of 1868 was signed. Jim Bridger occupied the room downstairs under the left gable, when stationed there. Monument to the right marks the place where the Oregon Trail crossed the site of old Fort Laramie. This monument was unveiled June 17, 1915.

the northern part of the Bozeman Trail became safe for travel and settlement.[137]

To illustrate the distrust that the Indians had for the word of our government that the hated forts should not again be used, is shown by the action taken upon the abandonment of the fortifications, for our soldiers were not yet out of sight of Fort Phil Kearney before the watching Indians raided it and set fire to the buildings, Old Little Wolf applying the torch.

With the surrender of the three forts to the ravages of the Indian, freighting on the trail ceased for a num-

---

[137] Leeson (M. A.) *History of Montana*, p. 199: United States Military Posts. The buildings at Fort C. F. Smith (to guard the Bozeman and Jacobs' route of 1863-1864) and of Fort Phil Kearney and Reno, in 1866-1867, afforded proof positive that the government was determined to check all hostilities, whether directed by Indians or white men, and to guarantee to the travelers or immigrants a safe road to the country beyond the mountains. The policy was effectual in a great measure, and if not discontinued would undoubtedly have had the effect of bringing peace into the territory. The treaty with the Indians, negotiated in 1868, provided for the evacuation of the three forts mentioned. No sooner was the faith of the government observed than the Sioux took possession of the buildings, gave them up to fire, and claimed sole dominion over the country and new settlers, irrespective of treaty stipulations. To remedy this false step, the War Department authorized the construction of defenses and barracks in addition to the posts, which were not evacuated, and to this order is due the reëstablishment of forts throughout the territory.

McClure, *Three Thousand Miles Through the Rocky Mountains* (1867). The proposed surrender of the Bozeman or Powder River route as an Indian reservation would be a stupendous folly; worse – it would be crime. Those who have advised its abandonment either want a war of extermination or know nothing of the value of the route. Those who say it is not needed have studied the west to little purpose, or belong to the white vampires of the plains. It is the natural route to Montana, and the only practicable route overland. By it Montana is reached without crossing the Rocky range; the overland routes south of the mountains must be crossed twice. It traverses the eastern base of the mountains, has fine streams and pasturage, and is the only route that has these priceless advantages. . . The mere abandonment of the forts and route by the national authorities would be of little consequence; but the effect to surrender it to the Indians by treaty and exclude the whites from it, as has been proposed, would be a foolish attempt on the part of the government to do an impossible thing.

ber of years; the emigrants sought a more safe though longer route to Montana. The dangers along the road in the late sixties and early seventies were infinitely greater than the days when the soldier guarded the road to the gold-fields. When the soldiers left the forts the Indians were in full and exultant control of their treasured possessions. The coming of the Union Pacific Railroad now made it possible to transfer freight over the iron trail which ran north of Bridger's Pass in 1868 and was completed in the following year. With the event of the railway the Powder River country and the Bozeman Trail were absolutely abandoned by the white man for a long time.[138]

That the abandonment of the Bozeman Trail was a disastrous policy is shown from the following quotation made by General Sherman, dated September 26, 1868:

> The motives of the Peace Commissioners were humane, but there was an error of judgment in making peace with the Indians last fall. They should have been punished and made to give up the plunder captured, which they now hold; and after properly submitting to the military and disgorging their plunder, they should have been turned over to the civil agents. This error has given more victims to savage ferocity. The present

---

[138] John Hunton, living at Fort Laramie most of the time since 1867 in a letter bearing date August 6, 1920, states: "After Reno, Phil Kearney, and C. F. Smith were abandoned in the summer of 1868 there was absolutely *no* travel over the Bozeman Trail between the North Platte and Big Horn Rivers until the Crook expeditions in 1876, by freighters or any other white men, except possibly one or two small mining expeditions going to or from the Black Hills into Montana." Furthermore, from 1868 to 1876, no traffic whatsoever was carried on north of the Platte. By the terms of the 1868 treaty, no white man was allowed to enter the territory north of this river. It is true, the Indians were allowed to meander at will to the south of the North Platte, stealing the white man's cattle and milch cows, but the arm of the law reached out to the white man if he dared attempt to rescue the stolen stock by crossing the river into the country north of the Platte. If the white man intruded into the Indian's country, he was arrested by soldiers from Fort Fetterman and placed in jail awaiting trial.

system of dealing with the Indians, I think, is an error. There are too many fingers in the pie, too many ends to be subserved, and too much money to be made; and it is to the interest of the nation and of humanity, to put an end to this inhuman farce. The Peace Commission, the Indian Department, the military and the Indian make a balky team. The public treasury is depleted and innocent people plundered in this quadrangular arrangement, in which the treasury, and the unarmed settlers are the greatest sufferers.

Article XVI of the 1868 treaty contains much that was the cause, by not observing same, either by our government or by Red Cloud's warriors, of the sacrifice of additional hundreds of lives, the loss of thousands of cattle and engendered hate and distrust of our government:

> The United States hereby agrees and stipulates that the country north of the North Platte River and east of the summits of the Big Horn Mountains, shall be held and conceded to be unceded Indian territory, and also stipulates and agrees that no white person or persons shall be permitted to settle upon or occupy any portion of the same; or without the consent of the Indians, first had and obtained, to pass through the same; and it is further agreed by the United States, that within ninety days after the conclusion of peace with all the bands of the Sioux nation, the military posts now established in the territory, in this article named, shall be abandoned, and that the road leading to them, and by them to the settlements of the Territory of Montana, shall be closed.

The passing of the years did not bring the desired peace, for both signatory parties to the treaty violated their trust. The rigid enforcement of the regulations in regard to reservation life, which in time (a long time) was put into force and effect, accomplished what treaties did not seem to be able to perfect.

The treaty of April 29, 1868, gave to the Indians the "Great Sioux Reservation," embracing approximately twenty-two million acres of land within the territory embraced in the lands west of the Missouri River, and between the forty-third and forty-sixth parallels and east of the one hundred and fourth meridian. Not only were these almost countless acres given to the Sioux within definite boundaries, but the Indian was granted the right to hunt and travel in unceded territory north of the North Platte and on the Republican Fork of the Smoky Hill River. This hunting and roaming was to continue as long as the buffalo in sufficient numbers lived on the prairies to supply the Indians with meat and robes. That there were at this time seemingly an unlimited number of the buffalo for the hunt is witnessed by the fact that in the summer of 1868 General Sherman and his command rode for three days through one continuous band of buffalo. When the Indians of the Sioux nation were thus given the right to hunt and travel over the alloted territory, they believed, by the granting of these rights, that they were the sole possessors of that country and acted accordingly. They were firm in their conviction that for the white man to go over this territory was an act of invasion.

The provisions of the treaty which prohibited the whites from settling on the Indian's land without his consent was constantly violated. The seekers of gold and home were the most flagrant violators of this provision. To mention the invasion of the red man's territory by individuals and officers in 1874 in the Black Hills country where gold had been discovered is to explain Custer's last battle. During that year General George A. Custer was sent on an extended scouting expedition into the Black Hills from where he reported that there were great riches to be found in gold mining. The report created a stampede into the new gold camp against which Red Cloud, in 1875, made an angry protest. Depredations as a result of this "invasion" became so numerous that the government decided that the roaming Indian should no longer have that liberty, but must be confined within reservations. Sitting Bull and Crazy Horse, leading chiefs, refused to leave their ancient hunting grounds and be confined within restricted districts. To force the Indians on the selected reservations, to drive them back to make room for the advancing white man with his family caused the tragedy of June 25, 1876, when General Custer, fighting against the Sioux, made his last stand. In this battle, as in that of December 21, 1866, "there were no survivors."

The old Bozeman Trail is marked at irregular intervals from the North Platte River to the northern boundary of Wyoming, the last stone being placed just northwest of Parkman. One substantial monument, erected by our government, marks the trail on Massacre Hill overlooking the battle field of December 26, 1866, the unveiling ceremonies occurring July 3, 1908, Colonel Carrington delivering one of the addresses. The monument is made of native boulders, with a large bronze shield bearing the following inscription:

ON THIS FIELD ON THE TWENTY-FIRST DAY OF
DECEMBER, 1866
THREE COMMISSIONED OFFICERS AND
SEVENTY-SIX PRIVATES
OF THE EIGHTEENTH U.S. INFANTRY AND OF THE
SECOND U. S. CAVALRY, AND TWO * CIVILIANS
UNDER THE COMMAND OF CAPTAIN BREVET
LIEUTENANT COLONEL WILLIAM J. FETTERMAN
WERE KILLED BY AN OVERWHELMING
FORCE OF SIOUX UNDER THE COMMAND OF
RED CLOUD
THERE WERE NO SURVIVORS

* The tablet gives four, but is in error in so doing.

The remaining markers, all of rough, unpolished granite, have been placed since 1913 under the supervision of the Wyoming-Oregon Trail Commission. Most of these stones along the old trail bear the simple inscription, "The Bozeman Trail," a number of them being located where the State Highway automobile road crosses the trail. Somewhat more substantial are the two stones that mark the sites of Fort Phil Kearney and the Wagon Box fight.

Along the Bozeman Trail there have been built no cities of considerable size east of Livingston, Montana;[139] the country has been and is occupied by stockmen, ranchmen and the farmer, the lands once of fierce combats being largely turned over to the peaceful possession of cattle and used for grazing and agricultural purposes. No north and south railroad in Wyoming has penetrated this land of the buffalo, deer, and antelope, the home and hunting ground of the peaceful Crows and the warring Sioux.[140] The site of Fort Reno, on the Powder River remains today much in the same condition as it was in the sixties – an open, unpeopled territory, the stock enjoying the sun-cured grass as did the buffalo, hunted by their enemies, the Indians. The battle ground of Fort Phil Kearney is today a productive alfalfa field, where the hum of the reaper has supplanted the war cry of Red Cloud's thousands of warriors. Fort C. F. Smith is in the heart of the Crow reservation, rich in its productiveness.

In Wyoming, the town of Buffalo, on Clear Creek, was, in 1879, the first to be established along the Bozeman Trail north of the North Platte. In 1881 the town of

---

[139] Just east of Bozeman Pass, on the west side of the Yellowstone River.

[140] The Chicago, Burlington and Quincy and the Northern Pacific Railroads, in Montana, cross the old Bozeman Trail in Carbon County, west of the Crow Indian Reservation.

Big Horn had its beginning, to be followed in the next year by the town of Dayton, exactly in the old trail. Just north of Dayton has been built the railroad station of Parkman, a few miles south of the Montana boundary line. The Crow Indian Reservation (Montana) contains the old trail to the Big Horn River and west to a point between Pryor's and Clark's Forks of the Yellowstone. Along this part of the road there are, of course, no towns – just homes of the Crow Indians. "The Crow Indian has been allowed to retain but a small portion of the hard fought for region; but his cultivated fields, his farm machinery, his top buggies, his automobiles, and, not least indicative, his baby go-carts, seen throughout the reservation, are evidence that education is telling, and that the next generation will be a new race." Elsewhere, though not on or near the hated trail to the land of gold, the Sioux Indians have learned some of the ways of making nature respond to toil, and have on their reservation been educated and trained in useful and profitable occupations.[141]

Of the fertility and productivity of the lands embraced in the country along the Bozeman Trail, from the Powder River to where the once isolated Fort C. F. Smith was doing its part in protecting the frontiersman in his endeavor to push civilization a few more miles farther to the west, we find excellent expression from the pen of one who has lived on or near the old road for the past third of a century.[142] "For the past thirty-five years I have been almost within sight of the Bozeman Trail. I conclude, from observation covering this long period, and from my travel over Wyoming and other northwestern states, that those who saw the coun-

[141] Two hundred trained Sioux soldiers were in the ranks of the American Expeditionary Force in France during the World War of 1917-1918.

[142] E. L. Dana, Parkman, Wyoming.

try as 'trail blazers' in the sixties must have been strongly impressed with the grandeur in earth and sky of that country lying along the Big Horn Mountains from Massacre Hill to Fort C. F. Smith. The soil through this area is a sandy loam that yields bountifully to the plow, and is of such fertility that abundant crops of hay, grain, and vegetables are raised wherever nature is properly assisted. Much of the land is, and more may be, irrigated from the numerous mountain streams, and, as in the northwest, it would seem that nature was not asking too much of man when she furnished everything and required of him the pleasant task of applying the water to the land.

"At a point about three and one-half miles northwest of Parkman the trail enters Montana from Wyoming, and from that point to Fort C. F. Smith, I judge it to be about forty-five miles. Through all this distance and reaching for miles on either side, there is no barren land, and little, if any, waste land. Most of it is susceptible to home building."

The Crows have, after years of conflict and combat with both the white man and the red man, regained possession of their coveted land on which their ancestors roamed, and over which their warriors hunted, through which other tribes wandered and lived, and for which our soldiers bravely and uncomplainingly paid the supreme sacrifice. The present condition of that section of land in Wyoming through which the Bozeman Road passed, duplicates itself in Montana. South of the Yellowstone River no cities of great importance have come into existence. There are but a few towns along the trail from Fort C. F. Smith to the city of Livingston. Bozeman and Livingston are the most important of cities along the trail from the North Platte to Virginia City. Among other small towns along the trail in the region of the Yellowstone are Prior, Bridger (on a cut-off), Eager, Boyd, Fishtale, Absarokee, Springdale, and Hot Springs. "An interesting feature by way of contrast is the fact that the Montana Agricultural College is located at Bozeman, and the peaceful pursuits of agriculture are now being taught on the very ground over which the red men raced and whooped in bloody foray, even in comparatively recent times."[143]

In the valley of the Yellowstone are prosperous farms and ranches. Stock raising, farming, dairying, flour milling, and manufacturing are the chief gainful occupations. The most productive crops being alfalfa, oats, flax, barley, corn, and wheat.

In place of the wrathful Indian with his guerilla warfare, fighting fiercely and savagely for what he honestly believed was his rightful inheritence, are now to be found peace and prosperity, the heritage of children born of the pioneer who fought for occupancy in the lands along the Bozeman Trail. In the neighborhood of the end of the trail, in the Beaver Head country where once tens of thousands of hectic prospectors rubbed shoulders with the outlaw, the murderer and the peaceful and honest homeseeker, where law and order were daily challenged, may be seen schools and homes; horses, sheep, and cattle in the forest reserves; orchards of apples and small fruits; fields of alfalfa, clover, timothy, wheat, oats, barley, rye, and root crops. Virginia City, with a new world at her feet in the sixties, her wide open camp with its frame buildings, saloons, gambling dens, and dance halls, now numbers her law abiding population only by the hundreds, a city

---

[143] Wheeler (O. D.) *The Trail of Lewis and Clark,* vol ii, p. 333.

with a fascinating past, with memories, and of historical significance.

Our national expansion has been a western movement, one that was the most romantic and most epochal in all of our written history. Change is the immutable law of progress. Men and women of energy, courage, and determination are the ones who have sought in the broad expanse of the west a refuge from social stagnation felt in the localities from which they have migrated. The freedom of the plains, the low death rate, of the territory surrounded by the pure, invigorating air of the mountain regions, the free lands west of the Missouri contributed to the cause of territorial expansion. "It has been a social movement of conquest, colonization and expansion, owing its birth to that passion of acquisition and possession of large tracts of virgin soil on which were no inhabitants, through which were no roads, and over which there was a limited government." It is a wonderful history of pioneer struggles, of privations, of hardships, conflicts with Indians, of long and dangerous journeys to unknown parts of our country, the subduing of mountains and streams, the making of trails over trackless prairies and through treacherous passes. Yet all of this was not in vain, for these hardships, dangers, and tribulations gave backbone, courage, hope, sinew, and mental power to our frontiersmen – to our nation builders.

It is the frontiersman with the pioneer spirit that builds a nation and founds commonwealths within that nation. This class of men and women have been our nation builders.

Index

Absaraka Indians: see Crow Indians
Absarokee: 265
Adobe Buildings: 122; at Fort C. F.
    Smith, 135, 136, 139, *footnote*, 140,
    footnote, 171; at Fort Laramie, 255;
    at Fort Reno, 127, 131 *footnote*; see
    also *Buildings*
Agate (Nebr.): 22, 182
Agriculture: 262–265; at Fort Phil
    Kearney, 99
Ambulances: 90, 101; at Wagon Box
    Fight, 69
American Expeditionary Forces:
    Sioux Indians in, 263
American Flag: at Red Cloud's home,
    192
American Fur Company: 216, 219; at
    rendezvous, 217
American Horse, Chief: 182; killed
    Fetterman, 188
Ammunition: 50, 51, 57, 60, 61, 83,
    92, 102, 131, footnote; at corrals,
    43; at Hayfield Fight, 162, 165, 168;
    at Wagon Box Fight, 74; scarcity on
    plains, 29; traded for furs, 217;
    traded by Indians, 143, *footnote*; see
    Artillery, Firearms
Amputation: necessary account of se-
    vere weather, 105
Amusements: at Fort Phil Kearney, 98
Andover (Mass.): 192
Antelope: 146; see *Game*
Anthony, D. R: 33
Apache Indians: campaign, 182
Arapahoe Indians: 31, 70, 143, 159,
    194, *footnote*, 245; kill Laramie, 233;
    mean war, 145
Arctic Ocean: 238
Arickaree Fork: 80

Arizona: 182
Army posts: see *Forts, Camps*
Arrows: 60, 62, 63, 76, 79, 93, 126,
    174; fire, 62, 78, 84, 166; number
    found in dead, 92; see *Bows and Ar-
    rows*
Artillery: 29, 79, 92; cannon, 69; Capt.
    Ten Eyck sends for, 101; howitzer,
    85; at Wagon Box Fight, 68
Ashley, Gen. William H: Bridger joins,
    206
Atlanta (Ga.): 72
Atlantic Ocean: 215

Backbone Mountain: 144
Bailey, Capt: 21, also *footnote*, 97, 98
Bair, *Private*: see *Blair*
Baker, Private William A: 71, *footnote*
Banner Ranch: 117
Barber Shop: at Fort Reno, 127
Barricades: at hayfield, 162; barrels
    used for, 55, 61, 63, 67, 74, 78; neck-
    yokes used for, 52, 61, 74; willows
    used for, 166
Barry, D. F: 12
Barton, Private Ashton P: 71, *footnote*
Bastions: 36, 125, 127, 172
Bear: 86, 146; account of Glass's com-
    bat, 209
Bear Creek: 115
Bear River: 210
Beaver: 220, prices of skins, 239
Beaver Creek: 117, 120
Beaver Creek Divide: 117
Beaver Head (Mont.): 265
Beck, Hon. George T.: 117
Beckton (Wyo.): 117
Beckwourth [Beckwith], James: 143,
    also *footnote*

"Bedlam": 23
Beecher Island: 80
Berdan's Creek: 120
Berthune, Frank: hired to guard camp, 171
"Big Bat": see *Pourier, Baptiste*
Big Boulder Creek: 120
Big Goose Creek: 117, 228
Big Horn (Wyo.): 113, *footnote*, 263
Big Horn Basin: 211
Big Horn Building: at Fort C. F. Smith, 143, *footnote*
Big Horn Country: 89, 121, 178, 179, 229, 235
Big Horn Crossing: 118
Big Horn Mountains: 26, 119, *footnote*, 128, 139, 228, 240, 254, 259, 264
Big Horn River: 106, 117, 118, 119, *footnote*, 120, 121, 122, 135, 136, 143, *footnote*, 145, 159, 160, 170, 178, 209, 219, 240, 258, *footnote*, 263; see also *Little Big Horn River*
Big Mouth, Chief: 178
Big Piney Creek: 47, 53, 55, 69, 178; see *Piney Creek, Little Piney Creek*
Big Piney Valley: 45, 58, 59, 65, 68, 69
"Big Sam": 109, 110
"Big Spring": 116
Bingham, Lieut. H. S: killed, 99
Black, Private William: 71, *footnote*
Black Canyon Creek: 144
Black Fork River: 220, 222
Black Hills: 258, *footnote*, 260
Black Horse, Chief: 140
Blackfoot Indians: 132, 217; attack fur trappers, 216; skirmish with Bridger, 218, 219; country, 216
Blacksmith shops: at Fort Bridger, 220
Blair, Private: 132, 155; killed, 126
Blizzards: 16, 24; see *Weather*
Blockhouses: 93; at Fort C. F. Smith, 141; at Fort Reno, 129, 172
Blue River: see *Big and Little Blue Rivers*
Bonanza Trail: see *Bozeman Trail*
Boulder River: 121
Bow and arrows: 53; see *Arrows*
Bowers, Sergt. C. R: killed, 99

Boyd, John: 232
Boyd (Mont.): 265
Bozeman, John M., 121; photograph, 4
Bozeman [City] (Mont.): 120, 121, 143, footnote, 264, 265
Bozeman-Jacobs route: 257, *footnote*
Bozeman Expedition of 1874: 118
Bozeman Pass: 121, 262, *footnote*
Bozeman Road: 179, 181, 253, 257, *footnote*, 264; see *Bozeman Trail*
Bozeman Trail: 4, 16, 35, 40, 81, 82, 114, 171, 172, 232, 257, 262, also *footnote*, 263, 265; abandonment of, 258, also *footnote*; forts on, ordered abandoned, 254, also *footnote*; marked, 261; route of, 113–148; towns on, 262, 263; see *Bozeman Road*
Bradley, James H: *Journal* quoted, 140, *footnote*
Bridger, Chloe: mother of James Bridger, 205
Bridger, Felix: 248, 251
Bridger, James: 81, 113, 121, 205–252; as guide, for Gen. Raynolds, 119, *footnote*; surveys Bozeman Trail, 119; sent to interview Crows, 40; travels entire length of Bozeman's Trail, 118
Bridger, Mrs. James: at Fort Bridger, 223
Bridger, James: father of Major Bridger, 205
Bridger, Josephine: 248
Bridger, Mary: 248
Bridger, Virginia: see *Waschman, Mrs.*
Bridger, William: 248, 251
Bridger-Bozeman race: 119, *footnote*
Bridger (Mont.): 121, 265
Bridger Crossing: 173
Bridger's Ferry: 37, 114, 151
Bridger Lake: 215
Bridger Pass: 252, 258
Bridger Road: see *Overland Trail*
Bridger's Trail: 121
Brooke, Gen. ——: 198
Brooks, Private Charles: 71, *footnote*

Brough, John C: 22, 33

Brown, ——: cook, 45, 62, 63

Brown, Private Alexander: 71, *footnote*

Brown, Private Denis: 71, *footnote*

Brown, Capt. Frederick H: 20, 135, 188; body mutilated, 101

Brown's Fork: 120

Brown's Spring Creek: 114

Buffalo: 146, 228, 260; furnished all Indians desired, 177; robes for sale at Fort Bridger, 223; traded for ammunition, 143, *footnote*

Buffalo (Wyo.): 115, 116, 131, 262

Buffalo Bill: see Cody, William F.

Buildings: at Fort Reno, 122, at Fort C. F. Smith, 136; at Fort Phil Kearney, 95; see *Adobe Buildings*

Bull Trains: 40, 52

Bullock, William G: 232

Bullwhackers: 55

Buntline, Ned: see *Judson, Col. E. B. C.*

Burial Grounds: see *Cemeteries, Graves*

Burnett, F. G: 113, also *footnote*, 114, 129, 131, *footnote*, 141, 163; quoted, 247–248; account of Fort C. F. Smith, 135, 136, 159–174

Burnot, Felix: in council with Red Cloud, 199

Burnt Fort: see *South Pass Station*

Buzzard, Private John: 71, *footnote*

Cache La Poudre River: 32

Cache La Poudre Road: see *Overland Route*

Caldwell, Kemp: sutler at Fort Reno, 171

California: 239

Camp, William: quoted, 166, *footnote*, 167, *footnote*

Camp Proctor: 41

Camp Rankin: see *Fort Sedgwick*

Campbell, Robert: 218

Canada: Bridger visited, 238

Caravans: 217; belonging to Sir George Gore, 225; see *Bull Trains, Pack Trains, Stage Lines*

Carbines: see *Firearms*

Carbon County (Wyo.): 121, 262, *footnote*

Carondalet (Mo.): 233

Carpenter, Col. ——: 34

Carrington, Frances C: affidavit relating to John Phillips' ride, 30; *Army Life on the Plains*, quoted, 231–232; see also *Grummond, Mrs. G. W.*

Carrington, Gen. Henry B: 19, 21, 23, 26, 30, 35, 39, 46, 52, 54, 71, 82, 89, 95, 99, 101, 113, 114, 119, 122, 135, 158, 159, 172, 178, 179, 229, 231, 232, 261; *Absarka*, quoted, 230–231; affidavit relating to Phillips ride, 28–30; orders to Capt. Fetterman, 180; goes after dead, 103; left Fort Phil Kearney, 40; orders women and children into powder magazine, 102; planned Fort Phil Kearney, 93, 94; portrait, 41; Red Cloud accuses, 178; report of Bridger's visit to Crows, 140; report regarding Indians, 143; sends for reinforcements, 20, 21; signals at Fort Phil Kearney, 81, *Some Phases of the Indian Question*, quoted, 119, *footnote*

Carrington, Mrs. Henry B: see *Carrington, Francis C.*

Carrington, James B: photograph loaned by, 11

Carson, Kit: 219, 234, 243; associated with Bridger, 218

Carter, Judge: sutler at Fort Bridger, 224

Casualties: caused by Sioux, 179; at Fetterman Disaster, 20; at Hayfield Fight, 168; see also *Indians—Casualties*

Catholics: 203; Red Cloud's faith, 195, 200

Cattle: 92; claims settled, 25

Cavalry: 147, *footnote*, 173; at Fort C. F. Smith, 169

Cayuse Indians: murdered Whitman, 217, *footnote*

Cemeteries: at Fort C. F. Smith, 139, *footnote*, 140, *footnote*; at Fort Reno, 128, 129, 131, *footnote*; at Crow

Cemeteries (*cont.*)
  Agency, 132; see also *Custer Battle-field National Cemetery, Graves*
Charges-At-or-Kills-Above, Mrs: 200
Chase Alone, Mrs. Fannie: 200
Chattanooga (Tenn.): 89, *footnote*
"Cherokee City": see *Latham*
Cheyenne (Wyo.): 25, 80, 81, 233, 234
Cheyenne Indians: 25, 28, 70, 80, 159; bring report to Col. Carrington, 140; disagree with Sioux, 160, 188; disliked Bridger, 231
Cheyenne River: 115
Chicago, Burlington and Quincy Railroad: 262, *footnote*
Chicago *Times*: correspondent with Gen. Crook, 127, 148
Chickamauga (Tenn.): Capt. Powell at, 72
Children: 57, 91; at Fort Phil Kearney, 16, 27, 38, 95, 231; Indians want to trade, 90; Indian, killed, 194; killed by Indians, 89; of Bridger, 248; of Red Cloud, 200
Chimney Rock: 114
Chittenden, H. M: *Yellowstone Park*, quoted, 211–214
Chivington Massacre: 194, also *footnote*; see *Sand Creek Massacre*
Cholera: see *Disease*
Chouteau, Pierre: 220
Chugwater Creek: 22
Civil War: 51, 89, 103, 162, 165; Bridger's son in, 248; Capt. Powell served in, 72
Clark, Hopkins: 232
Clark's Fork: 120, 263
Clarke, ——: 150, 151, 152, 154, 156
Claus, Frederick: 71, *footnote*; account of Wagon Box Fight, 82–87
Clear Creek: 116, 119, 262
Cody, William F: 250
Cody (Wyo.): 117
Cold Spring Creek: 120
Colorado: citizens at Chivington Massacre, 194
Colorado River: 217
Colter, John: 211, 212

Columbia River: 222
Colvin, Capt. D. A: 163, 168, 169; in charge at Hayfield Fight, 165
Colvin, Zeke: 162, 163, 165, 166
Condon, Private James: 55, 61, 62, 63, 67, 71, *footnote*, 74
Conferences: see *Laramie Peace Conference*
Conley, Corp. Paddy: 46
Connor, Gen. Patrick E: 122, 228, 229, 234, 235
Cook, Capt. James H: 22, 23, 185–192, 200, 203, 204; photograph, 183; Red Cloud's most intimate white friend, 182; valuable aid to government during Indian troubles, 182
Cooke, Gen. Philip St. George: orders Bridger discharged, 232
Corrals: 49, 50, 51, 58, 62, 63, 65–67, 69, 73–79, 83–85, 125, 126, 132, 149, 155, 156, 157, 161–163, 165, 166, 170, 235; at Fort C. F. Smith, 136; at Fort Reno, 129; made by wagon boxes, 43
Council Fire and Arbitrator: quoted, 199–200
Courthouse Rock: 114
Coutant, George: *History of Wyoming*, quoted, 33, 146, *footnote*, 147, *footnote*
Coyotes: 126
Crazy Horse, Chief: 189, 194, 261
Crazy Woman's Fork: 36, 90, 115, 116, 119, 178
Cromer (Creamer), Phil: Bridger apprenticed to, 206
Crook, Gen. George: 127, 171; at Fort Fetterman, 147, *footnote*; Indians had faith in, 197
Crook Expedition of 1876: 258, *footnote*
"Cross H" Ranch: 116
Crow Agency (Mont.): 132
Crow Indians: 103, 143, 162, 169, 214, 232, 262, 264; join whites to fight Sioux, 140; at council at Fort Laramie, 254; Bridger a friend of,

231; enemies with Sioux and Cheyennes, 177; friendly with Sioux, 159, 160; of today, 263; quarrel with Sioux, 145; Sir George Gore visited, 227; trade ammunition with Sioux, 143, *footnote*; warn whites of danger, 160, 161

Crow Indian Reservation, 118, 262, also *footnote*, 263

Crow King, Chief: 189

Cruse Creek: 117

Culbertson, Major: in command at Fort Union, 227

Curry, Bandmaster: 95

Custer, Gen. G. A: 132, 248, 260, 261

Custer Massacre: 189

Dakota Indians: 192

Dakota Territory: 39, 123

Dallas (Mo.): Bridger buried near, 251

Dana, E. L: 263, *footnote*, 264

Dandy, Gen. George P: 43; quartermaster at Fort C. F. Smith, 144

Daniels, Lieut. ——: 90; killed, 92

Davis, Lieut. ——: 156

Dayton (Wyo.): 118, 263

Deming, Private Nolan V: 46–48, 50, 71, *footnote*

Denver (Colo.): 234, 237, 246

Dillon, George: 21

D'Isay, Capt. I: 112

Dirge to the Pioneer: 7

Disease: at Fort Phil Kearney, 40, 107, 108

Dodge, Gen. Grenville M: quoted, 70, 251, 252; quoted, 250–251

Dogs: at Fort Phil Kearney, 45; with Sir George Gore, 225

Domestic Animals: at Fort Phil Kearney, 99

Doyle, Private Thomas: 52, 57, 58, 69, 71, *footnote*; killed, 61

Drips, Andrew, 216

Driscoll, Dennis: 143; wounded, 144

Dubois Creek: 120

Dull Knife, Chief: 140

Duncan, George: 163

Dye, Maj. William McE: in command at Fort Fetterman, 147

Eager (Mont.): 265

Elk: 146

Elkhorn Creek: 114

Elm Creek: 81

Emigrant Road: see *Oregon Trail*

Emmil's Fork: 120

Fenlon, Tip: 34

Fessenden, F. M: 89, *footnote*

Fessenden, Mrs. F. M: accompanied husband, 90

Fetterman, Capt. William J: 15, 16, 20, 24, 26, 71, 90, 100, 101, 261; fort named for, 147; killed by American Horse, 188, also *footnote*; sent to disperse Indians, 179, 180

Fetterman Disaster: 15, 20, 25, 26, 32, 34, 40, 49, 52, 71, 86, 101, 103, 104, 106, 147, 158, 172, 175, 180, 188, 194; monument erected, 261; Red Cloud took no active part in, 187; result of, 39

Fetterman Massacre Memorial Monument: 82

Fetterman Massacre: see *Fetterman Disaster*

Finerty, John F: 147, quoted, 148; *Warpath and Bivouac*, quoted, 127–131, 148

Firearms: 54, 60, 84, 91, 154, 169; at Hayfield Fight, 162, 168; at Wagon Box Fight, 77; breech-loading rifle first used on plains, 180; exchanged for pelts, 79; Indians demand, 253; Indians offer five ponies for revolver, 92; Indians own Winchester rifles, 173; new at Fort Phil Kearney, 43; owned by Indians, 48, 79; scarcity at Fort Phil Kearney, 20, 21; Springfield rifles, 47; used in Wagon Box Fight, 74; used by Indians, 53; see *Ammunition*

First Dragoons: 72

Fishtale: 265

Fitzgerald, ——: and Bridger agree to nurse Glass, 210

Fitzpatrick, Thomas: 210, 216, 218

Flathead Indians: 217; Bridger married, 248

Flynn, Dan: 51

Food: onions used to treat scurvy, 108; scarce at Fort Phil Kearney, 39, 40, 105

Foote Ranch: 116

Fort Berthold: 228

Fort Bridger: 220, 222, 224, 243, 248, 252; description of, 222–224

Fort C. F. Smith: 20, 106, 113–115, 118–122, 132, 135–147, also *footnote*, 151, 159, 174, 178, 229, 234, 254, also *footnote*, 257, *footnote*, 258, *footnote*, 262–264; plan, 137, 141; photograph of ruins, 133; sketch, 112

Fort Carrington: see *Fort Phil Kearney*

Fort Caspar: 37, 40, 147, *footnote*; see *Sweetwater Station, Platte Bridge Station*

Fort Connor (Reno): 122; see also *Fort Reno*

Fort D. A Russell: 233

Fort Fetterman: 25, 27, 83, 114, 146–148, 258, *footnote*; Bridger transferred to, 234

Fort Fred Steele: 234

Fort Kearney (Nebr.): 39, 73, 89, 95, 113, 114, 119, 121, 229, 237, 241

Fort Kiowa: 210

Fort Laramie (Wyo.): 16, 19–23, 25–27, 29, 31, 32, 36, 37, 39, 40, 73, 83, 90, 102, 104, 105, 113, 115, 119, 121, 128, 149, 151, 156, 172, 225, 228, 233, 234, 236, 239, 241, 254, 255, 258, footnote; Bridger at, 232 ff; Indian council held at, 177, 199, 230

Fort Leavenworth: 20, 73, 81

Fort Leavenworth Treaty: 194

Fort McPherson: 83, 114, 119, 121

Fort Mitchell: 114

Fort Phil Kearney: 15, 16, 19, 21, also *footnote*, 24–28, 30, 31, 33, 34, 35, 37, 40, 43, 46, 52, 54, 68, 71, *footnote*, 72, 73, 80, 81–83, 87, 89, 90, 92–95,

108, 109, 119, 121, 122, 125, 132, 143, 144, 147, also *footnote*, 151, 158, 159, 172, 175, 178–180, 187, 229, 231, 234, 254, also *footnote*, 257, *footnote*, 258, *footnote*, 262; distance from Fort C. F. Smith, 140; Indians burn, 257; invulnerable against Indians, 171; staff at, 16

Fort Rankin: see *Fort Sedgwick*

Fort Ransom: see also *Fort C. F. Smith*

Fort Reno: 20, 22, 35, 36, 37, 73, 83, 90, 92, 105, 108, 109, 113, 115, 119, 121–135, 147, also *footnote*, 149–158, 159, 171, 172, 234, 254, also *footnote*, 257, *footnote*, 258, *footnote*, 262; Carrington in charge of rebuilding, 178; Indians plan to destroy, 161; plan of, 129; see also *Fort Connor*

Fort Robinson: 189

Fort Robinson Treaty: 194

Fort Sedgwick: 73, 89, 108, 110, 113, 114, 119, 121, 144; child born at, 90; see also *Camp Rankin*

Fort Union: 220, 227

Fort Washakie (Wyo.): 113, *footnote*, 247

Fort Williams: see *Fort Laramie*

Fraeb, Henry: 210

Frank Leslie's Illustrated Weekly: correspondent for, killed by Indians, 96

Freeman, Gen. Henry B: 126, also *footnote*, 156

Fremont, General John C: 239, 243; Bridger disliked, 234

French Creek: 116

Friend, John C: 22, 33; telegraph operator at Horseshoe Station, 21

Fry, Col. James B: *Army Sacrifices*, quoted, 71–72

Fur Companies: see under various names of companies

Gallatin River: 120, 121

Game: at Fort C. F. Smith, 145, 146

Gangnier, Baptiste: 185, also *footnote*, 190; in conference with Red Cloud, 189

Garber, Mrs. A. L: 113, also *footnote*, 115, 122, 129, quoted, 131, *footnote*, 141; information regarding Fort C. F. Smith, 135, 136, 139

Garrett, Private John M: 46–48, 50, 71, *footnote*

Garver, Frank Harmon: *Early Emigrant Roads and Trails in Montana*, quoted, 121

Gaul, Chief: 189

Germany: Frederick Claus emigrated from, 83; Sergt. Listmann emigrated from, 72

Gervais, Jean Baptiste: 210

Ghost Dance War: 45, 182, 192; Red Cloud not active in, 190; Red Cloud's reasons for, 195–199

Gibson, Sergt. Samuel: 55, 71, *footnote*, 82; account of Wagon Box Fight, 39–71; portrait, 41; sketch by, 55; took part in Indian Campaigns, 70

Gilmore and Parker: 43; bull train at Fort Phil Kearney, 40

Glass, Hugh: companion of Bridger, 209, 210

Glover, Ridgeway: 96, also *footnote*, 97

Goose Creek: 119

Gore, Sir George: 225, 226, 227, 228; burns his outfit, 227

Grady, Private John: 46, 51, 53, 60, 61, 62, 63, 71, *footnote*

Grand Army of the Republic: 33, 34

Grand River: 209

Grass Lodge Creek: 120

"Gray Fox": see *Crook, General*

Great Falls: 211

"Great Medicine Road of the Whites": see *Oregon Trail*

Great Salt Lake: 211, 238, 239, 252; Bridger claims to have discovered, 210

Green River: 217, 220; rendezvous at, 217; see *Black Fork River*

Greene, Col.: arrives at Fort C. F. Smith, 169

Grinnell, G. B: *Fighting Cheyennes*, cited, 187

Groetgeers, Rev. H: 200

Gross, Private Henry: 71, *footnote*

Grouard, Frank: 116

Grummond, Lieut. George W: 19, 20, 30, 95, 99, 100

Grummond, Mrs George W: 19, 20, 40, 102; see also *Carrington, Frances C.*

Haggerty, Private Henry: 55, 58, 71, *footnote*; killed, 61

Haller, Private Mark: 71, *footnote*; wounded by bear, 86

Hamilton Ford: 116

Hanes, Billy: 163

Hannibal, ——: 95

Harris, ——: 48

Harris, P. C: 254, *footnote*

Harrison, Lieut. ——: 110

Hartz, Capt. Edward L: 137; goes for help, 167

Hayfield Fight: 139, *footnote*, 159–174, 253; plan, 163

Henry, Andrew: 206, 209; offers reward for nursing Glass, 209

Hines, Drummer: 45

Holister: see *Hollister*

Hollister (Holister) ——: 163; killed, 168

Holt, Private ——: buried at Fort Reno, 128

Holy Rosary Mission: Red Cloud buried at, 200; Jack Red Cloud buried at, 204

Hoover, Sergt. Frank: 55, 58, 60, 71, *footnote*

Hoover, Sergt. John M: see *Hoover, Sergt. Frank*

Horses: claims settled for, 25; kept saddled at Fort Phil Kearney, 94, 99; stampeded, 221; starve, 105; stolen, 179, 209; with Sir George Gore, 225; see also *Mules*

Horseshoe Creek: 114

Horseshoe Station (Idaho Terr.): 21–23, 33, 37, 46

Horton, Dr. Samuel M.: 69, 95

Hospital: at Fort Reno, 126, 127, 129

Hot Springs: 265

Hot Springs Valley: 121
Humfreville, Capt. Lee: *Twenty Years Among Our Hostile Indians*: quoted, 242–246
Humphrey's Camp: 37
Hunton, John: 24, quoted, 258, *footnote*
Hyde Park (Mass.): home of the Carringtons, 30, 82

Ice Water Springs: 120
Illinois: Forty-ninth Infantry, 89
Independence (Mo.): 233, 234
Independence Rock (Wyo.): 215
Indian agents: graft, 193, 196
Indian Territory: 248
Indians: 16, 19, 22, 29, 36, 37, 40, 43, 44, 46, 50, 51–53, 58, 60, 61, 63, 65, 72, 73, 76, 77, 83, 89, 91, 93, 95–98, 100, 106, 109, 110, 113, 118, 125, 126, 128, 132, 144, 145, 147, 155, 156, 168, 170–172, 206, 209, 218, 221, 222, 229, 230, 232, 235, 236, 238, 242, 248, 251, 257, *footnote*, 258, also *footnote*, 259, 260, 262, 265, 266; at winter quarters, 146; attack pinery, 47, 48; burn forts, 181; carry Spencer carbines, 48; casualties at Hayfield Fight, 168, 169; casualties at Wagon Box Fight, 70, 85, 86, 181; demand firearms from U.S., 253; depredations, 99, 261; at Fort Reno, 128; claims for, 25, 28; harrass trains, 143; harrass woodchoppers, 94; in war paint, 49, 76; casualties at Fetterman Disaster, 103, 188; mistaken for mail carrier, 157; mutilate dead, 71, 96, 101, 180; near Fort Phil Kearney, 20; number in Wagon Box Fight, 86; not treated fairly, 193–199; on reservation have rations reduced, 196, 197, 198; outnumber white men 100 to 1 in Wagon Box Fight, 80; pay frequent visits to Cook ranch, 191; prepared to wipe out forts on Bozeman Trail, 159; pretend to be friendly, 92; pursue John Phillips, 23; recover their wounded and dead, 57, 58, 70, 78; retreat at Wagon Box Fight, 67, 68, 69; signal with mirrors, 59, 81; skirmishes with, 91, 92, 245, 246; steal John Phillips stock, 28; surprised, 173; want to buy baby, 90; weapons, 54, 64, 66, 79, 84, 188; see also under names of various tribes

Jackson, H. H: *Century of Dishonor*, 194, *footnote*
Jackson Creek Valley: 117
Jefferson Barracks (St. Louis, Mo.): 72
Jefferson Forks: 211, 216
Jenison, Col. ——: 34
Jenness, Lieut. John C: 52, 55, 58, 62, 69, 71, *footnote*, 83, 132; killed, 61, 78, 84
Johnson, W. G: *Experiences of a '49er*, quoted: 222–224
Johnson County (Wyo.): 116
Johnston, Gen. Albert S: 224, 252
Jones, Private Philip C: 72, *footnote*
Jonesboro (Ga.): Capt. Powell wounded at, 72
Joseph, Chief: 175
Judd, ——: accompanies John Phillips, 46
Judson, Col. E. B. C: 250
Jule, Father: 195, 198
Julesburg: 73, 89, 109, 236, 237

Kansas: 33; Fifth Cavalry, 34
Kansas City (Mo.): Bridger's remains removed to, 251
Kansas City *Journal*: 212
Kelly, Corp. James: 126
Kessler, Charles N: 11
Kilberg, ——: 48
Kinney, Col. N. C: 135
Kiowa Indians: mean war, 145
Kirkendall, Hugh: 92
Kirtland, Lieut: 92, 150, 151, 154–156
Kittredge, ——: 48

La Prele Creek: 114, 147
La Ramée, Jacques: see *Laramie, Jacques*

La Ramie, Jacques; see *Laramie, Jacques*
Laggin, Private: buried at Fort Reno, 128
Laidlaw, ——: 221
Lake De Smet: 119
Land of the Crows: see *"Absaraka"*
Land of the Sioux: see *Powder River Country*
Lang, ——: 48
Laramie, Jacques: 233
Laramie Peace Conference: 230, 254
Laramie Peak: 239
Laramie River: 25, 114, 218
Laramie Valley: 233
Larpenteur, Charles: *Forty Years a Fur Trader on Upper Missouri*: 221, also *footnote*
Laughlotts, ——: 95
Leeson, M. A: *History of Montana*, 143, *footnote*, quoted, 257, *footnote*
Leighton, A. C: 159, 169; sutler at Fort Reno, 125; sutler at Fort C. F. Smith, 136
Lightle, Marie Louise: great-grand-daughter of Bridger, 251
Lincoln (Nebr.): 82, *footnote*
Link, Lieut. ——: 91
Link, H. H: 122, *footnote*, 131, *footnote*
Liquor: used as medicine, 69
"Little Bat": see *Gangnier, Baptiste*
Little Big Horn River: 118, 120, 121; Indians winter near, 146; see also *Big Horn River*
Little, Bob: 163
Little Goose Creek: 228
Little Goose Valley: 117
Little Moon, Chief: see *Two Moons, Chief*
Little Piney Creek: 15, 45–48, 53, 62, 178, 180; see also *Big Piney Creek, Piney Creek*
Little Santa Fe (Mo.): 248
Little Wolf, Chief: 140
Little Wound, Chief: 182
Littmann, Max: 49, 55, 71, *footnote*; account of Wagon Box Fight, 72–82
Livingston (Mont.): 262, *footnote*, 264
Locomotive: first at Cheyenne, 80

Lodge Grass Creek: 118
Lodge Pole Creek: 114
Lodge Trail Ridge: 71, 180, 187
Longfellow: read to Bridger, 244
Louisville: 146

McCarthy, Lieut. Francis: 46
McClure, ——: *Three Thousand Miles through the Rocky Mountains*, quoted, 257, *footnote*
McCumber, Private ——: 46
McDonough, Private Jack: 45, 46
McKenzie River: 238
McNally, Private ——: 46
McQuarie, John H: see *McQuiery, John H.*
McQuiery, Sergt. John H: 44, 51, 53, 58, 61, 62, 71, *footnote*
McUlvane, Daniel: 33
Madison: 119, *footnote*
Madison River: 121
Magazine: at Fort Reno, 172
Mail: distribution at Fort Reno, 149–153; length of time between, 145
Makh-pi-ya-luta: 175, 203; see *Red Cloud, Chief*
Manderson (S. D.); 171, 190
Marsh, Prof. ——: called on Red Cloud, 185, 186
Marshal Station: 147
Massachusetts: 38
Massacre Hill: 52, 57, 116, 117, 261, 264; see also *Prairie Dog Divide*
Mather, ——: 116
Maurer, John: 95
Mead Creek: 117
Meadow Creek: 121
Meanor, William, Ranch: 117
Medicine Bow Station: 234
"Medicine Road": see *Oregon Trail*
Messiah Craze: 189
Mexican War: 135, *footnote*
Mexico: 222
Milk River: 220
Millard's Spring: 120
Mills, ——: 230
Missouri Fur Company: 206
Missouri River: 206 210, 211, 216,

Missouri River (*cont.*)
222, 227, 233, 236, 237, 260, 266;
Second Artillery, 248; see also *under various cities*
Monarch (Wyo.): 143
Mondell, F. W: 25
Monker, ——: 116
Montana: 32, 118, 119, *footnote*, 121, 132, 145, 181, 230, 257, *footnote*, 258, also *footnote*, 259, 262, *footnote*, 263, 264
Montana Agricultural College: 265
Montana Historical Society *Collections*: 113, *footnote*; quoted, 139, *footnote*, 140, *footnote*, 225, *footnote*
Montana Road: 128
Moonlight, Gen. Thomas: 34
Moore, Dave: 46
Moorehead, W. K: *American Indian*, quoted, 192–195; friend of Red Cloud, 192
"Mormon Road": see *Oregon Trail*
Mormon Trail: 220
Mormons: 227; disliked Bridger, 224
Mount Washington Cemetery: Bridger's remains removed to, 251
Mules: 78, 166; see also *Horses*
Murphy, Private ——: buried at Fort Reno, 128
Murray, ——: 95

Nebraska: 81, 175
Nebraska University: 191
New England: 38
New Haven (Conn.): Red Cloud visits, 186
Nez Perce Indians: 175, 217
Nine-mile Creek: 115
Niobrara River: 22, 182, 191
North, Major Frank: 229
North Platte River: 73, 114, 119, *footnote*, 146, 147, 220, 258, *footnote*, 259, 260, 261, 264; see also *Platte River*
North Platte Route: see also *Oregon Trail*
North Platte Trail: 176

Northern Pacific Railroad: 262, *footnote*

Obsidian Cliff: 213
Ogallala Sioux Indians: 28, 203; Red Cloud, their chief, 175
Ogden's Hole: 211
O'Hara, Theodore: 7
Ohio: 107; Eleventh Cavalry, 234, 236
Old Little Wolf, Chief: 257
Old Pioneers of Wyoming: see *Wyoming Old Pioneers*
Omaha: 22, 39, *footnote*, 82
Oregon: 216
Oregon Road: see *Oregon Trail*
Oregon Trail: 114, 121, 209, 215, 253
Orin Junction: 114
Osborne, Gov. Tom: 34
Ostrander, A. B: 22, 109, 110, 122, 129, quoted, 125–127, quoted, 140; account of John Phillips ride, 32–38; reminiscences of Fort Reno, 149–158
Overland Route: 252
Overland Stage Route: 253
Overland Trail: 37, 237, 241; see also *Oregon Trail, North Platte Route*

P. K. Ranch: 118
Pacific Ocean: 215
Pack trains: see *Caravans*
Palmer, Gen. Henry E: 122, 228–229
Parker, Rev. Samuel: *Journal of Exploring Tour Beyond the Rocky Mountains*: quoted, 217–218
Parkman (Wyo.): 261, 263, also *footnote* 264
Parmelee, Edward: 122, also *footnote*, 129, 131, also *footnote*, quoted, 132, 135, 154
Pass Creek: 118, 120
Pawnee Indians: 95, 229; enemies with Sioux, 177
Payne Ranch: 117
Peneau Creek: see *Prairie Dog Creek*
Peno Creek: 119
Perry, Capt. John A: 11, 112
Phillips, Private Freeland: 58, 72

Phillips, John: 15–39, 102, 108, 158, 172, 173; portrait, 17; presents robe to Mrs. Grummond, 20

Phillips, Mrs. John: receives compensation from United States, 25

Phillips, "Portugee": see *John Phillips*

Picket Point: see *Pilot Hill*

Pierre's Hole: rendezvous at, 215, 216

Pilot Hill: 81, 93, 100

Pine Ridge Reservation: 70, 175, also *footnote*, 182, 185, 189, 190, 192, 195; Jack Red Cloud dies at, 204; Red Cloud's daughters live at, 200; Red Cloud dies at, 200

Piney Creek: 71, *footnote*, 116; See also *Little Piney Creek, Big Piney Creek*

Platte Bridge Station: see also *Fort Caspar*

Platte River: 89, 113, 114, 121, 147, 160, 173, 175, 230, 234; see also *North Platte River, South Platte River*

Platte Road: see *Oregon Trail*

Platte Route: see *Oregon Trail*

Plum Creek (Nebr.): 81

Pomp Creek: 117

Ponies: see *Horses*

Porter, Mr.: 46

Porter, Corp. Riley: 46

Pourier, Baptiste: 171, 185, 190, also *footnote*; hired to guard camp, 171

Powder River: 37, 90, 108, 109, 115, 122, 125, 126, 127, 131, *footnote*, 177, 178, 225, 228, 262, 263

Powder River Country: 19, 89, 127, 146, 148, 178, 229, 253, 254, 258

Powder River Indian Expedition: 122

Powder River Road: 257, *footnote*

Powder River Valley: 149

Powell, Maj. James W: 44, 50, 53, 55, 57, 58, 67, 68, 70, 71, *footnote*, 73, 74, 83; compliment to, 71–72

Prairie Dog Creek: 117, 228, 229

Prairie Dog Divide: 116

Prior: 265

Prior Fork: see *Pryor Fork*

Prior River: see *Pryor River*

Proctor, Gen. ——: 36, 156; stockade around Fort Reno, 172

Pryor (Prior) Fork: 120, 263

Pryor (Prior) River: 120

Pumpkin Buttes: 119, *footnote*

Quively, A. M: *Yellowstone Expedition of 1874*, 140, *footnote*

Rain-in-the-Face, Chief: 45, 70

Ramé, Jacques de la: see *Laramie, Jacques*

Rawlins (Wyo.): 21

Raynolds, Gen. W. F: 118, footnote

Red Arm, Chief: 140

Red Buttes: 121

Red Cloud, Chief: 16, 26, 28, 29, 40, 45, 53, 66, 71, 86, 104, 175–204, 229, 230, 254, 259, 260, 261, 262; cunning, 15; in command at Wagon Box Fight, 65, 67; states loss at Wagon Box Fight, 70; council with Red Cloud, 199

Red Cloud, Jack: 200, 203; buried at Holy Rosary Mission, 204

Red Cloud Agency: 185, 188, 200

Red Cloud Buttes: 200, 201

"Red Napoleon of the Plains": see *Red Cloud, Chief*, 175

Religious Services: at Fort Phil Kearney, 98

Rendezvous: at Green River, 217

Republican River: 80, 260

Revere, Paul: compared with John Phillips, 19, 38

Revolvers: see *Firearms*

Reynolds, Peter, Ranch: 118

Richard, Mrs. Louisa: 200

Richmond (Va.): Bridger born at, 205, 207

Rifle pits: at Fort C. F. Smith, 139, 141

Rifles: see *Firearms*

Riley, Private: buried at Fort Reno, 128

Roads: to the West, see under various names

Robertson, Sergt. Francis: 52, 53, 62, 71, *footnote*

Rock Creek Valley: 116

Rocky Fork: 120

Rocky Mountains: 225, 233, 241, 246, 257, *footnote*

Rocky Mountain Fur Company: 211, 218; Bridger interested in, 210

Rosebud River: 120

Ross (Wyo.): 115

Rotten Grass Creek: 118, 120

Rotten Grass Valley: 118

Royer, Indian agent: ridiculed by Indians, 189

Sabille Creek: 233

Sackett, ——: 117

Sage Creek: 114

Sage Creek Station: 37

St. Joe (Mo.): 238, 239

St. Louis (Mo.): 82, 146, 225, 228, 246, 247, 248; Bridger family move to, 206; Sergt. Littmann at, 72, *footnote*

St. Peter's Rock: 224

Sand Creek (Colo.): 115

Sand Creek Massacre: see also *Chivington Massacre*

Sawmills: at Fort C. F. Smith, 136, 141, 144, 145; at Fort Fetterman, 147, *footnote*; at Fort Phil Kearney, 92, 93; at Fort Reno, 129

Schonborn, Anton: 112, 123

Scott, Sir Walter: read to Bridger, 226

Scott's Bluffs: 114

Scully, Mr: 222

Shakespeare: Bridger fond of, 226, 231

Shell Creek: 116

Sheridan, Gen. P. H: ride compared to John Phillips, 31

Sheridan (Wyo.): 82

Sherman, Gen. W. T.: 54, quoted, 258, 259, 260

Shields River: 121

Shoshone Indians: 217, 248

Shoshone River: 145

Shotwell, A. J: 234, quoted, 235–242

Shurly, Maj. E. R. P: sent to Fort C. F. Smith, 144

Sioux Campaign of 1876: 70, 148, 171, 182, 188

Sioux City (Iowa): 132

Sioux Country: 115

Sioux County (Nebr.): 22, 182

Sioux Indians: 16, 19, 25, 26, 30, 31, 49, 70, 79, 95, 128, 140, also *footnote*, 159, 160, 176, 177, 182, 185, 186, 187, 221, 230, 257, *footnote*, 259–263; at Pine Ridge Reservation, 185; attack caravans, 40; conditions of treaty accepted by U. S., 181; disagree with Cheyennes, 160, 188; disliked Bridger, 231; hunting grounds, 177; loss at Hayfield Fight, 169; mean war, 145; pretend to be Crows, 143; quarrel with Crows, 145; served in World War, 263, *footnote*; trade with Crows for ammunition, 143, *footnote*; see also *Ogallala Sioux Indians*

Sioux Reservation: 259

Sitting Bull, Chief: 175, 261

Slagle, Private ——: buried at Fort Reno, 128

Slow Bear, Mrs. Libbie: 200

Smith, Major ——: 69

Smith, Gen. Charles Ferguson: Fort C. F. Smith named for, 135, *footnote*

Smith, Jackson, and Sublette: sold Rocky Mountain Fur Co., 210, 211

Smith, Gen. John E: 144

Smith, Capt. John W: post trader at Fort C. F. Smith, 143, *footnote*

Smoky Hill River: 260

Snake Indians: Bridger married, 248

Soap Creek: 118

Soldier Creek: 118

Somers, Private John L: 55, 72, *footnote*

South Park: 245

South Pass: 209

South Platte River: 114, 220; see also *Platte River*

South Platte Trail: 176

Specimen Ridge: 214

Spotted Tail, Chief: 178; assassinated, 196

Spring Creek: 120

Spring Gulch: 135, 136

Springdale: 265

Stage Coaches: see *Caravans*

Stage Lines: 236

Stage Stations: see *under various stations*

Standing Rock Agency: 45, 70

Stanton, ——, Secretary of War: anecdote, 146

Stead, Jack: 95

Stephens, Al: 163

Sternberg, Lieut. ——: killed, 162, 163 [printed in error as Stromberg], 168

Stevens, Private Charles A: 72, *footnote*

Stillman Fork: 120

Stillwater River: 120

Stockades: 16, 21, 35, 93, 96, 99, 100, 122, 126–128, 136, 141, 145, 157, 170, 171, 179; at Fort C. F. Smith, 139; at Fort Reno, 131, *footnote*

Stone, A. L: 113, also *footnote*

Strache, Private Julius: 72, *footnote*

Stromberg, Lieut. ——: see *Sternberg, Lieut.*

Stubbins Watts Farm: Bridger buried on, 251

Sublette, Milton: 210, 218

Sublette, William L: 211, 218

"Sublette Cut-off": see also *Oregon Trail*

Sullivant Hill: 44

Sweetwater River: 119, *footnote*, 215

Ten Eyck, Capt. Tenedore: 71, 103; sent to relief of Fetterman, 101

Terrill Ranch: 117

Thompson, Capt. C. F: 143, 144

Three Forks: 211, 216

Tobacco: 58

Tongue River: 26, 118, 120, 226–229; Indian lodges along, 20

Tongue River Valley: 140

Trabing (Postoffice): 115

Treaties: 257, *footnote*; broken by U. S., 195–197; of 1865, 194; of 1867, 254; of 1868, 181, 258, *footnote*, 259, 261; with Sioux, 194; see also *Fort Robinson Treaty, Laramie Peace Conference*

Twenty-five Yard River: 120

Twin Creek: 118

Two Moons, Chief: 189

Two Ocean Pass: discovered by Bridger, 215

Tyler, President: Bridger a distant relative, 232

Union Pacific Railroad: 239, 253, 258; engineers consult Bridger, 246, 247

United States Army: see *under various regiments*

United States Congress: report of 1913, 26

—— Department of Interior: see also *United States Indian Department*

—— Government: broke faith with Sioux, 176; lease land from Bridger, 222; official recognition of John Phillips act, 25; promised medals to survivors of Wagon Box Fight, 82; report regarding John Phillips' claims, 25; want to build wagon road, 177

—— Indian Department: 198, 199 259; transferred to U. S. Department of Interior, 185; see also *United States Department of Interior*

—— Smithsonian Institute: 185

—— War Department: 254, *footnote*, 257, *footnote*; at cross purposes with Indian Department, 253

—— Peace Commission: 258–259

United States Second Cavalry: 34, 105

—— Fourth Infantry: 147

—— Seventh Infantry: 52

—— Tenth Infantry: 52

—— Eighteenth Cavalry: 261

—— Eighteenth Infantry: 28, 30, 39, 72, 83, 89, 131, 146, 159, 178; band, 40, 89, *footnote*, 107

—— Twenty-second Infantry: 45

—— Twenty-seventh Infantry: 32, *footnote*, 39, 72, *footnote*, 82, *footnote*, 83, 122, 126, 137, 149; at Fort Phil Kearney, 43; members of Company C, 71, *footnote*, 72, *footnote*; guard supplies en route to Fort C. F. Smith, 143

Utah Expedition: 224

Utah Mountains: 222
Utaw Indians: 217
Ute Indians: Bridger married, 248

Valley Forge: 105
Van Voast, Major ——: 109, 135
Van Volzah, ——: 151, 156, 158;
    killed, 108
Vanderburgh, Henry: 216
"Varina": see *Virginia City*
Vasquez, Col. ——: associated with
    Bridger, 218, 222
Vasquez, Mrs: at Fort Bridger, 222,
    223
Vehicles: see also *Wagons*
Vendome Hotel: 34
Virginia City (Mont.): 113, 119, also
    footnote, 121, 265; distance from Fort
    C. F. Smith, 140

Wages: paid Phillips by U. S., 27; paid
    Van Volzah, 152
Wagon Box Fight: 39–87, 132, 159,
    175, 181, 189, 253, 262; sketch, 55
Wagon Trains: 173, see also *Caravans*
Wagons: used as corral, 43, 44; used in
    Wagon Box Fight, 50, 51, 75, 84–85
Wands, Lieut. A. H: 90, 92, 95
War Man's Creek: 118, 144; see also
    Warrior Creek
War Man Hill: 118
Ward, Seth E: 232
Warm Springs: 120
Warren, Senator F. E: 11, 25
Warrior Creek: 135, 165, 166; see also
    War Man Creek
Waschman, Mrs: daughter of Bridger,
    248, 249
Washakie, Chief: friend of Bridger,
    248
Washington, Mr: 172
Washington, Mrs: 37, 172
Washington, George: 105
Washington (D. C.): 189, 193, 199,
    242; Bridger visited, 243
Washita: battle of, 194, also *footnote*
Water: alkali, at Fort Reno, 172; at

Wagon Box Fight, 61, 62; soldiers
    suffer for, 63, 78
Waukantanka: Sioux name for God,
    195
Weather: extreme, 15, 19, 23, 24, 27,
    39, 104, 105, 107; see also *Blizzards*
Wessels, Gen. H. W: 40, 104; takes
    charge of Fort Phil Kearney, 39
Western Frontier: 15, 205
Westgate, ——: 117
West Point: 240
Westport (Mo.): 251; Bridger died
    near, 207; home of Bridger, 212
Wheeler, Olin D: 265, *footnote*
Whiskey at Fort Bridger: 223
Whitman, Dr. Marcus: removes arrow
    from Bridger's back, 216–218; slain
    by Indians, 217, *footnote*
"Wichahpi Yamoni": see *Crook, Gen-
    eral*
Williams, H: travels entire length of
    Bozeman Trail, 118
Willits, Miss Vie: see *Garber, Mrs. A. L.*
Willow Creek: 114
Wind River: 115
Wisconsin: Red Cloud lived in, 177
Wolf Creek: 118
Wolves: 98, 126, 132
Woman's Dress (Indian scout): 190
Women: 57, 91; at Fort Bridger, 222,
    223; at Fort Phil Kearney, 16, 19, 27,
    38, 95, 231; colored servant at Fort
    Phil Kearney, 90; Indian shot by
    U. S. Troops, 194, *footnote*; killed by
    Indians, 89
Wounded Knee: battle of, 194, also
    footnote
Wounded Knee Campaign: 70
Wyoming: 30, 37, 38, 39, 104, 121,
    145, 147, 253, also *footnote*, 261–264
Wyoming Old Pioneers: resolution
    adopted on John Phillips death, 31,
    32
Wyoming-Oregon Trail Commission:
    262

Yale College: 185
Yankton Charlie: 190

Yellowstone Expedition: 118, *footnote*
Yellowstone Ferry: 120
Yellowstone Lake: 213
Yellowstone Park: 212–215, 252;
    Bridger's account of, 211
Yellowstone River: 41, 119, *footnote*,
    121, 206, 209, 211, 215, 218, 219,
    226, 227, 228, 234, 262, *footnote*,
263, 264, 265
Yellowstone Valley Road: 120
Young, Brigham: 239
Young-Man-Afraid-of-His-Horses,
    Chief: 182

Zachary Ranch: 118